D1566271

THE PSYCHOLOGY OF COMMITMENT

EXPERIMENTS LINKING BEHAVIOR TO BELIEF

SOCIAL PSYCHOLOGY

A series of monographs, treatises, and texts

EDITORS

LEON FESTINGER AND STANLEY SCHACHTER

Jack W. Brehm, A Theory of Psychological Reactance. 1966

Ralph L. Rosnow and Edward J. Robinson (Eds.), Experiments in Persuasion. 1967

Jonathan L. Freedman and Anthony N. Doob, Deviancy: The Psychology of Being Different. 1968

Paul G. Swingle (Ed.), Experiments in Social Psychology. 1968, 1969

E. Earl Baughman and W. Grant Dahlstrom, Negro and White Children: A Psychological Study in the Rural South. 1968

Anthony G. Greenwald, Timothy C. Brock, and Thomas M. Ostrom (Eds.), Psychological Foundations of Attitudes. 1968

Robert Rosenthal and Ralph Rosnow (Eds.), Artifact in Behavioral Research. 1969

R. A. Hoppe, E. C. Simmel, and G. A. Milton (Eds.), Early Experiences and the Processes of Socialization. 1970

Richard Christie and Florence Geis, Studies in Machiavellianism. 1970

Paul G. Swingle (Ed.), The Structure of Conflict. 1970

Alvin Zander, Motives and Goals in Groups. 1971

Stanley Schachter, Emotion, Obesity, and Crime. 1971

Charles A. Kiesler, The Psychology of Commitment: Experiments Linking Behavior to Belief. 1971

THE PSYCHOLOGY OF COMMITMENT

EXPERIMENTS LINKING BEHAVIOR TO BELIEF

CHARLES A. KIESLER

Department of Psychology
University of Kansas
Lawrence, Kansas

ACADEMIC PRESS New York and London 1971

ACADEMIC PRESS, INC.
111 Fifth Avenue, New York, New York 10003

United Kingdom Edition published by
ACADEMIC PRESS, INC. (LONDON) LTD.
Berkeley Square House, London W1X 6BA

LIBRARY OF CONGRESS CATALOG CARD NUMBER: 78-163910

PRINTED IN THE UNITED STATES OF AMERICA

TO SARA

CONTENTS

PREFACE

This book is essentially a research monograph. It has no other pretentions. As such, it focuses very specifically on a line of research on commitment that I have been involved with for several years in collaboration with my students. It is really a progress report, since our thinking and research continue. These hard-bound progress reports are appearing more frequently in psychology, and it is a trend I obviously endorse.

There are always several reasons for writing any book, but two in particular led me to the typewriter in this case. Most important were my graduate students who repeatedly urged me to bring all of the material together so that one could better assess the impact of the overall project. The necessary brevity of the usual journal article was hindering us from interrelating a goodly amount of material and thought about commitment. More pragmatically, a half dozen projects were completed at about the same time. Faced with the prospect of writing individual papers, the alternative of writing a longer report which would include most of the projects' data became more appealing.

The approach taken to the study of commitment is psychological in tone. A sociologist, with some justification, might consider the approach rather narrow. It is true that both the theoretical model that I present and our research have focused very specifically upon behavior and its relationship to attitude. It is essentially a "micro-theory." A number of more macro-theoretical approaches to commitment may be found in the sociological literature. For example, sociologists would distinguish between personal commitment (dedication to completion of a line of action) and behavioral commitment (factors which constrain one to continue a line of action). They suggest that behavioral commitment may be partialed into two types: social commitment (expectations, norms, and so forth, which affect continuation of a line of action) and cost commitment (how costly it is to change a line of action, e.g., marriage). The micro- and macro-theoretical approaches do not necessarily conflict; we have simply concentrated on what sociologists would consider one aspect of commitment, i.e., behavioral commitment, mostly of the social variety. The lack of an adjective to limit the type of commitment in this monograph is partly for ease of presentation, rather than ignorance or lack of acceptance of sociological treatments of the concept. Further, we are only in the beginning stages of our study of commitment, but thus far we have not found a more detailed analytic approach to be particularly helpful. That is to say, we have not yet found that different "types" of commitment have different empirical effects. Since this monograph adheres rather closely to the data, we have taken the liberty of ignoring the analytic treatment of commitment in the sociological literature. We do this not to offend the sociologist, but rather to indicate that we simply have not reached the stage where that conceptual treatment has been especially useful.

Whatever modest success this volume may have, a good part of the credit should go to the graduate students involved in the research at Yale. In particular, I thank Dr. Gordon Bear (now at the University of Wisconsin), Dr. James Jones (now at Harvard), Dr. Leslie McArthur (now at Brandeis), Dr. Michael Pallak (now at the University of Iowa), Dr. Jerry Salancik (now at the University of Illinois), and Dr. Mark Zanna (now at Princeton). They formed the core of the weekly research meetings, and many of the ideas presented here originated or were honed at those meetings.

I would also like to thank the American Psychological Association for permission to reprint material from articles previously published in the *Journal of Personality and Social Psychology*. All of the previously unpublished work presented in this volume and most of my previous work on commitment were funded by a grant from the National Science Foundation.

CHARLES A. KIESLER

THE PSYCHOLOGY OF COMMITMENT

EXPERIMENTS LINKING BEHAVIOR TO BELIEF

I

ATTITUDES AND BEHAVIOR

A good deal of the day-to-day behavior of the average person is in one way or another related to his attitudes or beliefs. He subscribes to a magazine of known editorial slant; he reads one article in the newspaper but not another; he contributes money to the solicitor for a children's home but refuses to sign a petition offered him in a downtown street; he moves to a certain neighborhood rather than another; he acts distantly with a new black co-worker, then lends money to a friend; he declines one party invitation, accepts another.

Each of these behaviors can be said to reflect an attitude. Attitudes are evaluative. The person may support the Vietnam war; favor government intervention in local school systems; and feel sorry for abandoned children. On a theoretical level, attitudes *guide* behavior. They are the impetus that leads a person to act one way and not another.

On the other hand, obviously, not all behavior is "produced" by an attitude. The principle of multiple determinants of behavior has been a traditional view in psychology and it is no less applicable here. Many things affect the way we behave. For example, there may be important higher level attitudes. A person may contribute money to a children's home because he feels sorry for abandoned children. However, feeling sorry for someone does not necessarily imply that one will, or even should, contribute money on their behalf. There must be a higher level attitude (or value, in Rokeach's system; Rokeach, 1968) that says one should help those one pities.

We may also have conflicting attitudes that affect behavior. Suppose we wish to contribute money to a children's home—we may even feel that one should do so, but we can't abide the person who is the director of the home. One cluster of attitudes impels us to contribute; a different set makes us very reluctant to do so. Our final behavior may be determined by the relative intensity of these two groups of attitudes.

Chance events also are an important determinant of behavior. The contribution depends on who asks for it, who is present when the request is made, when the last payday was, the amount asked for, and whether the benefactor is angry, sad, or happy—the last aspect perhaps determined by the events immediately preceding the appeal.

We have called these *chance* events. Of course, they can be manipulated (and they help to determine the final behavior), and in that sense they are not totally up to the gods. But they are chance events in several respects: they are either extra-attitudinal or, if attitudinally related, do not depend on an attitude specific to the question (charity); they are irregular and temporary; and they are often beyond the reach (and ken) of the canvasser. In short, these events help us to predict another's behavior, but they are largely irrelevant to the attitude in question.

Although denying the predictability of group behavior, the novelist Nabokov, in *The Eye* (1966), emphasizes the important role that chance events play in the determination of the behavior of an individual:

> It is silly to seek a basic law, even sillier to find it. Some mean-spirited little man decides that the whole course of humanity can be explained in terms of insidiously revolving signs of the zodiac or as the struggle between an empty and a stuffed belly; he hires a punctilious Philistine to act as Clio's clerk, and begins a wholesale trade in epochs and masses; and then woe to the private individuum, with his two poor u's, hallooing hopelessy amid the dense growth of economic causes. Luckily, no such laws exist: a toothache will cost a battle, a drizzle cancel an insurrection. Everything is fluid, everything depends on chance, and all in vain were the efforts of that crabbed bourgeois in Victorian checkered trousers, author of *Das Kapital*, the fruit of insomnia and migraine. There is titillating pleasure in looking back at the past and asking oneself, "What would have happened if . . . ," and substituting one chance occurrence for another, observing how, from a grey, barren, humdrum moment in one's life, there grows forth a marvellous rosy event that in reality had failed to flower. A mysterious thing, this branching structure of life: one senses in every past instant a parting of ways, a "thus" and an "otherwise," with innumerable dazzling zigzags bifurcating and trifurcating against the dark background of the past [pp. 36–37].

Later, we will discuss just how well we can predict behavior from attitude. Obviously, though, there is not a perfect relationship between attitude and behavior. We cannot know exactly what a person is going to do, how he is going to behave, simply by knowing what his attitudes are.

Chance events impinge on the flow of a person's life and affect his behavior and, as mentioned, we know what some of them are. Irrespective of attitude, we know that a person will be more likely to behave as we wish if we offer him a prize or some financial incentive for doing so, if we provide him with the model or example of another person behaving the same way, or if the person requesting the behavior has especially high status. There are many other such variables.

Because of these environmental pressures, as we shall call them, person A may act on his beliefs and person B may not, even though the prior beliefs and attitudes of the two individuals may be, for all intents and purposes, identical. Given that A acts and B does not, should we now expect them to differ in any way? Does attitudinally relevant behavior affect the individual's attitude or the way he reacts to related subsequent events in his life? It seems reasonable to suppose it does, and the When?, the How?, and the Why? are the focus of the present monograph.

We can state the main issue of this essay and the exploratory research to follow very simply. How does a person's behavior affect not only (*a*) his attitudes, but also the very stuff from which attitudes are formed: (*b*) the processing of other information from the environment, (*c*) the acceptance of influence attempts from others, and (*d*) subsequent behavior?

More typically, the question is reversed. People have asked how we can predict a person's behavior from his attitude. But behavior is affected by many variables besides attitude. If persons A and B, having identical attitudes, act differently because of chance events, is their behavior attitudinally irrelevant? No, because one's behavior itself is an event that affects later behavior. In this view, an act could be seen as a chance event which in turn affects the probability of subsequent attitudinally relevant behavior. Of course, whether the act is attitudinally relevant or not is important in determining how subsequent acts will be affected. In our research, we have looked at the later effects of certain attitudinally relevant behavior where, however, attitude itself was not the original determinant of the behavior. We have been interested in the chain of events that can determine: how a person makes an important decision; what he decides; drastic changes in belief; stubborn refusals to act; strong resistance to attack on one's beliefs; and so forth.

We will emphasize the primacy of one's behavior in determining the outcome of this sequence of events. However, to set the stage for this question properly, we first need to consider the concept of attitude in some detail and then to review briefly what others have found about the relationship of attitude to behavior. We will then reverse the question to consider the effects of behavior upon attitude and subsequent behavior.

The Concept of Attitude

Definition

"Attitude" is a theoretical construct. It is not something you can lay your hand on; it is inferred to exist from other information. Secord and Backman (1964) define attitude as ". . . certain regularities of an individual's feelings, thoughts, and predispositions to act toward some aspect of his environment [p. 97]." The principal aspect of an attitude is the degree to which it is positive or negative toward something.* The "something" can be almost anything: a group of people, whether the group is defined by race (blacks), economic position (the rich), vocation (college administrators), education (MD's), or physical proximity (my neighbors); or a single person (Mr. Nixon). It can be inanimate (the freeway that goes by my house) or animate (cats). It can be temporal (summertime), abstract (thrift), or concrete (a certain brand of deodorant or beer). All these examples have been used at some time or another in an experiment, attitude survey, or motivation research project.

Consistency among Components of Attitude

An attitude is said to have three components: the affective component (feelings), the cognitive component (thoughts), and the behavioral component (predispositions to act). And these components are presumed to be consistent within each individual and each attitude. That is, one should behave and think consistently with the way one feels about a given object.

Whether one does behave and think consistently with the way one feels is another question. Depending on the way the question is phrased, there has been either extremely little research on this issue or a great deal. The point is that the question has seldom been approached directly—seldom, that is, considering the centrality of the concept of attitude to social psychology and the importance of the theoretical issue. If we pose the empirical issue as What exactly is the nature of the relationship among the three theoretical components of attitude?, then evidence is sparse because people have not gone around asking that question of themselves. However, if we pose the

* Attitude, of course, has other theoretical dimensions besides positivity. Most textbooks consider as relevant dimensions such things as centrality, extremeness, intensity, complexity, connectedness to other attitudes, and so forth. These other dimensions, although relevant, need not concern us for the moment.

question as Is there any evidence related to the issue?, then the answer is yes—quite a bit.

One source of such evidence is the experimental model that is typically used in the laboratory investigation of changes of attitude. In this paradigm, the subject reads some information about an object, an issue, or another person. Typically, but not always, he then completes an attitude scale, assessing his feelings or affect toward the object (or whatever was used in the experiment). As evidence on the consistency issue, we simply assume that the information given the subject produced a change in the cognitive component of his attitude and that the subsequent test reflected a consequent change in the affective component of his attitude. This is reasonable, though indirect, evidence on the issue. However, the fact that a group was given certain information and the group as a whole (and on the average) changed their "affect" somewhat is only weak evidence of consistency. If one wished to approach the question directly, then he would want to look at individuals. Specifically, one would need some independent measure of the cognitive component, its change for each individual, and the same for the affective component. Further, it would be necessary to have proper control groups and measures of both components before and after the introduction of the experimental information. To approach the question directly, one should show that the two components were highly related before the advent of new information, that the new information produced a change in the cognitive component, and that the individual subsequently changed the affective component of his attitude so that it retained its original consistency with the cognitive component.

One should not take this as a criticism of the usual method for studying attitude change; it is not. The experimental paradigm assumes existence of a consistent relationship between attitudinal components. (Otherwise, how could one expect change in the affective component from the introduction of new, but not affective, information?) Since one does indeed see change in the average affect after new nonaffective information, this is evidence for consistency among components of attitudes. However, the evidence is indirect at best, and it does not indicate any particular degree of consistency, just some consistency.

A second source of evidence concerning consistency among attitudinal components derives from particular methods of validating the measurement of attitudes (see "Measuring Attitudes," Chapter I). A typical way of determining whether attitude scales or tests are measuring what they are presumed to measure (that is, have they validity?) is to relate them to attitudinally relevant behavior. If one has a test which is supposed to measure attitudes toward labor unions and their activities, then a host of behaviors is relevant.

If an individual scores highly on your test, i.e., he is very pro-union, then he should be more likely to belong to a union if he has a choice, more likely to be active in union affairs if a member, more likely to vote for political candidates favorable to unions, more likely to contribute money to pro-union causes, and so forth. He should be more likely to do these things but with two conditions: first, that your test is valid—that it does measure attitudes toward unions, and second, that there is a relationship or some consistency between these two components of attitude, affective and behavioral. Many scales are quite highly related to such simple behaviors as activity in union affairs (see Shaw and Wright, 1967). Evidence such as this indicates both scales validity and consistency among components, but one cannot separate the two. A weak relationship between the scale and designated behaviors could be due equally well to the lack of validity (or reliability) of the scale or to the lack of relationship between this attitude and these behaviors.* Of course, a high correlation between scale score and behavior suggests both scale validity and consistency among attitude components.

Both batches of data provide some evidence of consistency among components of attitudes. The attitude change paradigm indirectly concerns the relationship between the so-called cognitive component and the affective component. The method of validating attitude scales gives some idea about the connection of the affective component to the behavioral component. In the next section, we will argue that there are good theoretical and practical reasons why these relationships should not be perfect—why the obtained relationship between any two components would almost never be perfectly predictable.

The Relationship between Attitude and Behavior

Most psychologists who are interested in the study of attitude and attitude change assume that attitude and behavior are highly related. They do this, first, because it seems a very reasonable assumption to make, and second, because it lends an air of practical importance to the laboratory study of attitudes. The question of just how related attitudes are to behavior seems on the surface to be an open and shut case of dust-bowl empiricism, i.e., we simply go find out. But the question is not that easy and it opens a Pandora's Box of confusing elements.

Part of the problem is definitional, and part is a measurement issue. Included in the definition of attitude that we gave before was the phrase, "predispositions to act," and this leads us to a problem of circularity. How

* A separate problem is the a priori designation of the behaviors as relevant, but this is an issue which will be treated later.

does one measure a predisposition? Of course, one infers it from behavior or action itself. There must, by definition, be a powerful relationship between behavior and attitude, much like a part–whole correlation. (Indeed, if the components of the attitude are perfectly consistent and if there is a perfect relationship between predispositions to act and behavior, then, by definition, the relationship between attitude and behavior must also be perfect).

In this view, the attitude–behavior question becomes a pseudo-issue.* Behavior is part of attitude, and if the person doesn't behave as we expected from our guess about his attitude, well, then we simply conclude that our guess was incorrect, i.e., the person obviously doesn't have the attitude that we thought he did. Indeed, some theorists dispense with the affective and cognitive components of attitude and infer the attitude directly from the behavior itself. Campbell (1950), for example, says, "A social attitude is (or is evidenced by) consistency in response to social objects." and "An individual's social attitude is a syndrome of response consistency with regard to social objects [pp. 31–32]." Green (1954) adds, ". . . the concept of attitude implies a consistency or predictability of responses . . . [and its content] is determined by the responses which constitute it [p. 336]."

The question is also related to how the attitude is measured. The subject usually completes some kind of attitude scale, and making those marks on the scale represents a behavior of sorts as well. In discussing this issue, Kiesler, Collins, & Miller (1969) wrote,

> What has happened is that social scientists have, almost without exception, settled on pencil and paper or interview techniques for the *measurement* of attitudes while retaining a *theory* that specifies behavioral implications for attitudes. The properly pedantic title for this section should be something like "The Relationship Between Certain Kinds of Behavior, Arbitrarily Designated by Most Social Scientists as Measures of Attitude, and Other Kinds of Behavior which, According to Theory, Should be Influenced by the Attitude in Question" [p. 23].

The question must be rephrased then, but it still can be asked. What is the relationship between attitude scales, which are typically measures or open statements of affect, and behavior, which is supposed to be theoretically relevant to this affect? The data come mostly from studies of attitude *in situ*, particularly from attempts to validate attitude measures, as we suggested in the previous section. Most of these studies show a respectable relationship between "attitude" and behavior, regarding union membership, educational practices, racial prejudice, attraction toward particular others, being in-

* It becomes a pseudo-issue only because the two elements, attitude and behavior, are confounded. Since one is part of the other, they must be related. If one considers affect and behavior as two independent components of an attitude, the question can be more cleanly stated and loses its circularity.

noculated, voting preferences, and so forth. (This is not the proper place for a detailed review of all of these studies. See, instead, Kiesler, Collins, & Miller, 1969, or McGuire, 1969). The relationship is far from perfect, but there are a number of factors which can attentuate it in particular circumstances.

Attenuating Factors

A number of things affect the relationship between behavior and attitude and, in a sense, determine whether a person acts on his attitude in a given situation at a particular time. The first we have already mentioned. That is, there are forces, other than simply his attitude, acting on the individual, leading him to behave in certain ways. For example, the rules of decorum and social etiquette restrict our overt behavior in interacting with others. Other extra-attitudinal pressures for behavior include the chance events we discussed before, the particular interpersonal and environmental mist surrounding each piece of behavior.

Similar factors affect the *expression* of attitude. For example, one is not supposed to voice negative feelings about others, particularly directly. I have noticed a related effect in studies of interpersonal attraction. No matter how provoking a confederate may be in an experiment, it is almost impossible to get a subject to say, or even indicate on an attitude scale, that he dislikes the confederate. If the attraction scale runs from "like him extremely" to "dislike him extremely," the negative half of the scale is seldom used. The results can be neat and orderly, but the differences between conditions represent various degrees of positive affect. The subject retains his positive view of himself by liking everyone, but he reacts to the experimental manipulations by liking some more than others. (This, of course, could be due simply to a lack of experimental impact, i.e., weak manipulations, but I really doubt it. If that were the case, one would always have a few negative responses by chance.)

A third factor that affects the obtained relationship between attitude and behavior is the relevance of other attitudes to the behavior. Several attitudes may be associated with a given behavior, and the attitudes may have different implications for the behavior. For example, contributing to a political party should reflect one's political beliefs, but other variables affect this behavior as well. If one holds a position in government, then an important determinant of financial contributions (if we are to believe the allegations following every national election) is whether one holds a civil service position or one that depends on patronage. In this case, attitudes toward one's superior or toward one's opportunities for promotion may dominate the behavioral act and political belief may be only secondary. In general, when several beliefs are relevant to some behavior, the attitude either most salient at the moment or most intensely held is the one likely to affect behavior.

Some attitudes may not be monotonically related to behavior. A certain level of intensity or strength of attitude may be necessary to cue off the behavior. In such a case, no one below a particular level of attitude intensity would behave in the specified way, but everyone above that level would (sort of a step function with only one step). The relationship between attitude and behavior in a given sample of people would depend on the intensity of belief sampled. If the sample included people at only either extreme of intensity, one would find no relationship at all. That is, if the sample included only people at the low extreme, no one in the sample would show the behavior; if the other extreme, then everyone would be performing the behavior. But there would be no statistical correlation in either case.

In the example above, the measurement of behavior is dichotomous; the only statistic is whether the subject performs the behavior or not, not how much of it he engages in. When this is so, the correlation between attitude and behavior is restricted by the split or division existing in the population. Suppose, for example, that one were studying the efficacy of prayer as a form of persuasive communication. Subjects in one condition might hear a standard communication advocating charity toward one's fellow man. Subjects in a second condition could hear essentially the same communication but translated into "praying" form, with appropriate thee's and thou's and a smattering of begat's. A control group would hear no communication. Later, all subjects could be confronted by a canvasser requesting contributions to a charitable cause. A dependent measure might be the percentage of subjects in each of the three conditions that contributes to the cause. If our interest were change (in contributing behavior as a function of the change in attitude produced by the communications), then we would want the population level (the control group) to be low. If everyone in the control condition contributed to charity, then there would be little possibility for the experimental conditions to show any increase over this. Consequently, in an experimental setting, we would wish to select some behavior of an appropriately difficult level.

However, if we wished to study the relationship of *existing* attitude to charity behavior, the choice of level of difficulty of the behavior would rest on different grounds. Suppose we knew how often people went to church in the control group in our experimental example and we wanted to see if there was a relationship between the attitude indicated by church attendance (let's call it religiosity) and charity—whether the person contributed when faced by the request of the canvasser. A small percentage of people contributing in this group would not be desirable statistically. If the level of difficulty of the behavior selected is at either extreme, e.g., either too many or too few people contributing, the correlation would be restricted or attenuated, even though there might be a high correlation between religious attitudes and charitable behavior in general in the population.

In sum, there are two points of interest: The level of difficulty of the behavior selected for study can attenuate any possible relationship between attitude and behavior; the basis for the investigator's selection of a behavior to study can be quite different, depending on whether he is concerned with attitudes *in situ* and their relationship to behavior, or with attitude change and its relationship to behavior.

This is not an exhaustive list of factors that can attenuate the relationship between attitude and behavior, nor was it intended to be. The main point is that, even when there is a strong relationship between attitude and behavior in the population, factors such as salience of attitude, nonmonotonicity, conflicting pressures, and level of difficulty of the behavior can lower the relationship actually obtained in some samples.

The Effects of Behavior on Attitude

Why Act?

There has been a good deal of discussion in the popular press about the fact that people do not necessarily act on their beliefs: They do not sell their house to a black even though they profess a strong belief in equality; they are reluctant to sign a petition though they indicate agreement with the issue it represents. To any one who has stood on a street corner with a petition (or who has been robbed on the same corner), the failure of people to act comes of no surprise. We are all indeed reluctant to act on our beliefs. Before we consider what the effects of attitudinally relevant behavior are, we might think for a moment about what leads a person to act on his beliefs in the first place. Let us assume that a hypothetical person has a certain belief and that he is asked to act on this belief—to behave in a certain way that seems on the surface to be consistent with the belief. Why should he? What are the kinds of things that run through his mind as he considers consenting? In short, what are the positive and negative features of consonant behavior?

Positive Features of Consonant Behavior

It seems to me that there are very few aspects of acting on one's beliefs that are positive although each one may be very important to the individual. There are three main positive features of consonant behavior.

First, assuming the person has a positive self-image, he probably feels that his attitude is "correct." Consequently, he feels that the issue is valid, that something should be done.

Second, acting on one's beliefs enhances one's self-view. Acting because one believes gives one a feeling of personal integrity and courage, particularly when the belief is not a popular one. The picture of sacrifice for belief is part of the hero image of fiction, as well as popular history and biography.

Third, acting on a belief implies knowledge of the issues involved. Therefore, the actor is one who knows what he is doing. He is knowledgeable.

These are the three main reasons why one might wish to act on his beliefs. They are few in number, but it is trite to say that people find them important; thousands have died for less. The combination of rightness and the hero image can be strong indeed.

Negative Features of Consonant Behavior

There are many of these. They may not all be operable in any particular situation, or if applicable, they may not be very salient. Nonetheless, they are the sort of thing that people probably consider when faced with a request or other pressure for behavior.

1. In a complex world, it is very difficult to verify one's beliefs, and it is always possible that one is wrong. Many, perhaps most, attitudes are not well thought out. An attitude may be conditioned from a single dramatic experience or be a holdover from early childhood. The person might be very willing to express such an attitude while at the same time acknowledging to himself that he hasn't really thought through the issue and its ramifications. So the first negative aspect of consonant behavior that may occur to the actor is that he could be wrong and, hence, appear silly both to himself and to others.

2. Action is explicit and public (while an attitude can be both implicit and private). By acting, one leaves oneself open to possible attack or argument. An attack can be both embarrassing and effortful in defense. But to consider a possible attack forces one to acknowledge that others might think us wrong. Not to act dispenses with that uncomfortable thought.

3. There is always the possibility that, although the attitudinally motivated behavior costs the actor something in time, effort, and money, it may be to no avail. It may not help the cause. As a result, it may be not only a waste of time and energy, but it could also make the person look silly—a modern Don Quixote.

4. Since the action is explicit but derives from one's personal feelings, it can give the impression of being personally very revealing, of laying one's soul bare before others, a prospect that many would find uncomfortable.

5. Given that the behavior is a public acknowledgment of a private feeling, our relationships with others may be affected. That is, others whom one admires, respects, or must get along with may disagree strongly on the issue and, consequently, either dislike one or otherwise make the subsequent interaction more difficult.

6. The explicitness of the behavior also affects our relationships with others in a different way. In interacting with others we often either misrepresent our opinions or omit mention of them. We misrepresent our opinions and attitudes, not only to ingratiate ourselves with others on important occasions (Jones, 1964) but also to insure that ordinary interaction is smooth and uninterrupted by public discordance (Goffman, 1959). Public, attitudinally relevant behavior decreases our alternatives or degrees of freedom in future interactions with others (see Chapter VII).

7. There is always the danger that the issue will change in the future but that others will remember only the behavior out of context. The union leader who fought in the streets for the rights of laborers may have been both in the right and acting on his beliefs, but he may find himself remembered simply as a street fighter thirty years later, when people have forgotten the original impetus and context of the behavior. Alternatively, others' interpretations of the payoffs from the behavior may vary later. That is, a given action may have several consequences but others may relate the behavior to only one of them. One of the consequences of the union's struggle for power is that the workers are now paid much more than they were thirty years ago, but no self-respecting labor leader would appreciate the implication that he "fought in the streets for a couple of bucks" (nor, I might add, would it be a fair implication).

8. By publicly acting on one's beliefs, one may be in for more than the original bargain. People recognize that one act may lead to many acts and, as a result, are reluctant to agree to the simplest request for action. In this day of "name-selling," most know that a simple two dollar response to a mailed charitable request will lead to an inundation of similar requests within days, each organization selling its list of suckers to other such organizations. Indeed, in Connecticut, applying for an automobile driver's license or paying your property tax will lead to the same end. Up until recently, the state was not only willing to sell these names, but it was even willing to sell particular types of lists, i.e., those under thirty, owners of Cadillacs, etc. Such a high degree of communication leads one to be wary of even the smallest request for action.

9. Acting on one's beliefs requires a reasonable certainty that one is correct. Let's assume that the person suspects that one explicit act may lead to some unknown number and variety of other related acts (or at least requests

for them). He intuits that the act has hidden implications for the future, but he isn't certain how many or what they will be. The person must be very certain of his belief and feel strongly about the issue before these other implications lose their importance. We suggest that the person muses, "There may be other things required of me if I act. Do I feel strongly enough not to care what these other requirements may be?" For most issues, this thought would imply to the individual that he should defer acting until he has sufficient time to consider other implications. Of course, in many cases where action is required, such as the crisis or panic situations described by Latanè and Darley (1970), if one does not act immediately, then one tends not to act at all.

10. The last two points above have an additional implication when considered together. We have suggested that a person expects further requirements from his behavior and that he wonders whether he is that certain of his attitude (or believes that intensely). If people are going to act on their beliefs, they obviously want to do it on an important issue—something that makes a difference (or so anecdotal experience tells me). However, if it is true that one's certainty of opinion wavers under a direct request for action, this almost guarantees that some other issue will momentarily appear to be more important, leading to inaction. Many whose social consciences impel them to do something for some cause or other appear to go through precisely this sort of process. As each request for action appears, they discard it as being of secondary importance, and they wait for something "really important" to come along. In the meantime, perhaps forever, they do nothing.

In the popular literature there seems to be no difficulty recognizing why people act on their beliefs. Literature, history, biography, and folklore (as well as psychological theories of human behavior) are filled with examples of courageous individuals not only acting on their beliefs but also making great sacrifices in the process. However, there seems to be only bewilderment at inaction. Why don't people do something? we say, or, The majority believe so-and-so, why do they allow such terrible things to go on? Why don't people act? We have tried to suggest, by our phenomenological analysis of the person faced with a request for action, that there are a number of reasons why he might not act. In general, we have suggested that people are leery of explicit and attitudinally relevant behavior because it is *restricting* in its implications for the future. As a result of such behavior, in the future an individual may have to defend himself; his interactions with others may have slightly different overtones (ingratiation is more difficult) or undertones (others may not like him as much); he may be labelled by others in an uncomplimentary way, either now or much later; and he may have to forgo action in other spheres because of limitations of free time.

If people do feel that attitudinally explicit behavior is restricting in implication, then they are entirely correct, for that is precisely what the experimental research shows, as the next section shall document.

The Effects of Behavior

The notion that overt explicit behavior tends to restrict subsequent behavior and possible attitudes is not new. It is assumed to be true, directly or indirectly, in a variety of settings. In some types of therapy situations the client is urged to act as if he were a "new person," as if he had different attitudes than those he has shown in the past (Wolpe, 1958). It is assumed that this new behavior will be difficult to undo and that new affect will be structured around this new behavior.* In T-groups, participants are encouraged to act openly and honestly with each other. When the participants are from the same industrial concern, it is assumed that this behavior will solidify and perpetuate itself, leading to new lines and smoothness of communication within the company.

Certain rites have the same function. Whiting, Kluckholn, and Anthony (1958) hypothesize that male puberty rites are designed to break the child's dependence on the mother. The rites break the binds of the past by producing new ultramasculine behavior difficult to reconcile with any future interaction with older females. They were able to show that those primitive societies with severe puberty rites were also those in which the male child was extremely dependent upon the mother in the earlier years. Aronson and Mills (1959) and Gerard and Mathewson (1966) showed that severe initiation does produce the desired effect in the victim. The person justifies having undergone the severe initiation by enhancing the attractiveness of the group and the value of its product.

Lieberman (1956) studied the effects of certain role behavior upon attitude. In an industrial setting, he was able to inspect the subsequent behavior and attitudes of men who were promoted to either of two divergent positions: shop steward (a union man), or foreman (a company man). He found that the behavior and attitudes of the men changed to fit the new position. Further, if the men reverted back to their old position as ordinary worker, then behavior and attitudes reverted back as well. Although this is a complex situation in which it is difficult to tease out specific causes of change, it is reasonable to suppose that one contributory factor in the Lieberman study was that the new positions demanded new behaviors and that the new attitudes (not strictly demanded) followed from the new behavior.

* Wolpe, however, implicitly assumes that the new behavior will be rewarded by the environment and that repetition of the new behavior depends upon that reinforcement.

An equally complex situation prevails in studies of contact between minority and majority group members. For example, Deutsch and Collins (1951) showed that whites living in racially integrated housing projects were more likely to view blacks positively than were whites living in segregated housing, even though there was no evidence of any difference in attitude prior to contact. Star, Williams, and Stouffer (1958) found similar increased positive affect following inforced interracial contact in military companies during the Second World War. In the present context, one could suggest a possible contribution to these effects. In the day-to-day exigencies of living, the pressures of decorum and protocol induced whites to behave politely toward blacks in a variety of situations and in a number of instances. Polite behavior is positive behavior (although not extremely so), and attitudes became more closely arrayed with the behavior.*

A host of material about decision-making is relevant to the present discussion. Lewin (1947) posited that a decision is a form of behavior that is often irrevocable. It, in a sense, freezes one's cognitive world. Other more pliable aspects of one's life, such as attitudes, must be fitted around the frozen part. (Note the implicit assumption of consistency between behavior and attitude.) In this view, one may induce social change by forming the issue as a decision and then leading the person to participate in the decision (and, of course, to decide on a predetermined alternative). In a number of experiments, Lewin compared the results of people deciding on a particular course of action (e.g., giving cod liver oil to their babies) in a group setting, being led to this decision, of course, by a skilled group leader, with those of people given private instruction or hearing a lecture on the same topic. Lewin found the decision made in the group context to be much more effective than instruction in affecting subsequent behavior and attitudes. (Pelz, 1955, found that the decision made in the group did not necessarily have to be public in order to be effective.) Coch and French (1960) similarly found the decision in a group context to be more effective in producing workers' acceptance of higher production rates in a factory than a simple request or instruction.

Dissonance theory has also produced a variety of data on the issue. (See Festinger, 1957, 1964; Brehm & Cohen, 1962; Kiesler, Collins, & Miller, 1969. See, also, "Introduction to Dissonance Theory," Chapter I, for a definition and Chapter III for a more detailed discussion of the relationship

* Deutsch and Collins stress that the relationship must be one of equality since, presumably, the negative attitude would be reinforced under other circumstances. This is not inconsistent with the present discussion since polite behavior would not be forthcoming if the relationship were not relatively equal. Or, if occurring under inequality, it might be considered condescending or paternalistic.

of dissonance theory to the issue under discussion.) The best summary statement of this research is that attitudes change following a decision, in a manner that justifies the decision. If you choose object A over object B, then following the decision there is a tendency to distort the attractiveness of the two objects. The chosen object is seen as more attractive than before and the rejected object as less attractive (even without new information). Gerard (1965) notes a similar effect in an Asch-like conformity setting. Gerard stresses that the subject chooses to conform or not on the first trial of a series. In his terms, the subject is forced to take an Unequivocal Behavioral Orientation (UBO) toward the issue. Although a variety of factors may influence whether the person conforms on trial one or not, subsequent behavior is frozen by that initial decision, and the subject either always conforms on the series or never.

Freedman and Fraser (1966) found that if you want a person to do a big favor for you, the best technique is to induce him to do a small favor first. In their experiment, housewives were asked to place a large ugly sign on their front lawns extolling others to keep California beautiful. Those subjects who were first asked to put a small sign in a window, were much more receptive to the larger request later (whether or not the two requests were made by the same person or the two signs concerned the same issue). They concluded that the small behavior leads the person to have a new conception of himself as an activist or a "doer" so that the large request is subsequently seen more favorably than it would otherwise be.

Public behavior is particularly freezing in its effect. Hovland, Campbell, and Brock (1957) found that subjects who expected their initial opinions to be made public were more resistant to a persuasive communication than were those subjects who did not think that their opinions would be seen by others. In an Asch-type setting, Deutsch and Gerard (1955) found that when subjects wrote down their initial judgments of stimuli, they were later much less likely to conform when confederates made different (and false) judgments than if they had not previously written out their initial impressions. Indeed, resistance was increased even when first impressions were recorded on a "magic pad" and could be immediately erased.

Often, subjects need only to be reminded of their previous behaviors. Charters and Newcomb (1958) found that Catholic subjects were much less accepting of attitude items critical of formal Catholicism when they were reminded of their personal affiliation than when they were not. Kelley (1955) also found under similar conditions of salience of group membership that there was greater resistance to an anti-Catholic communication.

I don't wish to oversimplify the situation. The evidence for the attitudinal effects of behavior is somewhat weak, since direct attempts to study the effects of behavior by itself have been infrequent. The initial focus of the experiments discussed above was not on the issue at hand. However, if one thinks about the phenomenology of the person contemplating some explicit behavior, he should be struck by the degree to which people are wary of performing such behavior. Part of this wariness centers on how others will regard the behavior and whether others will now expect one to behave consistently. The demands by others for one to be consistent in behavior and attitude may be especially true for Western culture. Segalman (1968), for example, suggests that stress on the individual's responsibility for his actions may be an integral part of the Protestant ethic. Another aspect of explicit behavior is internal demands for consistency, that the individual is uncomfortable behaving inconsistently with how he feels. The person is not anxious to perform explicit but attitudinally relevant behavior because of possible conflict with attitudes that are not salient, which he cannot recall at the moment. A third aspect of such behavior is its implications for the future. The actions define the man, so to speak, and explicit behaviors not only lay one open to possible attack but also there is a sense of finality or irrevocability about them. If one is defined by some previous behavior, then one's freedom to grow and to accept new information is retarded.

Behavior is in this sense the real man. Attitudes, as affect, are often not well thought out (except probably for important ones). For example, in a presidential election we may favor one man over the other. But we cannot really know that one of them would be better than the other because there is literally no way to know. However, we do know that we voted for one of them, and that behavior is irrevocable.

Attitudes may be fluid and not terribly explicit; we cannot only change our attitude toward some object, but we can easily deny to ourselves that we ever thought that way to begin with. Behavior, if explicit enough, freezes one, in Lewin's terms. Explicit behavior, like an irrevocable decision, provides the pillar around which the cognitive apparatus must be draped. Through behavior, one is *committed.*

Chapter Notes

Measuring Attitudes

An attitude is an hypothetical construct. It neither can be seen and therefore categorized, nor does it have physical substance. Like all hypothetical constructs in psychology, it has translations or operationalizations that tradition and consensus lead us to accept and use. It may be helpful to review the three most popular methods of measuring attitudes, the Thurstone, Guttman, and Likert techniques. The first involves twenty or so declarative statements whose degree of pro-ness or con-ness on an issue has been determined by judges. The subject simply endorses those statements he agrees with and his score is the mean or median value of the endorsed statements. His score, his attitude, could as easily be considered to be the most positive or the most negative statement that he approves. However, subjects often affirm one extreme statement while the rest of their responses cluster around some moderate value. The extreme probably misrepresents their attitude, and the median, which is typically used in the Thurstone scale, minimizes the weight of a ratified extreme statement that stands off by itself.

The Guttman technique tackles this problem directly and the constructor of the scale attempts to arrange the statements so that they follow each other perfectly. Ideally, with the Guttman technique, if a person concurs with statement four in the series, then one knows that he has also consented to statements one, two, and three as well. The person's score or attitude value is the number of the last statement endorsed. When one knows which statement of the respondent is this critical one, then the whole set of responses can be reproduced without error. It is a very simple technique conceptually, but in practice one can almost never build a scale, a reproducible one, with such a perfect array of statements. One of Guttman's many contributions to attitude scaling is a quantification of how good a scale is. His "coefficient of reproducibility" tells us how close a scale comes to being perfectly reproducible for all subjects. It also tells us if the attitude is unidimensional, if it is simple with only one thread running through it.

To build a Guttman scale, one often gives a batch of subjects a large number of attitude items which one has derived on a priori grounds. Using a computer, one asks the question, What is the most reproducible subset of these items of size n or larger? However, if the set of original items is sufficiently large and the subset of the final scale items sufficiently small, one can end up with an attitude scale that is measuring something quite tangential to the investigator's original intention. If an issue is a very complex one, it is probably not unidimensional (almost by definition). With a complicated issue, the reproducible part may inadequately represent the broader context.

However, the technique forces unidimensionality, and it is difficult to ascertain whether the reproducibility thus derived is to some degree artificial.

The Likert technique has been the most popular in laboratory research. With this method, the respondent is offered several possible responses to each statement in the test. Variations of response run from "strongly agree" to "strongly disagree." There are usually five possible responses, including neutral or "no opinion." The assigned values, of course, run from one at one extreme to five at the other.* The construction of a Likert scale bears some resemblance to the other two methods. One starts with a reasonably large batch of a priori items, which subjects complete. Items are retained or discarded on the basis of the degree of relationship with other items (specifically item-total correlations). Like the Guttman scale, the defining quality for item retention is the internal consistency of the test as a whole. However, five responses per item allow for considerable variability, and one could demand, in addition to internal consistency, that each item relate to some external criterion as well, such as some particular behavior or variation in behavior.

The construction of a proper Likert scale is not appreciably less laborious than for the other two methods discussed. However, we have said that the Likert technique is the most popular in laboratory research on attitude change, and in that context the recommended labor is not expended (although perhaps without great cost to the investigator). Often at question in experiments on the change of attitudes is the general process involved or a specific theoretical issue. The content of the particular attitude issue that one uses for this purpose may be of little or no concern to the investigator. Attitude issues are often selected for an experiment on grounds that are peculiar to a given experiment, investigator, time, and place. I've picked issues because they were, I thought at the time, particularly hot on campus (e.g., the draft or premajority voting rights) and guaranteed subjects' involvement in the experiment, because they were appropriate to available subjects (e.g., den-mothers or seventh graders in a nearby school), because the test items had been used in other research and we could therefore be assured of a certain level of reliability, because a graduate student was interested in the issue and could regard the pretest as a preliminary survey of sorts, or because there was a known distribution of scores (e.g., bimodal or highly skewed) for my subject population. In short, the content of a particular attitude issue is only one of a number of considerations contributing to the final decision about a topic for an experiment.

The practice of testing subjects before and after an experimental manipula-

* Often, investigators allow the subject to place his mark anywhere along the scale (instead of just five alternatives). This technique allows fine gradations in score.

tion also limits the items one can use. It is the practice to keep a subject unaware that the investigator is primarily interested in attitude change, for fear that this knowledge would make him behave in ways that he otherwise would not. Giving the subject a 24-item Thurstone scale twice within the usual experimental hour is a dead giveaway. Consequently, a typical attitude "measure" in an experiment consists of one, two, or three Likert items that the experimenter made up the night before. This practice has been roundly criticized on a number of occasions, and longer, more reliable tests are suggested. This criticism could also be applied to several experiments in the present monograph in which very brief a priori tests are used. It is instructive, therefore, to consider the efficacy of the short test in some detail.

Short A Priori Tests

What's wrong with a three-item a priori test in an experiment? Three criticisms are usually mentioned: lack of reliability, lack of validity, and misleading results. All three criticisms are often inappropriate when applied to experiments *and* when the alternative is simply a longer and better constructed test of attitude. There is no question that a three-item test is less reliable than a longer test when other things are equal or held constant. However, possible systematic variation in a test score or an item score is limited by its reliability. If a test has zero reliability (as, for example, when there is no relationship between scores on the same test taken on two separate occasions), then systematic differences between experimental conditions are impossible. Increasing reliability allows for greater possible systematic differences between conditions. Put another way, if two populations differ on some trait or value x, then the greater the reliability of the measuring instrument, the greater the probability that two samples, one drawn from each population, will also differ. In short, an experimenter who is trying to test for predicted differences between two experimental conditions is simply cutting his own throat when he uses an unreliable measuring instrument.

However, suppose the experiment comes out precisely as predicted: differences between conditions as expected and statistically significant. In this case we can reason backward and conclude that whatever the reliability of the scale or test used, it was reliable enough for the populations tested. Given the argument in the preceding paragraph, if one wishes to argue that the reliability of the test is low, then he must also conclude that the differences between the populations must be huge. Thus, low reliability is not a cogent argument against the experiment in which the data are arrayed as expected and in which the differences between conditions are statistically significant. Experiments using unreliable measuring instruments have a low probability of statistically coming out as expected, but when they do, one cannot use the argument of low reliability to dispense with the results—quite the opposite.

The question of validity is different. Here one is saying that the three-item test is either invalid or of unknown validity. The former one can dismiss out of hand. One cannot say that something is invalid, without knowing what the validity is. The proper argument is that the three-item test is of unknown validity and, moreover, that its validity is less than that of a longer test. This is an argument that is not easy to deal with. The items are selected because they have face validity (they look as if they would measure what they are supposed to). The results come out as they were expected to on theoretical grounds, giving the short test some appearance of construct validity. However, unless the items have been used before in another experiment (lending greater construct validity) or are known to relate to some external criterion, that is the gist of the defense of the three-item test. What would the longer test give us? Nothing, necessarily. The longer test is more reliable and hence allows for greater validity, but it does not guarantee it. The items in the longer test have surely been also selected for their face validity as well, but again, that by itself does not guarantee greater resulting validity.

In sum, the longer test can make the claim of greater validity only if such validity has been demonstrated, as with an external criterion, for example. However, as even a glance at the compendium of Shaw and Wright (1967) would show, very little attention has been given to questions of validity in the construction of the typical attitude scale (long or short). Often, when there has been some attempt at external validation, the criterion is weak indeed. For example, suppose we are constructing a test of conservatism–liberalism. If we use as a validating criterion the person's political preference—whether he voted for a Republican or a Democrat in a particular election, then we have not aided our cause much. If the test is valid, then predictive accuracy in voting should be the absolute least we should expect from the test. Even if the validity of the test is very low, we should at least be able to make decent predictions of voting preferences. The one-item test "Are you a registered Republican?" probably predicts voting behavior with about 90% accuracy. Validating a test of conservatism–liberalism requires several other steps and criteria than just voting behavior. And if voting behavior is all we have, then we don't have much. It is a weak criterion.

It is only fair to add that the longer test is probably more valid than our hypothetical three-item test if it has been properly constructed. But if it has been validated only with weak criteria, it cannot be said that it is demonstrably more valid. From the point of view of the experimenter beginning a research project, there is often little in the question of validity that would lead him to abandon the three-item test of his own invention in favor of a longer test invented by someone else.

The third criticism of the three-item test is that it may produce misleading results. The usual meaning of this is that either the short test can be easily faked or that it is subject to transitory fluctuations in the person's mood. It seems to me that both of these objections can be dismissed quickly. It is true that the short test can be faked if the person wishes, and it may be true that it is subject to momentary variations in mood, but it does not follow that the longer test is any less open to criticisms of this sort.

The traditional method of measuring attitude is with a formal attitude scale. The short scales used in research have been criticized on the grounds of length alone. We have suggested that the main drawback of the short scale, as opposed to the longer, better-constructed ones, is that it produces too many null results. Too many experiments do not give significant results when real differences exist in the populations, i.e., when the hypothesis was correct. However, when the experiment does produce the expected results, then criticism of the experiment on the grounds of scale length is not valid.

This defense of the short scale relative to the longer one in experimental research should not be taken as a defense of the short scale per se as a measure of attitude. I quite agree with others' recommendations of multiple measurement, indirect and unobtrusive measures (Webb, Campbell, Schwartz, & Sechrest, 1966), and both behavioral and "behavioroid" measures (Aronson & Carlsmith, 1968) applied to attitudes.

Introduction to Dissonance Theory

Most readers of this monograph will, I assume, be quite familiar with dissonance theory and the research related to it. For those who are not, however (and especially for those of them who wish to understand Chapter III), I append this brief introduction to the theory. (Also, see Festinger, 1957, 1964; Brehm & Cohen, 1962; or Kiesler, Collins, & Miller, 1969).

Dissonance theory deals with cognitions: bits of information or knowledge about oneself, one's behavior and opinions, and the environment. The knowledge that you are reading this chapter note could be considered a cognition. Further, the theory goes on, a person is uncomfortable when any pair of cognitions are inconsistent and he is motivated to do something about it. This motivated, uncomfortable state is called dissonance.

How motivated the person presumably is to reduce his discomfort depends on how important the cognitions are to him, how many of them are involved in the inconsistent relationship, and the degree of inconsistency. By dissonance, Festinger does not mean *logical* inconsistency, but rather, *psycho-*

logical inconsistency. Thus, the inconsistency might depend upon cultural values, previous learning, and so forth. The cognitions "I am a good father" and "I change our baby's diapers" are not really logically related. However, depending on the culture and the individual, they might be either consistent or very inconsistent.

There have been two main experimental models for the study of dissonance phenomena. One is called the forced compliance paradigm, and the other, the free choice paradigm. In the forced compliance experiment, a subject is induced to behave contrary to his beliefs. The degree of dissonance aroused depends on other justifications for the counter-attitudinal behavior: The less the justification, the greater the dissonance. For example, Festinger and Carlsmith (1959) induced subjects to lie to a confederate. They were led to tell the stooge that an extremely dull task was really quite enjoyable. Some were paid one dollar for the lie and some were paid twenty dollars. The smaller payment theoretically produced greater dissonance, and presumably, these subjects were more motivated to reduce the inconsistency. Since the behavior was explicit and undeniable, it was predicted that the one-dollar subjects would change their opinions of the prior task to make them fit more closely with their behavior. Indeed, as expected, subjects paid one dollar for lying about the task rated the task as more enjoyable later than did subjects paid twenty dollars.

In the free choice setting, a subject merely chooses between two or more alternative objects or courses of action. As implied in our text, dissonance would be aroused by positive features of the rejected alternative and negative features of the chosen alternative—the degree depending upon the importance of the choice for the subject. Consider, for example, two conditions of an experiment by Brehm (1956), who had subjects choose which of two objects they were to keep for their own. By arrangement, the more attractive of the two objects was rated nearly equally in both conditions. But Brehm varied the attractiveness of what was to be the rejected alternative. The more attractive the rejected alternative is, the greater dissonance should theoretically be. Brehm hypothesized that subjects would distort the attractiveness of the objects on a second rating, but how much they distorted should depend how the degree of dissonance aroused. The results were as expected. When the two alternatives were relatively close in attractiveness, subjects enhanced the attractiveness of the chosen alternative and deprecated the attractiveness of the rejected alternative. In each case, the change was greater than that for subjects whose rejected alternative was initially unattractive.

Dissonance theory has inspired a great deal of research and provoked its share of controversy, and this is not the place for a lengthy review of either category. The interested reader is referred to Brehm and Cohen (1962) for a review of the literature up until then; to Abelson *et al.* (1968) for a discussion of current issues in consistency theory in general and dissonance theory in particular; and to Kiesler, Collins, & Miller (1969) for a critical review of same.

II

COMMITMENT

Psychologists worry a lot about definitions of their main terms. There are two main requirements for a useful definition of a psychological term. First, obviously, the *literary* definition should be clear and precise; the words should mean something. But a clear and precise literary definition is often not enough for a research oriented psychologist. We must also have an *operational* definition, specifying the set of (experimental) operations which define the concept. Without the literary definition we cannot relate the concept to other constructs and issues of theoretical interest. Without the operational definition, which allows us to use the concept in an experiment, we cannot test the implications of the theoretical issues. To have any dialogue about the concept, it is imperative that we agree on both definitions.

Suppose two psychologists are discussing the concept of reinforcement. One uses the term to mean anything that, when following a behavior, will increase the probability of future occurrence of the behavior, and the second intends reinforcement to imply something that reduces a drive; an old pseudo-issue in psychology and one familiar to all. However, if the definitional differences are not made clear, each discussant might say some things about reinforcement which would astound the other. The connotations of the separate definitions can be quite different. A term like commitment raises special problems in this regard.

Commitment is a term that many of us are accustomed to seeing in a variety of circumstances. It is often used not only by social psychologists but also by sociologists, anthropologists, psychiatrists, and popular writers.

In short, it is in the everyday language of our society, with all the emotional overtones, special meanings, and hidden implications that suggests.

There are three main definitions of commitment listed in Webster's Collegiate Dictionary (*5th* Ed.). The third is the one in current vogue. The first definition refers to the consignment or entrusting of something to someone else, especially in the sense of transfer or delivery. The second refers to the accomplishment of some act, as the commitment of a crime. It is the third definition that has relevance to the present discussion and reflects the most popular usage today. The third definition of commitment incurs the pledging or binding of oneself, as in committing oneself to a course of action. It is this meaning of commitment, for example, that Meyerson (1966) refers to when he says that today's protesting student ". . . likes to think that each member is totally committed to the cause (p. 727)." It is this definition that Kenniston (1965) prefers in his book, *The Uncommitted*, a discussion of the unfettered youth of today; it is often what is meant in discussions of the alienated, those who are not tied or bound or connected, in short, those who are uncommitted either to a course of action or to others around them. It is also this definition that inspires the current writer's research interest.

The first requirement of testing the effects of commitment in the laboratory is that we be able to manipulate it, that we be able to vary it experimentally. Actually, very little experimental work has been done on commitment, in spite of the popularity of the term. Part of the problem has been in pinning down a clean definition of commitment. We must be able to operationalize the concept without other variables intruding. A concept which has overtones or connotations that vary from instance to instance is not only vague but also provides a major obstacle to precise implementation.

In the case of commitment, these varying connotations are particularly important. Some aspects of commitment involve things that psychologists already know something about. Indeed some uses of commitment sound strangely like old and well-researched variables in social psychology. If the term is to have any technical meaning whatsoever, then it is imperative that it can be distinguished from other variables and terms about which something is already known. Let me give you a couple of examples of the way the term commitment has been used, and perhaps you will see what I mean.

A volume by Moore and Feldman (1960) discusses issues of labor commitment. By labor commitment, they mean the extent to which one is committed to a job. For example, one could look at labor commitment among natives. Alverson (1968) did just this. He was interested in situational and background factors that contribute to the morale of the Bantu tribesmen working in industry. For Alverson, commitment refers to the extent to which the Bantu is committed to the idea of an industrial position. The term implicitly or explicitly includes such divergent things as the type of job the tribesman has in industry, whether or not he has a family, whether he had to sell his house and cattle before he came to take the job, how much he is being paid for the job, whether the job is clean or dirty, and so forth. Actually, Alverson's dissertation is an excellent piece of anthropological work, but I think we can agree that commitment is used a little loosely. A clean job and the sale of one's house and cattle may imply quite different psychological variables, even though their effects on morale are similar. In this case, we have difficulty in pinpointing a definition of commitment, indicating what is committing and what is not, or even if commitment is supposed to be an independent, intervening, or dependent variable. Let's take a very different example.

Suppose we have a group of people with a similar opinion; say that they are all against the war in Vietnam. Suppose, further, that some of these people are willing to carry signs indicating their opinion publicly and some are not. Could we say that the sign-carriers are committed and the non-sign-carriers are not? Certainly such an assertion would be consistent with several current definitions of commitment in social psychology, so perhaps we could. However, there are probably several other differences, besides commitment, between the two groups, even leaving aside the question of personality differences.

When we focus upon people who happen to carry signs and those who happen not to, there are a number of intruding or confounding variables. The sign-carriers and the non-sign-carriers could differ in a number of respects, many of them obvious. The two groups could differ in (*a*) the extremeness of their attitudes on the issue, both against the war but one group more than the other, (*b*) familiarity with the attitude issue (depth of knowledge about the surrounding circumstances of the war, leading some to be more confident of their opinion and more willing and able to defend it publicly), (*c*) social support for the attitude (degree of affiliation with others advocating such a stance, rendering opinions seemingly more or less popular and more or less likely to be attacked), and so forth.

Each of these variables, extreme attitude, familiar issue, and social support, is well researched. That is, in specific situations, such as willingness to volunteer for some act or reaction to counter-communications, we can predict with some success how the subject's behavior and attitudes will be affected. If the overt difference between our two hypothetical groups,—carrying a sign—merely reflects an underlying difference on some well-known psychological dimension, then it is superfluous to speak of the difference as one of commitment.

It would not add much merely to equate commitment with one of the variables involved, such as extremeness of attitude. If we limit commitment to mean simply extremeness of attitude, then we have just added a completely redundant term to the literature.

On the other hand, it is not useful to define commitment arbitrarily as some combination of variables, unless one is suggesting and, preferably, can demonstrate some qualitative or typological distinctiveness. That is, suppose one arbitrarily defined a committed individual as one who has all of the following: an extreme opinion on some issue, familiarity with the facts and background surrounding the issue, *and* social support for his opinion. We might then assert that the sign-carriers are committed because they have all three characteristics. This would be a useful typology if, and probably only if, all three characteristics were necessary to affect the behavior of sign carrying. To use the logically extreme case, if a person who had an extreme opinion, was familiar with the issue and had social support would *always* carry a sign if requested, and a person who had an equally extreme attitude, equal familiarity, but less social support would *never* carry a sign, then we would have excellent evidence of some qualitative distinctiveness. In that case, some particular combination of the three variables would be necessary to affect the behavior in question. However, as long as each variable affects the behavior independently,* the typological term is redundant. It adds little.

So the person who simply uses a complex behavior to point to as his definition may not help us much. When he says that by a committed person he means one who would carry a sign if requested, then he has not given us a definition that will provoke much thought or research.

In short, when we select our subjects nonrandomly, we run into many difficulties. However, random selection does not free us of all difficulties. This point is probably not so obvious. Let us take the next logical methodological step. Let us manipulate the behavior, experimentally. Suppose that we induce people to carry anti-war (Vietnam) signs and that we randomly assign people to these two experimental conditions. Would this be some sort of "pure" manipulation of commitment? What expectations would we have about such an experiment (aside from the ethical issues involved)?

First, we can say something about counter-attitudinal behavior. If the person carrying the sign is initially pro-war, then the act of carrying the anti-war sign should produce dissonance. With knowledge of the contingencies and incentives involved, we should be able to predict whether the act itself will affect the person's attitudes about Vietnam (see the next chapter for a more complete discussion of dissonant behavior).

* If they are independent, then when we hold any two of the three variables constant and increase the third, it should increase the likelihood that the subject will carry the sign. If we increase the second variable, the probability will increase even further. If the variables are independent, then they are, in a loose sense, additive in effects.

Second, we have some relatively clear notions about the person who is against the war and whose attitude is extreme. The act of carrying the anti-war sign should be consistent with his attitude and, other things being equal, should produce no dissonance. Even so, other things are often not equal and this case is not as simple as it sounds. The effects of carrying the sign depend on the circumstances surrounding the act. I will return to this point later.

The third point is more important for the moment. What can we say about the person who carries the sign and is against the war but whose attitude is not very extreme? To use the jargon of the typical attitude scale, and grossly oversimplify our case, let's call these people the two's and three's of the seven point scale. The question is, if the person has a mildly negative attitude and he is induced to carry an extremely negative sign publicly, would we expect any systematic effects on attitude? The answer is yes. We would expect such behavior to systematically affect attitude. Indeed a number of theoretical perspectives, involving role-playing, incentives, dissonance, and attribution, would all predict some change in attitude as a function of a behavior that is more extreme than one's attitude.

In our uncontrolled example, which involved no random assignment of subjects to condition, some of the difficulties were obvious. Several variables intruded, which would prevent any precise conclusion regarding a variable such as commitment. On the other hand, in our more carefully controlled example in which people would be induced to carry the signs, there are still several difficulties of a not dissimilar nature. The manipulations could systematically affect the attitude of the subject, leading the sign-carriers ultimately to have a more extreme attitude. Any subsequent differences between the two groups could as easily be due to the difference in attitude as any other variable, such as commitment. If we do not wish to equate commitment with extremeness of attitude, then a difference in attitude between two experimental groups blurs our picture of commitment.

These examples illustrate the difficulties of attempting experimental research with a concept which, like commitment, is used in the everyday language. It is not a simple task to strip the term of its superfluous aspects and control for other known variables without also discarding everything initially interesting about the topic. Indeed, with a concept like commitment, there is no a priori guarantee that there will be anything left after such a methodological strip.

The present monograph reports research in which we tried to control for intruding variables of the type we have just discussed. Although these variables are undoubtedly correlated with commitment in uncontrolled settings, we can demonstrate the independent status of commitment. We show the effects of commitment under highly controlled, "greenhouse" conditions.

Lucid presentation of the research requires that we make explicit our preliminary working assumptions about the variable. Subsequently, we will bring focus to our discussion by detailing an experimental example.

Preliminary Assumptions about Commitment

It should be made clear that what follows is not a theory, except in the picayune sense that any restricted set of not inconsistent assumptions make up a theory. The following statements might best be regarded as organizational assumptions that merely allow one to nose around in the empirical world. However, they should be made as explicit as possible to assist critical discussion.

Working Definition

For the purposes of discussion, commitment shall be taken to mean the *pledging or binding of the individual to behavioral acts* (Kiesler & Sakumura, 1966, p. 349). Except for the behavioral part, about which more shall be said later, one can see that this is a straightforward extrapolation from the dictionary. It is a reasonable, albeit somewhat unusual, point of departure for a psychological model—the naive psychology of the day, a dictionary definition.

Underlying Scale of the Variable

I assume that commitment is a continuous variable, rather than a dichotomous one. That is, people are referred to as more or less committed to some behavior, rather than being simply committed or not. This is a simple assumption but one which should be made explicit. Its theoretical and methodological importance shall become clear later.

Assumption 1

> The individual attempts to resolve inconsistencies between the attitudes he holds and behavioral acts which he, for one reason or another, is induced to perform. This assumption is quite similar, if not identical, to the main assumptions of the 'consistency' models proposed by Festinger (1957), Heider (1958), and Osgood (1960), and hence is supported by evidence related to those theories. We assume that to resolve the inconsistency one may change either the attitude or the act (including the psychological implications of the act) [Kiesler and Sakumura, 1966, p. 349].

This assumption merely allows one a point of contact with dissonance and other consistency theories prevalent in social psychology and has no other significance.

ASSUMPTION 2

"The effect of commitment is to make an act less changeable [Kiesler & Sakumura, 1966, p. 349]." This assumption is the most critical one of all, and at once betrays both the focus and the bias of the investigator. As discussed in the following chapter, a reasonable corollary to this assumption would be that commitment also makes the cognition representing the behavior more resistant to change as well. This corollary allows a point of contact between the present collection of assumptions and a variety of other models of cognitive consistency. We shall refer to this as the *cognitive corollary*. More detail on the justification and implications of this assumption will be presented later in the chapter.

Briefly, we will argue that explicit, attitudinally relevant behavior is something that the person must accept as integral to self, and on occasion, he must deal with it. The degree of commitment tells us how closely some behavior is tied to self and how easily it is to dispense with if necessary. To "unbind" himself, the person might deny to himself and others his having behaved that way, or he might reinterpret the act, compartmentalizing it and divorcing it from other behavior and belief, or he might change the implications of the act for self, perhaps asserting that he was forced to behave that way. However, to the extent that a person is bound to some explicit and attitudinally relevant behavior, he must accept it as integral to himself, to his self-view, and other attitudes and beliefs must be accommodated accordingly.

Assumptions 1 and 2, considered together, lead to two general hypotheses. First, if the act should be inconsistent with the subject's previous belief system, then commitment to the act leads the person to change his attitudes toward greater consistency with the act. It should be emphasized that there is no implication here that commitment alone leads to attitude change. I do not assume that commitment is an active mechanism (unless shown otherwise). Let's keep an open mind on that until we look at more evidence. We begin by positing that commitment is inert, and we shall see where that assumption leads us. The motivational force underlying the attitude change posed in this hypothesis is presumed to be the striving for consistency (or, alternatively, the desire to reduce inconsistency). It is what many would call dissonance.

Given inconsistency, the notion of commitment tells what the person will do. It provides the pillar around which the cognitive apparatus must be draped. In short, with the concept of commitment, we can specify what can be changed and so, presumably, what will be changed (given some motivation to change in the first place). Given some level of dissonance, for example, the greater the commitment to the dissonant act, the greater the expected change across subjects, because it is more difficult to "undo," reinterpret, or otherwise change the act and its meaning for the person. Dissonance equal, but present, the person should accommodate to whatever is most difficult to change in his cognitive world. (See Chapter III for a more complete discussion of the relationship of commitment to dissonance.)

The second hypothesis follows a similar reasoning. If the act is consistent with the subject's previous belief system, then commitment to the act should make the person more resistant to subsequent attack on his beliefs. Suppose the person carries out some explicit and attitudinally relevant behavior and he is committed to the behavior. (We haven't said how that happens yet.) The person, by assumption, is stuck with the behavior and its implications. If he accepted the attack on his beliefs and changed his attitudes on the issue, he would be in an uncomfortable position. He would have a new attitude, granted, which would relieve him of being under attack. However, he would still be tied to an explicit bit of behavior that would conflict with his new attitude. Of course, exactly what the person will do should depend logically on how committed he is to the behavior (how easy it is to rid oneself of the implications of the behavior) and how powerful the attack is. This interactive view of commitment and attack is the subject of Chapter IV.

In general, then, if the behavioral act is counter-attitudinal, then greater commitment should lead to greater attitude change so that act and attitude become more consistent. If, however, the behavioral act is consistent with one's current views, then commitment should have no (necessary) immediate effect upon belief but should produce greater resistance to change if the belief (and by implication, the act) should come under subsequent attack.

Assumption 3

In order to work with the concept of commitment, we need to make some working assumption about the relationship between the degree of commitment and the effects of commitment. The simplest assumption is an ordinally mapped relationship; in short, the greater the commitment, the greater the effect. Or, more formally, the magnitude of the effect of commitment should be positively and monotonically related to the degree of commitment. By implication, then, the greater the commitment to some behavior, the greater the attitude change when the act is inconsistent with the person's prior belief and the greater the resistance to subsequent attack when the act is consistent with prior opinion.

Assumption 4

Finally, we have to make some assumption about how one may manipulate commitment—a translation into operational terms. This translation of course is necessary before any research can be done. The operationalization of concepts is a step fraught with peril for any theory since it connects the abstract universe with the concrete one. I have rather blatantly assumed that one can manipulate commitment in several ways. Most of the techniques presented below as translations of commitment have been derived from other research; the remaining ways seem to fit intuitively into the same schema. I hypothesize, then, that one may increase the degree of commitment by increasing one or more of the following.

1. The explicitness of the act, e.g., how public or otherwise unambiguous the act was (cf., Hovland, Campbell, & Brock, 1960).
2. The importance of the act for the subject (cf., Sherif, Sherif, & Nebergall, 1965).
3. The degree of irrevocability of the act (see Gerard, 1968, for relevant discussion).
4. The number of acts performed by the subject (see Chapter IV). We must assume for the moment that the acts are additive in some way. They could be repetitions of the same act, or they could be separate behaviors that are closely connected in some way. (Obviously, this can get a little complicated here, given our definition of commitment, but the issue will be discussed in greater detail later.)
5. The degree of volition (or freedom or choice) perceived by the person in performing the act (cf., Freedman & Steinbruner, 1964). This requires a little explanation. This seems complicated, but anyone knowledgeable about dissonance theory will recognize that this is a simple extrapolation from typical manipulations in dissonance experiments. In short, it seems eminently reasonable to assume that the less the pressure put on a person to behave in a particular way, the more he is tied or bound to the behavior (the more he is committed to it in present context). Extrapolating from the dissonance literature, then, we view volition to be inversely related to the degree of external pressure or inducement. For example, the more money offered to a person to behave consistently with his beliefs, the less committed he would be to the act, and presumably, the less resistant he would be to any attack on this belief (as compared with someone who had received less money for the same act).

The Kiesler and Sakumura Experiment

The topic of commitment intrigued me. After thinking about it a bit, I made some preliminary assumptions to work with. The next conceptual step was to decide whether the assumptions were useful at all. (Should, for example, some or all of them be discarded?) The question of usefulness depends on a series of questions: Are the assumptions logically consistent? Do they help to organize existing data? Do they have interesting implications for research? In answer, they are logically consistent and these are not many data to organize. The implications for research are the topic of this monograph. The question of whether they are interesting or not is properly left to the reader.

It may be helpful in clarifying the issues to present an experimental example. This is a published experiment by Kiesler and Sakumura (1966). It is a simple experiment, but illustrative. Afterwards we shall return to a more theoretically oriented discussion, but using the experiment as a point of focus.

From the previous discussion it should be clear that the less one pays a person for performing an act consistent with his beliefs, the more committed he will be to the act. The greater the commitment to consonant behavior, the greater the resistance to subsequent attack on related belief. The Kiesler and Sakumura experiment tests specifically this hypothesis: The less the payment for some consonant behavior, the greater the resistance to subsequent attack on belief. The experimental design is presented in Table 2-1.

TABLE 2-1

EXPERIMENTAL DESIGN OF THE KIESLER AND SAKUMURA EXPERIMENT[a]

Sequence of events	Experimental		Control	
	$1	$5	$1	$5
Pretest	X	X	X	X
Consonant speech	$1	$5	$1	$5
Counter-communication	X	X	0	0
Posttest	X	X	X	X

[a] X indicates that subject received that treatment; 0 indicates that he did not.

Briefly, after a pretest of attitude, all subjects were induced to tape-record a speech consistent with their beliefs. All of the subjects were paid for making the speech, but half received one dollar and half received five dollars. Subsequently, each experimental subject read a counter-communication on the same issue, attacking his belief. Lastly, the attitude of each subject, experimental and control, was measured. The dependent variable was the amount of attitude change that each subject showed as the result of reading the counter-communication. Since the five-dollar subjects were presumably less committed to the consonant behavior than the one-dollar subjects, they should be less resistant to the attack. In other words, the five-dollar subjects should show greater attitude change than the one-dollar subjects.

The experimental procedure deserves a little more detail. The attitude issue that we selected for this experiment was that the legal age of voting should be lowered to eighteen. We used this item for a particular reason. I had used the same item as a filler item in other attitude change research and had noticed a bimodal distribution of scores (for sophomores at Ohio State University, the population from which the subjects for the Kiesler and Sakumura experiment were drawn). That is, people were not neutral on this issue, but were either for it or against it. As you shall see, such an item fit our purposes quite well.*

When a subject arrived at the appointed place, he was told that he was actually going to be in two separate and unrelated experiments during the hour. (This was not unusual at O.S.U., and subjects invariably accepted the information without comment.) Each subject first completed an attitude scale, expressing his opinions on a number of issues. Then,

> The experimenter covertly noticed whether the subject was pro or con on the key issue. The experimenter assigned the subject the communication consistent with the subject's position and asked him to read it into a tape recorder, identifying himself by name. The subjects were told that Dr. *E* would pay them $1.00 or $5.00 for doing this, depending on condition [Kiesler & Sakumura, 1966, pp. 350–351].

Each subject believed that his speech was to be used in a study of regional accents in demonstrations and seminars throughout the country. To justify the amount of money given, the experimenter drew an explicit analogy to residuals for television commercials. To wit, even though subjects were not ordinarily paid for experiments, it was justified in this experiment since the speech would be used several times. Note that this comment could justify either one dollar or five, and it had the advantage of allowing us to say the same thing to subjects in both conditions.

The subject was handed a prepared speech, and he went over it several times (to smooth out possible performance differences between experimental conditions), and then read the speech aloud into the tape recorder. When he had finished, he was told that that was the end of the first experiment. To separate the two portions of the experiment, the subjects were given a short break, during which the experimenter signed the subject's credit slip for the experiment and carried on a casual conversation.

The second part of the experiment was introduced following the break. This part was portrayed as being, of course, a second experiment but also supervised by a different faculty member (the experimenter was a graduate

* It perhaps would have been even better if we had used an attitude issue on which subjects held uniform opinions. Such an issue was not readily available, however.

student). Further, each subject was led to believe that he was the first person to participate in it. Pressed for time, the graduate student had not had time to discuss the "second" experiment with the relevant faculty member; he read the instructions from a paper and maintained that he was unable to answer any questions. The subject was then handed a counter-communication to read, and this was followed with a "personal inventory." The personal inventory had been duplicated by a different process than the scale used for the pretest, and the items were not only of different content, but they also had different formats, as well. However, the crucial item was repeated in identical form.

To summarize, experimental subjects completed an attitudinal pretest, then were induced to read a consonant speech into a tape recorder for which each was paid either one dollar or five dollars. They then took a short respite, read the counter-communication under a different pretext and, finally, completed the attitudinal posttest. Control conditions were additionally necessary to test for possible effects of the consonant act itself, without the impact of the counter-communication. Subjects in the two control conditions filled out the pretest, read the consonant speech into the tape recorder (for either one dollar or five, depending on condition), and also took the short break; but they were then given the posttest and never saw the counter-communication.

TABLE 2-2

RESULTS OF THE KIESLER AND SAKUMURA EXPERIMENT[a]

Condition	Payment	
	$1	$5
Experimental *Ss*	.14	.76
(*N*)	(32)	(36)
Control *Ss*	−.025	−.15
(*N*)	(20)	(17)

[a] Dependent variable is attitude change in the direction advocated in the counter-communication.

The results from this experiment are presented in Table 2-2, and are arrayed as expected. First, notice the two control conditions. Payment had no differential effect on these conditions. The change in the five-dollar control condition was very similar to that found in the one-dollar control condition (−.15 vs. −.025; a slight intensification of attitude in each case towards greater extremeness, although neither condition approaches being significantly different from zero change). The five-dollar subjects did not become more or less extreme than the one-dollar subjects as a consequence of simply making the consonant speech.

The experimental conditions also have the expected effect. We expected greater resistance to the attack on belief in the one-dollar condition than in the five-dollar condition, presumably as a result of the one-dollar subjects being more committed to the behavior of making the (explicit and attitudinally relevant) speech. The one-dollar subjects showed very little change (+.14 on a seven-point scale) and were very similar to the controls in that respect. The five-dollar subjects evidenced considerably greater change (that is, less resistance to the counter-communication), an amount that is significantly different from both the control conditions and the one-dollar experimental condition.

There are two summary conclusions to be drawn. First and foremost, the less the financial inducement for a consonant behavior, the more resistant a subject was to attack on a related belief at a later time. This is the main implication of this experiment for the study of commitment. But there is a second point which, as we shall see, has both methodological and theoretical implications: Differing degrees of commitment to the behavior had no (differential, at least) effect on existing attitude. The commitment merely determined one's reaction to the subsequent attack.

An Alternative View

Gerard (1968) has argued that the difference between the one-dollar and the five-dollar conditions in the Kiesler–Sakumura experiment is unrelated to commitment. He distinguishes between the concept of commitment and one he calls "conviction," and he argues that the difference between the one-dollar and the five-dollar conditions in the Kiesler–Sakumura experiment is one of conviction, not commitment. He goes on to say that the subject in the high-commitment (one-dollar) condition, because of minimal pressure to perform the consonant behavior, added "justifications" for having agreed to advocate the opinion in his speech. These justifications, Gerard argues, increased the subject's depth of conviction in his opinion. I ask merely that, if the subject did add justifications in the high commitment conditions, what is the evidence for such a process? Semantics aside, this assertion logically implies that there should be a systematic difference between the commitment control conditions. That is, if one adds justifications as a function of payment (and changes one's attitudes as a result), then the one-dollar control condition should be more extreme in attitude than the five-dollar control condition.

Of course, we observed no such difference, and Gerard's explanation of the data would appear to be relatively implausible.*

The purpose of the control conditions in the experiment was to assess possible alternative explanations of the data, which are based on possible combinatorial effects of consonant behavior and payment. Kiesler and Sakumura mention specifically two such explanations: (*a*) that a small payment for consonant behavior produced a greater "strengthening of belief" than a larger payment for the same behavior, (*b*) that a small payment somehow made the belief more important (or less important, for that matter) than the larger payment. Both of these classes of explanations, or rival hypotheses, would lead one to predict a corresponding difference between the commitment control conditions. There is no such difference, thus rendering these explanations ineffective.

A Methodological Note

The commitment manipulations by themselves produced no differences in attitude (as evidenced by the lack of difference between control conditions). However, we did not think that this lack of difference was accidental; we worked very hard for it. The main function of the control conditions was to avoid (at worse, assess) other possible variables which the performance of consonant behavior could involve. As mentioned earlier, differential degrees of dissonance could be produced between conditions even though the behavior is superficially consonant. Differences in the satisfaction with the job one has done in reading the consonant speech (especially so, if it is not a prepared speech but instead something that the subject prepares, such as an essay on the issue) or differences in the embarrassment one has incurred in doing so are also possible in this situation. Any such variables (and I have not given an exhaustive list) could produce systematic differences in attitude between conditions even though the subject is performing some behavior that is presumably consonant with his beliefs.

Further, I think it no difficult task to produce a difference between conditions involving consonant behavior. Using such variables as task satisfaction, task effort, or biased scanning of arguments (Janis & Gilmore, 1965) one could make the five-dollar control condition either more or less extreme in attitude than the comparable one-dollar condition. It is naive to assume that any old consonant behavior is committing.† In the Kiesler–Sakumura exper-

* Further discussion of the "depth of conviction" notion is presented in the next chapter. Of course, the explanation is not completely ruled out since the effect might possibly be mediated by some variable that does not affect the measurement of attitude and so is undetected by it.

† I do not mean to suggest that I am only interested in those consonant behaviors clearly involving commitment.

iment, we made an explicit attempt to keep other relevant variables constant between conditions. The fact that there were no differences in attitude between the two control conditions suggests that we were successful and allows greater specificity in the inferences one can draw from the difference between the experimental conditions.

Metatheoretical Considerations

The set of assumptions elaborated earlier represents, in a sense, a view of commitment without really being a theory of commitment. It is a model that attempts to describe the process underlying commitment. It focuses principally on behavior but, as we shall see in later chapters, need not do so to the exclusion of other considerations (recall the cognitive corollary). The Kiesler–Sakumura experiment supports the initial set of assumptions. An alternative way of looking at this experiment is to think of it as a demonstration—a demonstration that, when one strips from the concept of commitment such notions as importance, extremeness of attitude, involvement, dissonance, social support, conviction, and what have-you, there is something left. It is a something obviously of interest since it dramatically affects one's reaction to an attack on one's attitude, without in the meantime affecting the attitude itself. It appears to be an empirical representation of the cognitive "freezing" of which Lewin spoke.

On the other hand, an experiment of this sort does not answer a number of important questions. Why exactly does the one-dollar group show greater resistance than the five-dollar group? What is the process that an individual enmeshed in such a situation goes through in order that we obtain these data? How does this happen—what psychological factors could produce or justify a statement that someone is more or less tied or bound by his behavior? These are questions that will receive considerable discussion later in the monograph, but they also deserve preliminary consideration now. First let us speculate about the process that the subjects might be going through.

The Process: A Phenomenological Guess

The skeleton that we have to explain is almost magical in bare outline: Incentives for performing consonant behavior do not affect one's attitude at the time, but they do determine one's reaction to subsequent influence attempts. It's as if the person did not critically evaluate the incentive at the time of action, but it becomes crucial later. I say "as if," but I suspect this is probably what happens. After all, there is no necessary reason why consonant behavior should be terribly disturbing to its originator. We mentioned in the last chapter that there are many circumstances under which explicit, attitudinally relevant behavior *is* disturbing to the individual, and he is often wary of being inveigled into such behavior. Perhaps such behavior is even usually disturbing, but certainly not always; and in the Kiesler–Sakumura experiment we tried to remove such caution provoking elements as differential satisfaction, dissonance, fear of attack, and other implications.

To behave consistently with one's beliefs, for whatever amount of money, need not produce much discomfort or psychological work for the individual. A committing act, therefore, would not necessarily initiate any active process (other things being equal). In a sense, the attack provokes the active process. One way to deal effectively with a counter-communication is to change one's opinion. The nice thing about opinions and attitudes is that they are private. Hence, the person need not admit, perhaps even to himself, that his attitude has been changed. For example, consider two people in a discussion. In response to the other's effective argument, a person may not have to admit that his opinion has been changed by the other. He may simply say, "That's an interesting view and I quite agree with it." He *agrees*, but he hasn't been *changed.** Face-saving? Perhaps. But as we shall argue later, face-saving can be just as important privately (i.e., to oneself) as publicly.

In an extreme case a person cannot agree. The labor leader who has sacrificed his chances for wealth and an easy life would have a difficult time accepting the premise that a worker should have no voice in determining working conditions and incentives. A person who believes that the angels have told him that the world is coming to an end and who, in that belief, gives up his job, sells his worldly possessions for a pittance, and abandons his friends to flee to a safe mountain would reject any argument that angels do not exist.

Everyone might agree that both the labor leader and the prophet cannot accept the new arguments because they are committed. But why? Perhaps because they each have an explicit behavioral past that is difficult to deny or to undo or to reinterpret. They have to live with this prior behavior, and it is much more difficult to renounce the past than it is to dismiss disagreement. What, then, is the typical reaction to disagreement?

I am convinced that in an everyday situation (outside of the laboratory), the first reaction to an opposing opinion is to ignore it. People do not ordinarily have to face up to attitudinal discrepancies in the real world (see, for example, Hovland, 1959, for a discussion of the differences between conditions in the laboratory and the field). Life progresses in a stream of behavior, to use Barker's term. If one wishes to respond to an opposing view

* We assume that people don't like to admit changing their opinions. Although suggesting open-mindedness, change also has overtones of being wishy-washy and lacking in initial knowledge.

such as overhearing a remark in a bus, reading some view expressed in the newspaper, or catching a snide aside in the conversation of one's superior, then one must break out of the ongoing stream to do it. And one must do it immediately, or, metaphorically speaking, one is swept beyond the point of simple response. In short, ordinarily one does not have to do anything in response to opposition. One is simply still, and it is then too late to do anything. The situation resolves itself without any effort or energy expended by the individual.

I think of this process as analogous to the research carried out by Latanè and Darley (1970). They find that in reactions to crises, whether fires, others' fits, or whatever, people react immediately or not at all. It's as if there were only one choice moment, and if one does not respond then, the opportunity is lost forever. Whether one responds or not depends upon a number of situational and background factors, but most people don't respond. The same thing could be true of response to attitudinal challenge. A number of situational and background factors would affect whether one responded in a given instance, but if one does not respond immediately, then the opportunity (and the necessity) to respond is lost.

Sometimes, however, one is forced to respond to attitudinal attack. What then? It seems reasonable to suppose that the first response is a combination of Is it me he is talking about? and What do I think? If a communication argues forcefully for one point of view, then there is a subtle implication that someone would be silly to hold the opposite view. Hence, Is it me he is talking about? To determine that, one has to ask What do I think?

I think that one's first impulse is to agree with a communication. (In communication studies in the laboratory, for example, almost anything will produce attitude change.) Suppose one simply tries agreement on for size. One asks, Can I agree? There are a number of reasons why one perhaps could not agree with an opposing view, but one of them is his previous behavior and its contingencies, i.e., the circumstances under which the actor behaved. One's own behavior, as we shall argue in more detail in the next section, is an important part of one's definition of self.

One has to live with prior behavior in some way. One can deny having behaved that way, which is often difficult, particularly to one's self. One can distort the behavior in some way, adding extra shades or emphasizing particular details at the cost of others. Or one can reinterpret the meaning of the behavior. All we are saying is that the greater the commitment to some behavior, the more difficult it is to deny, distort, or reinterpret the behavior.

In the Kiesler–Sakumura experiment, one of the properties of the behavior of recording the speech is that there was money associated with it. The more money accepted, the easier it would be for the subject to discard the meaning and implications of his behavior, by simply telling himself that he did it for the money. It is therefore more difficult for the high-commitment (one-dollar) subjects in the Kiesler–Sakumura experiment to accept the new opinion since it would then leave the subject in the uncomfortable state of having an opinion that conflicts with undeniable behavior.

This trying-on-for-size notion leads to an intuitive understanding of the Kiesler–Sakumura results. An inferring-one's-attitude-from-one's-behavior notion (Kelley, 1967; Bem, 1965; Kiesler, Nisbett, & Zanna, 1969) leads to a similar conclusion but with an added assumption. That is, suppose one infers one's attitude from one's behavior and its dispositional properties. The less the outside pressures for one's behavior, the more likely one is to infer that the behavior reflected one's true attitude. (We shall discuss these issues in detail later in Chapter VIII.) In the present experiment we must assume that there is some reason why this inference did not take place for the control conditions. Perhaps it was because the behavior was so innocuous that there was no reason to reflect on its attitudinal properties. It is only later, when faced with the counter-communication, that one must think about his attitude. At that time then, one assumes that when one was paid very little for recording the speech, the speech must have represented one's opinion. That was the reason for the behavior. On the other hand, the five-dollar subjects infer instead that the motivation for recording the speech was financial—that they did it for the money. The trying-on-for-size and the inferring-one's-belief notions might be thought of as reflecting the questions Is it me he is talking about? and What do I think?, respectively. In that sense they do not necessarily constitute rival hypotheses about the commitment process but may instead reflect different aspects of the same process. In both cases the emphasis is on behavior and its meaning for the individual.

The Behaving Self

In the Kiesler–Sakumura experiment, we suggested that subjects were differentially committed to an explicit and attitudinally relevant behavior. As a result of varying levels of commitment, possible responses to a subsequent attack on attitude were different also.

This view implies a pre-eminence to behavior (over attitude) that may strike the reader as slightly exaggerated. The emphasis in American social psychology has been directed more toward cognition and the behavior that follows *from* it. After all, our more philosophically oriented critic might maintain, Descartes did say, "*Je pense, donc je suis,*" not "*J'agis, donc je suis.*" In that view, the defining character of one's behavior is only a peripheral aspect of self, dependent upon a suspicion that others expect our attitudes and behavior to be consistent, and that they might observe our behavior.

The question then is whether the effects of commitment to behavior reflect merely the person's desire to appear consistent before others.

We maintain here that one's behavior is closely related to, is indeed an integral part of, one's self-image. One's self-view or self-concept is not completely stable, even for adults. Marlowe and Gergen, in reviewing this literature in the *Handbook of Social Psychology* (1968), emphasize the temporary modifications and fluctuations in self-descriptions and self-ratings. I interpret this to mean that one's view of oneself is somewhat fluid and difficult to be precise about and, hence, that the person's view of himself is partially dependent upon his interpretation of his own behavior. Deutsch (1968), in his discussion of Lewin's theory in the same handbook, makes a similar point:

> The person in the life space or "the behaving self," to borrow a more expressive term employed by Tolman . . . , is the individual as related to the other entities in his life space . . . the behaving self may be thought of as the individual's perception of his relations to the environment he perceives. The psychological environment and his behaving self are interdependent components of the life space [p. 424].

Sarbin and Allen (1968) also think that private behavior has important implications for one's self-view:

> We should also view the performer as observing and evaluating his own role behavior; in this case the performer forms a one-person audience for his own role enactment. According to Mead (1934) the "me" is the role performance viewed by the person. The "I," as used by Mead, is close to our use of the term self or self conception. The "I" (self) serves as observer and reacts toward the "me" as another person, thereby serving as an audience [p. 529].

Heider (1958), Kelley (1967), and Bem (1965) also all discuss situations in which the individual makes inferences about self on the basis of his own behavior, whether these inferences involve responsibility for behavior, self-attribution of "dispositional properties" or attitudes, respectively. (The Heider, Kelley, and Bem views have implications also far beyond the present point and will be discussed in some detail at an appropriate later point.)

The research to be presented later will empirically justify the metatheoretical point now being made: The effects of commitment to some behavior do not depend simply on the individual's desire to appear consistent before others. The person's view of himself, his social identity, depends partly on his own behavior and his interpretation of his own behavior.

The Behavior in a Larger Context

Lewin and Grabbe (1945) make the point that behavior does not occur in isolation; it is always related to something else in a larger context. Not only is it related but it is interpreted by the individual in a larger context, perhaps being fitted into some unit of cognitive organization, such as Kelly's (1955) *construct* or Harvey, Hunt, and Schroeder's (1961) *concept*. In short, each act may be related to other acts, connected with other dispositions, and interpreted within a larger frame of reference. As a result, one should not take Lewin's notion of the "freezing" property of behavior too literally or in the absolute sense. When a person is induced to perform some behavior for a particular amount of money, he is only committed to the behavior relative to some other level of inducement. He is not committed in the absolute sense, not left to dangle forever on the petard of a single indiscretion. A single act, or several, are not irrevocable, only more or less so compared to something else. One should therefore not expect too much.

For example, consider some recent work on treatment intervention by Caplan (1968) on street gangs. Caplan has derived a multiple stage model on the progress of treatment. One of these he calls the *commitment* stage, in which

> The boy commits himself verbally to the adoption of the new behaviors required to meet the objective and does not deter the worker from instituting a variety of preparatory arrangements and pragmatic intervention steps to facilitate the behavior change. He appears ready for a conscientious effort to modify his behavior along lines which are often at variance with past or established behavior [pp. 67–68].

This is perhaps a necessary step in the progress of treatment, but this verbal agreement is a very low level of commitment, against which are pitted the whole repertory of previous behavior. Consequently, one would not expect a very powerful freezing effect to take place. And it does not. Caplan computes the direction and frequency of movement from the commitment stage, either upward to the *success* stage or downward, backsliding to some previous stage. He found that 57% of the subjects reaching the commitment stage subsequently abandoned their verbal commitment and new behavior and moved backward in the treatment process. What is important then is the level of commitment, not just some commitment.

The Case of Behavior Tesserae, or, Are Only the Star Acts Entertaining?

Barker (1963) differentiates between naturally occurring behavioral units and behavior tesserae. A behavioral unit is a naturally occurring segment of behavior, part of the ordinary stream. Behavior tesserae are artificial pieces or bits of behaviors that are selected or instigated by an investigator and are a consequence of research methods which cut off or isolate a segment of behavior from its place in a naturally occurring stream. The concept of behavior tesserae is a compelling one and has two main implications for the Kiesler–Sakumura experiment under discussion and other similar research.

The first is a possible criticism. That is, some might say that the behavior in the Kiesler–Sakumura experiment is so minor and innocuous that one wonders whether it has anything to do with the dramatic aspects of commitment that one is accustomed to associate with that term: sacrifice, dedication, extreme behavior, and so forth. Is the tiny difference between conditions really commitment? Would the situation be qualitatively or only quantitatively different with so-called "real" behavior—part of the natural stream. In other words, are only the star acts entertaining or just more so than the secondary acts? This is actually a different way of approaching a question already addressed. We concluded that having a small difference between conditions represents both a theoretical and a methodological advance; it allows a more precise conclusion by stripping the process of possible contributing variables. We cannot but conclude that putting the more dramatic aspects which the layman associates with commitment back into our experiment would only produce a more dramatic difference in the dependent variable.

However, that is not to say that one may extrapolate from the operations used in an experiment and expect that they would have the same power if used outside of the laboratory. This is another implication of the concept of behavior tesserae for laboratory research in general. Any behavior produced in the laboratory is cut off and bounded from the ongoing stream of behavior, just as Barker suggests. Being cut off and bounded, small behaviors in the laboratory are likely to have a more powerful effect than they would if they were immersed in an ongoing stream. Behavior in the stream is much more fluid, lending itself less readily to interpretation by the performer and demanding less of his attention. For that reason, we do not suggest that a difference in incentives of one dollar and five dollars would have a large effect in a more complex setting. Any effect obtained, we maintain, would be in the hypothesized direction, but outside of the laboratory one needs a much larger difference in the independent variable to effect the comparable difference on the dependent variable.

III

COMMITMENT AND DISSONANCE

In the last chapter, we reviewed some popular ideas about commitment, offered a working definition and a few preliminary assumptions, described a pivotal experiment, and discussed some of the implications and issues raised by this study. In so doing we ignored the source of the most frequent usage of the concept of commitment: dissonance theory. In the current chapter we will try to rectify this intentional oversight, by examining the typical uses of commitment by researchers of dissonance theory, relate these to the present view, describe an experiment on the interactive effects of commitment and dissonance, and end with the ubiquitous discussion of issues.*

With regard to dissonance theory, the term commitment most frequently appears in papers concerning forced compliance and decision-making. Festinger (1964) says that "a decision carries a commitment with it if the decision unequivocally affects subsequent behavior . . . that the decision has clear implications for the subsequent unrolling of events as long as the person stays with that decision [p. 156]." Secord and Backman (1964) also equate commitment with an "irrevocable choice situation [p. 150]." Brehm and Cohen (1962), in an often quoted statement, say,

> We assume that a person is committed when he has decided to do or not to do a certain thing, when he has chosen one (or more) alternatives, and thereby rejected

* Most readers of this monograph will be, I suspect, thoroughly familiar with dissonance theory and will need no reintroduction or review. For those who are not, a note at the end of the first chapter offers a brief review and the basic theory.

> one (or more) alternatives, when he actively engages in a given behavior or has engaged in a given behavior. Any one or combination of these behaviors can be considered a commitment [p. 7].

These definitions of commitment by dissonance theorists sound straightforward enough. However, I would argue that, used in this way, commitment really becomes a "throw-away" concept. Why?—two reasons, both specific to dissonance theory. First, it ultimately leads to equating commitment with a firm decision. Second, the situational definitions of commitment also theoretically define the presence or arousal of dissonance. One is confident that dissonance has been aroused only when there has been an irrevocable decision, because it is only then that one can a priori say that one cognition implies the opposite of another. In neither case does commitment have any independent status. Let me detail the argument a bit.

The dissonant relationship between two cognitions, when one cognition implies the obverse of the other, is a major input for dissonance theory. However, the question of psychological implication has been a major metatheoretical thorn. (For relevant discussion see Abelson, 1968; Aronson, 1968; and Kiesler, Collins, and Miller, 1969.) A decision has been used as the prototype for the presence of dissonance; that is, as the example par excellance of psychological implication. When a person makes, for example, a choice between two objects (he buys a Ford, rather than a Chevrolet, say) then it is relatively simple to assess what implies what. Everything positive about the Ford and everything negative about the Chevrolet is consistent with the choice made: Ford-positive and Chevrolet-negative imply "choose Ford." On the other hand, things negative about the Ford and positive about the Chevrolet are inconsistent with the choice; they imply the opposite decision and, therefore, theoretically create dissonance.

But a decision is necessary to create dissonance, in this context. It is not until one rejects the Chevrolet and its fine points and accepts the Ford with the occasional negative feature that a question of psychological implication arises. Theoretically, merely prefering the Ford does not have the same impact: One does not have to deal with the negative aspects of the Ford nor give up the positive features of the Chevrolet.

For dissonance to be present and for any question of psychological implication, one has to *buy* the Ford, thereby *rejecting* the Chevrolet. However, to say that one is then committed to the decision is, to my mind, simply another way of saying that one has decided. And this is one reason why I think that this usage of the term makes commitment a "throwaway" concept. One is using it redundantly. The second statement is sneaked in the back way. Commitment not only means having made a firm decision, it also indicates the presence of dissonance, since there is no dissonance until a decision is made. This dual implication could and, as we shall discuss later, does lead to confusion.

But does the term not have its uses to describe perhaps different types of decisions (or decisions on different dimensions)? For example, the difference between a person telling his wife that he has decided to buy the Ford and actually buying it? Perhaps, but decisions differ on a number of dimensions, and simply using commitment to cover all the possibilities not only does injustice to an otherwise useful concept, but probably obscures quite important dimensions of decisions and the decision-making process. Decisions do vary in the extent to which they have "implications for the subsequent unrolling of events." However, they also differ in how easily they may be revoked (a rich man versus a poor man buying the car, for example); they differ in how public they are and how much and in what detail one has to account for them to others; they may only affect oneself or a number of other people; they differ according to how much one has to give up to obtain the chosen alternative; and so forth. Does each of these variations have the same psychological meaning? No, I don't think so, and using one term to cover all this and indicating the presence of dissonance as well glosses over much contextual richness and important detail.

Fortunately, dissonance theorists also use commitment in a second way, one that is quite similar to the definition that I have given here. Of course, behavior is not mentioned since behavior is not an input for dissonance theory. The relevant inputs for dissonance theory are cognitions and cognitive elements, but this still leads to an easy extrapolation. The behavior, making a speech against reducing the voting age, becomes in dissonance terms the knowledge or the cognition that "I made a speech against reducing the voting age."

Brehm and Cohen (1962) say that "in addition . . . commitment increases the resistance to change of an element (or set of elements) and therefore affects the kinds of attempts to reduce dissonance that may occur [p. 8]." Cognitive resistance is much closer to our definition of commitment than is an irrevocable choice. We defined commitment as the degree to which one is bound or tied to some behavior. As mentioned, it is useful to add the simple corollary to our set of assumptions that one of the effects of commitment is to make the cognition representing the behavior more resistant to change.

There are those that find such formality fatuous. However, mention the word commitment to a social psychologist and one of his early associations will be something to do with dissonance theory. To discuss commitment sensibly, one must be prepared to make some point of contact with dissonance theory, preferably both conceptually and empirically. The purpose of this chapter is just that, to discuss the relationship of commitment to dissonance.

However, the issues are very complex and entangled, and it is best to proceed as simply as we can. The first step is to present a study which provides a connection between commitment to consonant behavior and the typical dissonance experiment.

The Interactive Effects of Commitment and Dissonance: An Experiment

Recall that in the Kiesler–Sakumura experiment subjects were more or less committed to a behavior consistent with their belief and that then that belief was attacked. One way to think of this experimental design is that commitment was varied, while dissonance (created by the attack) was kept constant. In the experiment to be reported below (Kiesler, Pallak, and Kanouse, 1968), commitment and dissonance were varied independently.

Description

The sequential analysis of this experiment is presented in Table 3-1. As shown there, there are three important points in this procedure. In the first time period, the subject was induced to perform a consonant act, and the degree of commitment to the act was varied. Later, in the second time period (and independently of the first), the subject enacted a dissonant behavior and the degree of dissonance was varied. The two behaviors, consonant and dissonant, were logically related; that is, the dissonant behavior was also inconsistent with the belief associated with the consonant behavior. Finally, at point 3 in time, the subject completed a posttest, assessing his attitudes on both issues.

TABLE 3-1

Sequential Analysis of the Kiesler, Pallak, and Kanouse Procedure

Time Periods[a]	Behavior or Variations
1. Consonant behavior (Topic 1)	Public, private, or control speech
2. Dissonant behavior (Topic 2)	Subject writes dissonant essay under high or low choice; control subject writes irrelevant essay
3. Posttest	All subjects complete posttest

[a] Each time period was handled by a different experimenter.

The experimental aspects of the study can be represented by a 2 × 2 factorial design. It is as if the subject first took part in a consonant commitment experiment, and then participated in a typical (forced compliance) dissonance experiment. The subject first recorded a speech, consistent with his attitude, against raising tuition at his university (a large state university with low tuition). Commitment to this act was manipulated by varying the future use of the speech. In the high-commitment condition, the subject expected the content of his speech and his association with it to be made public in the future, whereas in the low-commitment condition, the subject expected to remain anonymous.

Later, in what was presumably a second study, each subject went through the dissonance part of the experiment. To avoid suspicion, we decided to use a logically related issue for the creation of dissonance, rather the identical issue used for the commitment manipulations. Each subject was induced to write an essay in favor of making public universities more like private universities, either in a condition of high choice (high dissonance) or low choice (low dissonance). It was suggested to each subject that making public universities more like private ones would, of course, necessitate a tuition increase, among other things. In short, the subjects were uniformly against a tuition increase: They first performed a behavior consistent with this opinion and subsequently acted dissonantly with the same opinion (although specifically on a different issue). This leaves us with a factorial design with two levels of consonant commitment and two levels of subsequent dissonance.

Control groups are imperative in this case because we need baselines to assess the effects of commitment without dissonance, and vice versa. The addition of a set of conditions without commitment and another set without dissonance enlarges the design to 3×3. Note also, that this design allows us to assess the joint effects of commitment and dissonance on two issues: one specific to the manipulation of commitment and the other specific to subsequent dissonance arousal.

Since the procedural details of this experiment are very complicated, the method section of the Kiesler, Pallak, and Kanouse article is reprinted in its entirety below.

Subjects and Design. A total of 161 male and female undergraduates at Michigan State University volunteered and were each paid $1.50 to participate in a study on "regional speech accents." All subjects were run individually. A total of eight subjects were dropped from the analysis because they indicated suspicion to the post-tester. Another four subjects elected to leave at the choice manipulation. One subject did not fill in his final form completely and another worked on the local newspaper (invalidating the manipulation explained below), leaving a final sample of 147 subjects.

The basic experimental design was a 2×2 after-only, factorial design comparing public versus private commitment to a consonant position and high versus low choice to perform a subsequent dissonant act. In addition, the design necessitated three sets of control conditions: public and private commitment only without subsequent dissonance, high and low dissonance only with no prior commitment, and one condition involving no commitment and no dissonance. The control conditions were necessary to provide base-line levels against which to compare the experimental conditions.

Procedure. When the subjects arrived the experimenter explained that the study was investigating "regional speech accents" by having students make a taped speech. He went on to say that the best way to do this was to have students read a prepared speech containing a number of key words and phrases on a very familiar topic. Since there were presumably to be a number of prepared speeches, the subject was to be the only student who read "this particular speech." The speech which each student read opposed tuition increases at Michigan State. The experimenter told the subject to read the speech twice aloud as naturally as possible, for practice.

Commitment Manipulation. Commitment was varied by telling the subject that the speech, which advocated a position consistent with the subject's own, would be made public or would remain anonymous. In the high-commitment condition the experimenter stated that the subject's tape would be a part of a nationwide study; that "in cooperation with Michigan State" the tape would be used in several classes for instructional purposes; hence the subject's speech would have a wide audience. In addition, the subject was asked to include his name, age, and campus address on the tape. Finally, the experimenter stated, "Oh, by the way, I suppose students who hear your tape will probably think it represents your personal opinion—this typically happens but, as I mentioned earlier, we're interested only in speech accents."

In the low-commitment condition the subject was told that his taped speech would be a part of a nationwide study, and that the tape would be used in classes. However, the experimenter stated that no one would recognize the tape since "for our own analysis and presentation, these tapes are literally chopped up, and individual words and phrases are juxtaposed with words and phrases from other samples of accents. Thus your tape will be completely anonymous. No one will know who you are." In the three no-commitment-control conditions (high, low, and no dissonance) subjects recorded under conditions of anonymity a speech advocating remedial classes in English and mathematics.

After the speech was recorded the experimenter explained that normally the project took an hour, but since not all the equipment was set up, the subject was finished. He added, however, that the University was interested in interviewing all students participating in the project. Accordingly, the subject was to go to another building to be interviewed by "the graduate assistant to the dean." The experimenter said that he had spoken shortly before to the graduate assistant to the dean, who unfortunately had indicated that he was ½ hour behind schedule. The graduate assistant to the dean had suggested that the subject fill the waiting time by participating in a survey being conducted by a graduate student at Michigan State. The experimenter explained that he did not know anything about the survey, but that it obviously would not take long.

Dissonance Manipulation. Dissonance was varied by manipulating the degree of choice in writing a counter-attitudinal essay. The first experimenter had been blind to the ensuing choice condition up to this point, but now randomly assigned the subject to either the high-choice (high-dissonance) or low-choice (low-dissonance) condition by referring surreptitiously to a table of random numbers.

In the high-choice condition the experimenter then continued,

Now I want you to understand that you don't have to do this unless you want to—

your obligation is finished and you have been paid. Since it's probably more interesting than sitting around, however, why don't you see what it's all about?

In the low-choice condition the experimenter said, "Now I want you to understand that, since you've been paid for the hour, you may use up the unexpired time by participating in this survey." In this manner the first experimenter (Experimenter 1) was able to structure the choice manipulation used in the subsequent dissonance task, without being aware of the subsequent choice condition while commitment was being manipulated.

At this point another experimenter (Experimenter 2), allegedly the anticipated graduate student, entered the room and introduced himself to Experimenter 1. Experimenter 1 explained that everything was arranged for Experimenter 2 to use the subject in his survey. He then turned to the subject and reemphasized the choice manipulation. To high-choice subjects, Experimenter 1 said, "I want to emphasize that you don't have to do this. You have already completed your obligation for the $1.50." To the low-choice subjects, Experimenter 1 said, "You understand, then, that this will fulfill your obligation for the $1.50. You kind of have to do it."

Experimenter 2 explained to the subject that his office was in the student services building (on the other side of campus, approximately ½ mile away). He noted that this was too far to walk, and suggested that they try to find an empty classroom nearby. Experimenter 1 helpfully suggested a classroom at the end of the hall which he "thought was free."

On arrival at the classroom, Experimenter 2 explained to the subject that he was a graduate student working with "the Student Committee for the Study of Educational Issues," and that he was attempting to get advanced student reaction to a topic which would be debated on campus later that summer, namely, public versus private university education. At this point Experimenter 2 pointed to a large poster he had been carrying, headed "Campus Debate: Public vs. Private University Education." The campus-wide debate was presumably to involve classroom discussion, a running forum in the campus newspaper, and a series of public lectures and debates later in the summer. The purpose of the survey, Experimenter 2 explained, was to "sample student opinion" and "crystallize the issues which students feel are most important" in advance. Accordingly, students participating in the survey were being asked to write a brief essay on some aspect of the general issue. Experimenter 2 added that students had been writing down anything they wished, but it had become necessary to "narrow it down," since some sides were better represented than others. The subject was then asked to write a paragraph or two arguing that public universities should become more like private ones.

Experimenter 2 explained that the essays would be published by the committee in an initial forum in the campus newspaper, which would launch the debate and give people concrete opinions to agree or disagree with in subsequent debating. Experimenter 2 added that he recognized that it might be very difficult for the subject to organize his thoughts in just a few minutes' time, and consequently a memo had been prepared for the subject, "to help you get started organizing your own ideas." Experimenter 2 handed the subject the memo, which listed five implications of "making public universities more like private ones," one of which was the implication, "sizable tuition increases for state universities."

After the subject had read the memo Experimenter 2 reiterated the choice manipulation. To high-choice subjects he said, "As Mr. Pallak explained, you don't have to write the essay. You're not obligated in any way to do this." To the low-choice subjects, he said, "As Mr. Pallak explained, you do have to write the essay, and when you finish you will have completed your obligation for the money he paid you." The subject was given paper on which to write his arguments, headed "Public universities should more closely resemble private universities." After the subject had completed and signed the essay Experimenter 2 gave him detailed instructions on how to reach the office of the graduate assistant to the dean. The no-commitment control subjects, who had previously recorded a speech favoring remedial classes in English and mathematics, also wrote the essay favoring public universities over private universities.

In the no-dissonance control conditions the subjects wrote an essay on remedial classes in English and mathematics. However, in the condition with double controls, subjects first gave a speech favoring remedial classes in English and mathematics for the commitment manipulation, and in the subsequent situation wrote an essay on allowing cars on campus.

Posttest and Debriefing. To get to the office of the bogus graduate assistant to the dean the subject had to go down four flights of stairs, traverse approximately a block to a building entitled Olds Hall, and go up three flights of stairs to the office of the graduate assistant. The office was one normally occupied by a full professor, and was very comfortably furnished. The third experimenter (Experimenter 3) introduced himself to the subject as the graduate assistant to the dean, and asked the subject to sit down. He explained that Michigan State was very interested in obtaining student reactions to studies being carried out on campus. He said that he had several questions he would like to ask the subject about his experiences that day.

Experimenter 3 was "also very interested in obtaining some student reactions to broad topics of interest to undergraduates" and asked if the student would mind filling out an opinion questionnaire before the interview actually begun. He gave the subject a questionnaire, consisting of 10 70-point a priori Likert-type items with labels of extremely opposed, somewhat opposed, somewhat in favor, and extremely in favor. Included in the questionnaire was the item "as regards the proposition to greatly increase tuition at Michigan State University, I am personally: . . . ," and the item, "as regards the proposition that public universities should be more like private universities, I am: . . ." Other items concerned topics of interest to undergraduates, for example, holding evening classes, raising entrance requirements, lengthening the football season, and permitting alcoholic beverages in dormitories and fraternities. Upon completion of the questionnaire Experimenter 3 leafed through his files and produced a mimeographed form entitled "Regional Accents" with the name "Pallak" on it. This form contained four questions asking about the subject's perceived choice in making the speech, the topic of the speech, whether the speech included his name and address, and how much he liked the experimenter. When the form had been completed, Experimenter 3 produced another form entitled "Survey" with the name "Kanouse" on it, which asked three questions about the dissonance situation: the degree of perceived choice in writing the essay, the topic of the essay that the subject wrote, and how much he liked the person conducting the survey. The experimenter then asked if the subject were an in-state student, and obtained information relevant to the socioeconomic status of the student's parents.

The subjects were then completely debriefed, including an explanation of the study and the hypothesis involved, and some notions about expected results. We emphasize that when the subject completed the attitude items and the posttest, the posttester had no information concerning the subject's experimental condition. Thus the posttester was completely blind to the prior manipulations.

In summary, the subject made either a public or private speech consistent with his attitudinal position, and subsequently wrote an essay contrary to his attitudinal position, under conditions of high or low choice. In the consonant speech he argued against raising the tuition at his university. In the subsequent dissonance situation he wrote an essay arguing that public universities should become more like private universities. These two issues seem to be logically related, and indeed correlated .56 in a pretest sample ($p < .05$; $N = 19$) The salient features of the design and method are: adequate controls for both commitment and dissonance were included; two different experimenters were used for the primary manipulations; these two experimenters were unaware of the other condition the subject was in, that is, each was blind on the other dimension of the design; evaluation apprehension (Rosenberg, 1965) was avoided by separating the posttest from the rest of the experiment, both in terms of the person giving the posttest and in terms of the place in which it was given; the posttester was not aware of the subject's experimental condition; suspicion was minimized by manipulating commitment and dissonance on two logically related issues rather than one issue.

The basic results are presented in Tables 3-2 and 3-3.

Discussion of Results

The data for the item specific to dissonance arousal (i.e., public versus private universities) are presented in Table 3-2. First we should see if commitment by itself had any effect on this item. This may be determined by looking at the last column in the Table, the dissonance control conditions. These three conditions reflect prior commitment, but without any dissonance. As you can see, there are no differences among these conditions. Thus, the commitment manipulation had no effect on the dissonance item, a fact that is consistent with what we found for the control conditions in the Kiesler–Sakumura experiment.

The data reflecting the arousal of dissonance are arrayed properly although they are a little weak, statistically speaking. The high-dissonance manipulation was clearly effective, however, and each of the high-dissonance conditions is significantly different from the overall control mean. After writing the counter-attitudinal essay under conditions of high choice, these subjects (regardless of prior commitment) changed their attitudes on this issue, bringing their attitudes more into line with their behavior.

There was somewhat more change in the low-dissonance conditions than one might ordinarily expect in a forced compliance experiment (there seldom is any change in the low-dissonance conditions under these circumstances). Overall, the low-dissonance subjects became more favorable towards making public universities more like private ones, as compared to the control conditions. The difference between the high- and low-dissonance conditions is of only marginal statistical significance.*

TABLE 3-2

THE INTERACTIVE EFFECTS OF DISSONANCE AND COMMITMENT ON THE DISSONANCE ITEM[a]

Degree of Prior Commitment	Degree of Dissonance[b]		
	High	Low	No
High	35.28	29.68	24.25
	(21)	(19)	(12)
Low	35.35	37.70	27.92
	(20)	(20)	(12)
No	39.94	32.12	26.0
	(16)	(16)	(11)

[a] The higher the score, the more favorable the subject toward the item "Public universities should be more like private universities [from Kiesler, Pallak, & Kanouse, 1968]."
[b] *N*'s are in parentheses.

The results from the attitude issue specific to dissonance arousal look very similar to those found in the typical dissonance experiment. Following the counter-attitudinal behavior, subjects in the high-dissonance condition changed their attitudes, making them more consistent with their behavior, and this change was greater than that of subjects undergoing the low-dissonance manipulation or those in the control condition. Intuitively, one might expect that the commitment manipulation would have an effect on this issue, but there was none. On the item specific to commitment, however, the expected effect did take place. Those data are presented in Table 3-3.

Again, first look at the effect of the commitment manipulation by itself, as evidenced by the three means in the dissonance control column. Obviously, as one can see there, commitment to consonant behavior did not by itself systematically affect subjects' attitude on this issue.

Before looking at the other data, recall quickly what our expectations are.

* Part of the problem appears to have been sex related, and subjects had been assigned to condition without regard to their sex. An internal statistical analysis of these data showed that the dissonance manipulation had little or no effect on the females, perhaps because females tended to be much more positive than males towards making public universities more like private ones (ergo, they should have had less dissonance). For example, the relatively high mean in the low-commitment, low-dissonance condition appears to be due to the fact that the majority of the subjects in this condition were, by chance, females. Considering the data from the males separately, the results are quite clear. High-dissonance subjects changed more than low-dissonance subjects, who in turn changed more than the controls. In no analysis did the degree of dissonance interact with the degree of commitment.

The two attitudinal issues, public universities vs. private ones and raising tuition, are logically related. Therefore, an act that is inconsistent with one's attitude on the university issue should also be dissonant with one's attitude on the tuition issue. Consequently, with little or no commitment involved we should expect high-dissonance subjects to change their attitudes on the tuition issue also, much as they did on the university issue.

TABLE 3-3

THE INTERACTIVE EFFECTS OF DISSONANCE AND COMMITMENT ON THE COMMITMENT ITEM[a]

Degree of Prior Commitment	Degree of Dissonance		
	High	Low	No
High	11.05 (21)	13.53 (19)	12.58 (12)
Low	19.10 (20)	9.15 (20)	10.00 (12)
No	16.25 (16)	7.25 (16)	13.45 (11)

[a] The higher the score, the more favorable were subjects toward the item, "Tuition should be increased [from Kiesler, Pallak, & Kanouse, 1968]."

[b] *N*'s are in parentheses.

As Table 3-3 shows, the dissonance manipulation did have the expected effect on the issue specific to the manipulation of commitment. High-dissonance subjects changed more than low-dissonance subjects, both under conditions of no prior commitment (16.25 vs. 7.25) and low prior commitment (19.10 vs. 9.15). Put another way, performance of a counter-attitudinal act not only affected the attitude specific to the behavior, but other related attitudes as well. Note that this expected spread of effect gives us added confidence in the power and successful implementation of our dissonance manipulations.

With high prior commitment, however, the dissonance effect was obliterated. There was no spread of effect from one issue to the other when the subject was firmly committed to the consonant behavior. Under high prior commitment, the high-dissonance subjects did not show greater attitude change than the low-dissonance subjects. Indeed, there is a small difference in the opposite direction.

Consider the three commitment conditions under high dissonance for this issue, and relate them to the Kiesler–Sakumura experiment. This gives three levels of commitment, an attack of sorts (high dissonance), and the dependent measure is the issue specific to the commitment manipulations. The data also replicate those found by Kiesler and Sakumura: greater resistance to the attack by the high-commitment subjects than either the low-commitment subjects or those in the control condition. This provides nice support for the generality of the Kiesler–Sakumura experiment: Commitment is manipulated in a different way; the issue is different; the attack is quite different; but the results are the same.*

On the other hand, although the commitment manipulation affected the issue specific to commitment in the predicted way, we note that it had no effect on the issue specific to dissonance arousal. In other words, high prior commitment negated the effect of dissonance for the issue specific to commitment even though typical dissonance results were obtained on the issue specific to dissonance. Consider the subject in the high-commitment, high-dissonance condition. He is in a curious position. He is committed to a consonant behavior. But he is subsequently induced to behave quite inconsistently with his attitude on a related issue. An awkward position, of course, but what does he do? He changes one of his attitudes so that it more closely represents his behavior, but his attitude on the related issue remains as before. This would still be a peculiar position to be in, unless one somehow divorced the two issues or compartmentalized them in his own mind, in a sense no longer seeing them as related.

Compartmentalization appears the most ready explanation of these data. On the other hand, one cannot conclusively point to this process as the determining one since we did not measure how each subject perceived the relatedness of the two issues (neither before nor after the manipulations). We only know that the subject changed on one item and did not change on the other and that in other conditions changes on these items went hand in hand.†

Given that the process is compartmentalization, there is an interesting implication for dissonance theory and the generality of its results, at least, perhaps, when the issue is important to the subject. When a subject is induced to behave counter-attitudinally on an important issue, theoretically a lot of dissonance is produced. The subject is very strongly motivated to justify his behavior in this circumstance. If he is also committed to other consonant behaviors, which he is likely to be if the issue is important, change becomes

* One has a conceptual replication of the Kiesler–Sakumura experiment if one considers the following four conditions: high and low commitment by high and no dissonance. Of course, the results are the same, whichever way they are considered.

† Other data were gathered on the essay and the speech (e.g., length, favorability, quality) and also on the attractiveness of the two experimenters involved in the manipulations. None of these data provided any clues to the compartmentalization process, either for or against. We add that they do not suggest any alternative explanation of the data either.

very difficult. One possibility (although, perhaps a last resort to preserve one's self-image as one who is in control of his behavior and acts on his beliefs) is to drive a psychological wedge between the two attitudinal issues or sets of behaviors:

> . . . to divorce the issues specific to dissonance arousal from other attitudinal issues he previously thought to be related. Metaphorically speaking, the individual may occasionally burn cognitive bridges to protect important attitudinal areas from the inroads of change. If so, the results of the present study suggest that individuals are more likely to burn bridges connecting with attitude areas to which they are highly committed [Kiesler, Pallak, & Kanouse, 1968, p. 338].

Dissonance had no effect on the commitment item when subjects were highly committed. On the other hand, it is equally valid to point out that commitment had no effect on the dissonance item either. However, this may partly be due to the specific issues that we used and the grounds for their selection.

To study the interactive effects of commitment and dissonance, we had two main methodological considerations in mind. First, it was necessary to show that the dissonant act did actually produce dissonance, at least in the sense of producing typical dissonance results. Minimally, we needed a situation where we could be relatively confident of dissonance results in the replication conditions, to wit, a difference between high- and low-dissonance conditions on the dissonance issue, with either little or no prior commitment.

The second methodological consideration in the selection of topics was that they be cognitively related. In short, we wanted the dissonant act to be theoretically dissonant with the subject's attitude on both issues. If the items were completely unrelated, a study of the interactive effects of commitment and dissonance would be silly, i.e., there would be no reason to expect them to interact. Consequently, we wanted to be able to expect a corresponding difference between the high- and low-dissonance conditions on the related issue (again with little or no prior commitment). We were not completely confident (and still aren't) that we would get the spread of the dissonance effect with simply two related issues. From the dissonance point of view, we had a situation with three cognitions. We were asking, If cognition A is dissonant with cognition B, when is it also dissonant with cognition C? The answer was that A is also dissonant with C, when C is logically subsumed by B (see, for example, Festinger, 1957, p. 14).

These considerations forced our final decision on method and the issue of which topic would be assigned to which condition. We searched for two topics for which we could be relatively certain of the subjects' opinion beforehand, and with the added proviso that one topic could be subsumed by the other.

Having found them, of course, the narrower topic had to be assigned for consonant commitment and the broader one to the dissonance manipulation.

I am suggesting that as a result of this difference in topic breadth, there may have also been a difference in *directional impact:* that if A subsumes B, then implications of A vis à vis B are more salient, obvious, clear, straightforward (psychologically), and apparent than the implications of B vis à vis A. The dissonance issue had greater directional impact than the commitment topic in this view. If we had reversed the assignment of the topics, consequently, we would have expected the dissonance manipulation to have had less spread of effect and the commitment manipulation to have had greater spread of effect.*

We had a similar type of methodological problem when we chose the dissonance manipulation. The main problem was that theoretically we may as easily speak of commitment to dissonant behavior as consonant. This is not only a central feature of the assumptions presented in the last chapter, but it also seems reasonable on several other grounds as well. However, if we speak of commitment to dissonant behavior, then we must conclude that the dissonance manipulation in the Kiesler, Pallak, and Kanouse experiment is confounded with degree of commitment. After all, we assume that the greater the choice in performing any behavior, whether consistent or inconsistent with ones's beliefs, the greater the commitment to the behavior. When the subject behaves dissonantly under high choice, he has more dissonance than the subject under low choice, but he is also more committed to the dissonant act than the low-choice subject. From this perspective, even if dissonance were theoretically equal between these two subjects, we would expect greater attitude change from the high-choice subject because he would have greater difficulty in denying, distorting, or reinterpreting the act itself.†

Why not select a paradigm in which this obvious confound would be eliminated? Two reasons. First, the situations where degree of dissonance would not be confounded with degree of commitment are suspect on other grounds. For example, we could have varied dissonance by varying the strength of a counter-communication or varying the extremeness of the position advocated in a counter-communication (instead of using the forced compliance paradigm). However, these are not impeccable methods of varying the degree of dissonance. In fact, some (see Kiesler, Collins & Miller, 1969) maintain, with some justification, that these situations are

* There was a powerful spread of effect for the dissonance manipulation. In fact, dissonance results for the commitment issue were statistically more significant than for the issue for which dissonance was manipulated. This would seem to support the idea of an imbalance in directional impact between the two items.

† This is one of the reasons that I have preferred to concentrate my research on commitment to consonant behavior.

irrelevant to dissonance arousal and dissonance theory. Second, the main point of the experiment was to establish contact with dissonance theory, and this demands at least momentarily living within the premises of the theory. This led us to use a typical–reliable method of producing dissonance (that is, a paradigm which everyone accepting the theory would also accept as producing dissonance) even though it conflicts with some of our own assumptions. All is not lost, however. The experiment still gives an empirical connection between commitment to consonant behavior and a typical dissonance paradigm and a theoretical connection between commitments to consonant and dissonant behaviors.

In sum, we allowed the confound to remain in the Kiesler, Pallak, and Kanouse experiment on grounds of (*a*) empirical utility: We wanted to look at the parameters of the commitment manipulation interacting with a typical dissonance manipulation and (*b*) theoretical utility: Alternative dissonance manipulations that we could have used are not regarded by others as theoretically pure themselves.

The Theoretical Relationship between Commitment and Dissonance: A Review of Implicit Statements

Earlier, we mentioned that there is some confusion in the literature about commitment and the way it is supposed to be related to dissonance theory. At the time we were discussing definitions of commitment. However, explicit definition and implicit usage are not the same thing. One may formally define a term in one way, but then use it as if it meant something slightly different. But something slightly different may have vastly different implications. This is especially well illustrated in the present case by the implicit assumptions that investigators appear to make about the relationship of commitment to dissonance. In reviewing the literature, I found that varying uses of the term commitment led to three quite different implications about its theoretical relationship to dissonance. It is instructive to consider these in more detail.

1. One implicit assumption about the relationship of commitment to dissonance is that *unless the person is committed, one cannot make an unequivocal prediction from dissonance theory.* The statement is implied by our definition of commitment* and emphasizes the notion that commitment affects the resistance of some cognition to change. Consider that dissonance is presumably produced when two cognitions are inconsistent. One of the favored methods of reducing dissonance should be to change one of the

* Given, of course, our cognitive corollary that commitment to some behavior affects the resistance to change of the cognition representing the behavior.

cognitions. It is a truism that the one to change is the cognition that is less resistant. Knowledge of the committing circumstances would allow one to predict which cognition would change. This is apparently what Brehm and Cohen (1962) intended when they said that commitment "affects the kinds of attempts to reduce dissonance that may occur [p. 8]." Given our cognitive corollary, the statement that commitment aids in specifying how dissonance will be reduced is true by definition. We obviously cannot tell which of two cognitions will change unless we know which is the less resistant to change. Ordinarily, of course, one does not try to determine differential commitment within a given subject. The subjects perform some dissonant behavior. One docs not try to determine the difference between commitment to that behavior and some other behavior, an almost impossible task given the state of the art. Instead, one determines the difference between conditions in commitment to the dissonant behavior—quite a different thing, but leading to the same prediction, namely, that subjects in one condition will change more than subjects in another.

2. A second view of the relationship of commitment to dissonance is the following: *Unless the subject is committed, there may be no dissonance.* Of course, this is a much different implicit definition of commitment than that contained in the first statement above, and it is related to a different aspect of dissonance theory. As mentioned previously, this view of commitment brings in the question of psychological implication, or How can we tell when dissonance is present? This point does not need further discussion here, but I add only that Gerard has suggested a term which is quite useful, in these circumstances, as an alternative to commitment. He suggests that this stance be called a "unequivocal behavioral orientation" or "UBO." Perhaps there may even be theoretical degrees of UBO, but the first modifier suggests not. In their glossary, Jones and Gerard (1967) define UBO as "An orientation of the person toward his decisions and commitments that permits effective and nonconflicted action. As a consequence of this orientation, foregone alternatives tend to be deprecated and the value of the chosen course of action enhanced [p. 719]." In short, with an unequivocal behavioral orientation, dissonance is present; without UBO, dissonance is not present. The term commitment in this second sense becomes redundant, and its need is obviated.

3. There is yet a third view of commitment in the dissonance literature: *The more the subject is committed, the greater the dissonance.* Take the following example. Suppose we have an experiment in which we have varied the degree of volition in carrying out some counter-attitudinal behavior and the investigator, in describing his data, used the clause "the greater commitment engendered in the high choice condition." He could intend this clause to mean either of two things. It could mean simply that there is greater commit-

ment in the high choice condition, without any further implications (and this we would agree with). More likely, however, such clauses are intended as simple alternatives to the clause "the greater *dissonance* in the high choice condition." If so, the investigator is implying that the greater the commitment, the greater the dissonance (or worse, equating commitment with dissonance).

These three statements of the relationship of commitment to dissonance are quite distinct, and they have rather different theoretical implications. Consider the problem from the point of view of philosophy of science. Each statement involves a theoretical assumption (in this case, implicit) stating the relationship of one theoretical variable to another. If one enjoys thinking of theories as axiomatic systems (as I do), then obviously one could plug any one of the statements into the theory. Of course, you would have three different theories, depending on which of the assumed relationships you are prepared to accept. What one can say about dissonance as a theoretical construct is affected by its assumed relationship to other constructs, whether commitment, volition, emotional arousal, or what-have-you.

Of course, I don't think the situation is all that serious. I am unabashedly pushing the first statement: commitment as a resistance phenomenon. The second statement, regarding questions of psychological implication and the presence of dissonance, seems tailor made for Gerard's concept of unequivocal behavioral orientation. The third statement seems to me to be patently silly. Occasionally commitment is implicitly equated with dissonance, but I prefer to believe that it is not premeditated.

One of the attractive features of the resistance view of commitment is that it is totally independent of dissonance, conceptually speaking. It should neither affect the degree of dissonance nor the presence or absence of dissonance. Of course, it is a relevant input for dissonance theory and an aid in predictions derived from the theory. But it has an existence independent of dissonance. Commitment is only a customer of dissonance theory, not its mistress.

The fact that commitment and dissonance are conceptually independent does not necessarily mean that it is easy to keep them separated in an experiment. In dissonance experiments, the resistance view implies that commitment and dissonance are often confounded, particularly in forced compliance experiments. With regard to commitment experiments, I draw your attention to a methodological discussion of the Kiesler–Sakumura experiment in the last chapter. There we stressed that there are a number of possible sources of dissonance in the performance of behavior that is ostensibly consonant with one's attitude.

The two experiments described here indicate that the performance of consonant behavior and different degrees of commitment to consonant behavior need not affect the subject's existing attitude. This not only shows that there is something left to the concept of commitment after everything else is stripped away, but it also demonstrates that adequate control conditions are possible in the study of consonant behavior. I add that the presence of such control conditions are necessary—indeed, imperative—as well as possible. We cannot conclude that our variable had the predicted effect unless we can demonstrate that our operationalization is uncontaminated with other relevant variables. In the case of commitment, the range of possibly contaminating variables is not small.

The Question of Motivation

Is commitment motivating? I don't think so, not by itself anyway. Consider, for example, the control conditions discussed above. Simply performing consonant behavior doesn't necessarily affect one's existing attitude. Differential levels of manipulated commitment do not affect existing attitude either. In both cases, however, commitment does determine both the way one reacts to attacks on attitude and the effects of dissonant behavior. Given these facts alone, the obvious conclusion is that commitment does not have any motivational component. Commitment doesn't compel us to do something; it is inert. However, because of its binding or freezing properties, it does influence our response to other forces or situations that do compel us to do something, e.g., to move somewhere or react in some way.

However, the layman's view of commitment includes a motivational aspect. Once committed, one then does something active; one forges ahead, grimly determined, with one's spirit renewed, and assorted other clichés which imply some increased motivation. In most of these cases, though, I see other aspects of motivation in the situation besides simply commitment: One perhaps has taken an unequivocal behavioral orientation, perhaps producing dissonance, and consequently one justifies his past behavior with other action. Or perhaps one expects to be attacked, and knowing that he is bound to the behavior and cannot change it or its implications, the person actively prepares for the coming attack. (See, for example, Chapters IV and V for further discussion and research on the effects of impending attack on one's beliefs and its relationship to commitment.)

Cofer and Appley (1964) pose the concept of an Anticipation–Invigoration Mechanism (AIM) to describe situations where the invigoration of behavior is enhanced by learned anticipations. As we discussed in Chapter I, explicit, attitudinally relevant behavior has many possible negative implications, and most of us are reluctant to perform such behavior, however consonant it may be with other beliefs and considerations. In other words, we have learned to anticipate certain other, usually negative, demands or implications from consonant behaviors. From the anticipation of these possible negative events, we are motivated, we prepare for them. But such learned anticipations depend on past experience and should be situation-specific. In one situation the committed individual will be very aroused; in another situation, not at all. The concept of AIM can be applied very neatly to the quasi-motivating properties of commitment. But again, commitment alone doesn't provide the motivation. One must be both committed to some behavior and, on the basis of past experience and specific to a particular situation, anticipate that other things are also going to happen. Commitment alone is not enough for this invigoration to occur. The fact that the motivating properties of commitment are not always there, that they are only quasi-motivating, does not make them any less interesting. But if we are to use the concept of commitment to make any predictions about behavior, then we should try to specify what commitment by itself does and what other things are necessary for alternative things to happen. One such other variable to keep in mind is the Anticipation–Invigoration Mechanism.

IV

THE RESISTANCE EFFECT OF COMMITMENT: NEW EVIDENCE

We have discussed, in detail, two experiments involving different sets of operations for varying commitment to a behavioral act: amount of incentive offered for the act, and whether the act is public or not. In each case, greater commitment led to increased resistance to change, whether the change was advocated in a counter-communication or implied by subsequent dissonant behavior.

Replications of effects across diverse sets of operations and measurement techniques give us increased confidence in both the utility of the theoretical concept and the reliability of its presumed effects. In discussing the import of multiple operations, Webb, Campbell, Schwartz, and Sechrist (1966) state,

> Once a proposition has been confirmed by two or more independent measurement processes, the uncertainty of its interpretation is greatly reduced. The most persuasive evidence comes through a triangulation of measurement processes. If a proposition can survive the onslaught of a series of imperfect measures, with all their irrelevant error, confidence should be placed in it [p. 3]. When multiple operations provide consistent results, the possibility of slippage between conceptual definition and operational specification is diminished greatly [p. 5].

These considerations are especially important in the early stages of research on a theoretical variable. There are a number of sources of error regarding measurement and implementation, and also situation-specific factors, such as a particular topic, subject population, or setting (e.g., the laboratory). The multiple-operation, multiple-measurement principle is useful both to zero in on the concept and to generalize about its effects.

In the present chapter, we report two more implementations of the commitment concept and alternative measures of its effects. These studies are important on a priori grounds because they represent further triangulation on the concept. But there is an added plum: We found a reliable, but unexpected side effect in both studies that has interesting implications. More about that as we go along.

The first experiment was carried out by myself and Roberta Mathog and is not reported elsewhere in the literature.

Resistance to Influence as a Function of Number of Prior Consonant Acts: A Test

In Chapter II, we hypothesized that the greater the number of consonant acts performed, the greater would be the commitment engendered. This experiment tests the implication of this postulate, namely, that the greater the number of acts, the more resistant the person will be to subsequent attack on attitudes related to those behaviors.

This proposition rests, of course, on the premise that the behaviors and their implications are intimately related. If each of the acts performed were unrelated to any other behavior, increasing the number should have little effect on the individual. One way of thinking of this issue is in terms of the cognitive corollary: Commitment to behavior increases the resistance to change of the cognition representing the behavior. These behavioral cognitions should cluster with cognitions representing attitudes consistent with the behavior, and the whole cluster should consequently be more resistant to change.

The proposition is not a simple one to test. The difficulty stems from the fact that the number of behavioral acts is closely related to other theoretically relevant variables such as degree of social support, extremeness of attitude, and so forth. If we wish to test the effect of the number of acts in isolation, then we must be prepared to rule out, by experimental design, these other variables which would contribute to plausible alternative explanations of the data.

In the present case, we tried to build an attitude by experimentally providing the subject with a relevant set of experiences. We used a game with which the subject was unfamiliar and for which there were possible several clearly defined strategies. Subjects were induced to play a particular strategy either zero, one, or three times. Half the subjects then received a counter-communication, arguing against the efficacy of the strategy in question. The dependent variable was the degree to which subjects were influenced by the counter-communication.

The gain in precision provided by the game setting is somewhat offset by the lessening of experimental impact on the subject. With such limited impact, we might expect little difference between zero and one act. For this reason and for convenience, the hypotheses below are stated in the form of comparing the three-act group with the other two. The major hypothesis is that the three-act group will be more resistant to influence than either the one-act or zero-act groups. More specifically, after attack, the three-act group should (in comparison with the zero- and one-act groups) (*a*) subsequently choose the attacked strategy more often when offered the opportunity, (*b*) indicate less agreement with the counter-communication, (*c*) evaluate the attacked strategy more positively.

Method

Subjects. One-hundred-and-fifty females from an introductory psychology course at Southern Connecticut State College volunteered to participate in a study on game strategies. Twenty-five were randomly assigned to each of six conditions. Three subjects took part in each experimental session, each in a different condition.

Overview. Each subject played a game ("Racko") three times. For each game, each subject was assigned a strategy to use. One independent variable was the number of times a subject was assigned the particular strategy, "Guide Line play": Each subject used this strategy either zero, one, or three times. Cross-indexed with this variation, half of the subjects subsequently received a counter-communication arguing against the efficacy of this particular strategy. The rest of the subjects received an irrelevant communication. The dependent variable was the subject's acceptance of this counter-communication.

Procedure. The experimenter introduced the study by saying, "This study is on the effectiveness of game strategies. The game you will be playing is a card game. We could program a computer to play the game using different strategies, but what we are interested in is how real people will play the game and how much they will like the different strategies." The game was then described to the subjects. In this game, each person has 10 numbered cards (0–60) placed on a rack. The object of the game is to replace one's cards with cards from the deck or discards of the other players so that as many of the numbers as possible are in sequence.

So that subjects would be uncertain of their performance, two additional rules were imposed. First, the scoring system was to take into account not only the number of cards in sequence but also the number and magnitude of cards out of sequence. It was therefore possible to have five cards in sequence and receive a higher score than someone who had seven cards in sequence due to the complicated way in which the cards were scored. Secondly, each game consisted of each player making only eight plays rather than playing until someone obviously won.

To increase the importance of the games, subjects were informed of a tournament for prizes to be held later and to which approximately the top quarter of the players would be invited. It was emphasized that all subjects in a given group could qualify.

Strategies. The four strategies, each printed on a 3 × 5 card, were then given to the subjects. The experimenter read them aloud and discussed them until she felt the subjects understood them. The crucial strategy, Guide Line play, involved placing the cards according to the number on the rack and, in pretesting, was rated second best of the four. The subjects then rated each strategy on a Likert scale, with seven points identified.

For a given game, strategies were assigned with a separate deck of 3 × 5 cards, each card with a strategy printed on it, and in a previously determined order. Subjects were told each strategy appeared in the deck twelve times, and it was therefore possible that a given player *by chance* could get a particular strategy all three times or not at all. To insure that the subjects played the assigned strategy (although *E* could see if they did) without producing a feeling of extreme pressure, subjects were told they should not feel forced to play the strategy. However, if they chose not to play the assigned strategy, they could not play the other three or a simple variation, and they had to write down in detail what strategy they made up to use. All subjects played the assigned strategies. One-third of the subjects were not assigned the Guide Line strategy at all; one-third played it once; and one-third played it three times. Of those who played it once, half played it in the first game, half in the last game (of three).

Counter-communication. Subjects were told that only the first three games would count toward the total score. After these games were finished, the experimenter informed the subjects that they would be asked to rate the strategies again in light of their experience with the game. She also said, "I will be passing out to you a written statement by another person on a particular strategy. Since you have had some experience with the game now, we would like you to rate this other person's impression of the strategy she wrote about. By having you rate this other person's opinions, we can get a better idea about how realistic her assessment is and, thus, a better idea about the effectiveness of this strategy." "The other person's opinions" represented either a strong attack against the efficacy of the Guide Line strategy, or a filler communication. The filler communication delivered innocuous opinions about the least preferred strategy, as determined in a pilot study. Subjects then filled out the posttest.

The overall design is a 3 × 2 factorial (pretest–posttest) with three variations in number of times the game was played (0, 1, 3) cross-indexed with either a counter-communication or no counter-communication.

Results

Choice. One question on the posttest asked, If you had your choice, which of the four strategies would you play? We computed the proportion of subjects in each condition who elected the Guide Line strategy and these data are presented in Figure 4-1. We performed the analysis of variance of proportions, using arc-sine transformations, suggested by Gilson and Abelson (1965). The data are arrayed as expected and the interaction is significant ($F = 3.39$; $df = 2,144$; $p < .05$). As can be seen, the counter-communication decreased the proportion of people choosing the Guide Line strategy in both the zero- and one-act conditions (considered together, CR $= 2.20$; $p < .05$). For the three-act condition, the situation is reversed. There, reading the counter-communication actually increased the proportion of subjects who would choose the Guide Line strategy (.84 vs. .64; CR $= 1.68$; $p < .10$). Of course, within the counter-communication condition, the three-act subjects were much more resistant to the counter-communication than either the one-act or zero-act subjects, as predicted (CR $= 3.96$ and 5.36, respectively; $p < .001$ in each case). We may regard our hypothesis as confirmed regarding choice of strategy.

Agreement with the Counter-communication. Another question on the posttest asked of the counter-communication, Do you agree with this person's opinion of this strategy? Of course, this question is only relevant to the counter-communication conditions. The zero- and one-act means for this question (on a 24-point scale) were 13.48 and 13.92, respectively. The three-act subjects indicated much less agreement (M $= 7.32$) with the counter-communication than either the zero-act ($t = 4.31$; $df = 48$; $p < .001$) or the one-act conditions ($t = 4.62$; $df = 48$; $p < .001$). Thus, the second hypothesis may also be regarded as confirmed.

Attitude Change. There were no differences among conditions on the pretest rating of the Guide Line strategy (F's < 1.0). Consequently, the posttest answer to the question, How good do you think the Guide Line strategy would be for winning the game? was used as our measure of attitude. These data are presented in Figure 4-2.

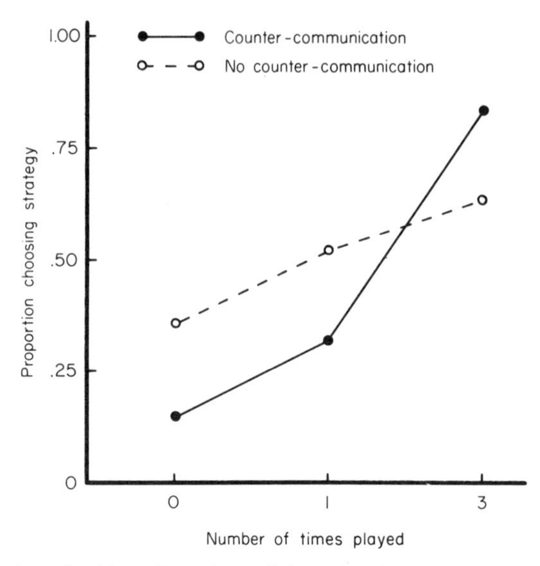

FIG. 4-1. Proportion of subjects in each condition who elected the Guide Line strategy.

As may be seen there, the data are similar to those on choice. However, they are not as statistically significant. The overall interaction is not significant ($F = 1.98$). However, the data are clearer if one controls for the evaluation of the other strategies. If we take as our dependent measure the attitude toward the Guide Line strategy minus the attitude towards the others, the interaction is then significant ($F = 3.40$; $df = 2{,}144$; $p < .05$). One could respond to the counter-communication in two ways: by lowering one's evaluation of the Guide Line strategy or by raising one's evaluation of the others. Apparently our subjects did a little of each. Considering the counter-communication conditions alone, the three-act group is significantly different from either the one-act condition ($t = 3.80$; $df = 48$; $p < .01$) or the zero-act group ($t = 2.68$; $df = 48$; $p = .01$). Thus, one might consider the third hypothesis also to be supported.

Other Measures. There were no significant differences in actual performance at the game (as recorded by the experimenter at the end of each game). If anything, the one-act subjects tended to do better than the other two (significantly better in one of the three games). Performance was however unrelated to feelings of success as measured by the two questions: How good do you think your score was? and, What do you think your chances are of being selected to return? The three-act, no counter-communication condition had a higher feeling of success than any of the other conditions (smallest $t = 2.15$). The other five conditions were all approximately the same.

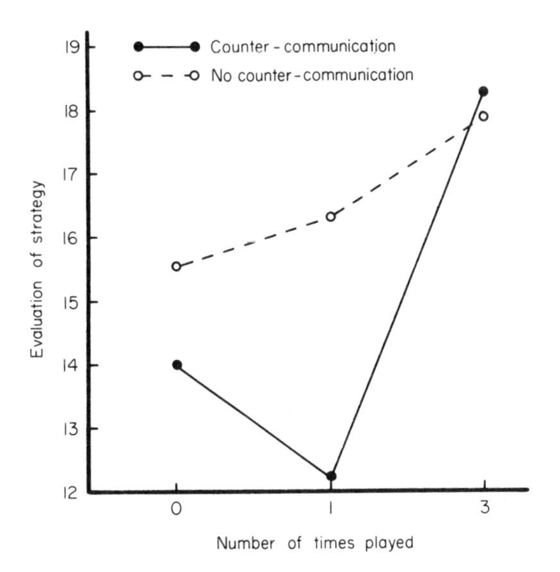

FIG. 4-2. Attitude based on posttest answers to the question, How good do you think the Guide Line strategy would be for winning the game?

DISCUSSION

The major hypothesis was supported: Subjects performing three consonant acts were much less susceptible to subsequent counter-attack than those performing either one act or no acts. After attack, the three-act subjects chose the disputed strategy more often, agreed with the counter-communication less, and evaluated the attacked strategy more positively than did either the one- or zero-act subjects. In short, our basic notions about commitment are further supported by the fact that an entirely different implementation of the commitment concept led to similar results. It gives us more confidence that the thread running through the three main experiments discussed thus far must be the same variable, one which I choose to call commitment. Given the general resistance phenomenon observed in these studies, the view of commitment as binding or freezing appears to be very reasonable. In all of these experiments, variables which others have seen as either commitment itself or some crucial part of commitment (such as dissonance, resolve, dedication, and various motivational constructs) do not seem to play a role.

That is not to say, of course, that these other variables are not important in their own right. Simply that these variables have been controlled in these experiments and, consequently, do not offer themselves as plausible alternative explanations or rival hypotheses for the data.*

The critic, on the other hand, might suggest that placing significance on the number of acts seems out of place in a discussion that views commitment as the binding of the individual to some particular behavior. What, this argument goes, has it got to do with the number of behaviors? In a broader context, this would be a telling criticism, but for the present experiment it is largely obviated by a simple assumption. The behavior of interest in this experiment, I would argue, is that of agreeing to play the critical strategy. Consider the process that we suggested goes on when the committed person faces an attack on his beliefs. We posed that commitment confers increased resistance because the individual must live with his previous behavior; commitment makes it more difficult for him to deny, reinterpret, or distort his own behavior. In this case, the number of acts represents the number of times that the subject chose to play the strategy. The person finds it more difficult to discard this previous behavior, when faced with the attack on the strategy, after doing it three times than when he has only done it once or not at all. The increased number of times chosen implies greater responsibility for the behavior, greater volition in accepting that strategy.

How would commitment relate to the number of acts when the behaviors in question were not identical? Intuitively, this should depend on how closely the behaviors (or their implications) were related or connected for a particular person. We are arguing, in a sense, that commitment can summate across behaviors. But the summation must not be of apples and oranges. The person must recognize the connection between the separate behaviors (although, not necessarily when the behavior takes place). Think of the issue in terms of the cognitive corollary; commitment increases the resistance of the behavior to reinterpretation and increases the resistance to change of the cognition representing the behavior as well. To the extent that the individual sees the two cognitions as related to one another, commitment will summate across the two behaviors. At one level, it is the difficulty in reinterpretation that is adding up. When two behaviors are cognitively connected, then if one is to rid himself of the meaning of one of the acts, he must do it for both.

Consider an experiment in which the subject is induced to carry out a series of small, relatively innocuous behaviors. Although each of these acts may have little import for the individual and not cause him to think twice while

* Of course none of these considerations imply that the term "commitment" is a meaningful way to describe the variable that runs through these experiments. X would suffice as well, a point that will receive some discussion later.

performing it, the collection of behavior may have an intense freezing action. Indeed, similar to the Kiesler–Sakumura experiment, the full import and the connections among the separate behaviors may not occur to the person until he is forced to review his attitudinal position and past behavior by an attack. National behavior can reflect a similar process, in the following sense. Often the behavior of our government, both militarily and diplomatically, consists of a series of relatively small, discrete acts, each of which is a specific response to a specific situation, unimportant by itself and not dictated by larger policy. However, later when a crisis appears on the scene, the government finds itself with a policy that is dictated by these smaller actions, even though none of the smaller actions was itself derived from any broad long-term policy decision. One can think of the smaller actions as commitments which, although innocuous at the time, summate to freeze one's position when the crisis (as an attack of sorts) forces a review of official policy.

Perhaps the most interesting finding in the Kiesler–Mathog experiment (the plum referred to earlier) is the boomerang effect, in which the attack merely intensified the subject's attitude. First, subjects with little or no commitment responded in the typical way following the attitudinal attack. After reading the counter-communication, subjects in the zero- and one-act conditions became less positive towards the attacked strategy and said they would choose it less often if offered the chance in the future. On the other hand, the attack increased the percentage of subjects in the three-act condition who said they would choose that strategy if free to do so.

This finding gives us some insight into the concept of commitment. The committed subject is indeed bound by his previous behavior. His future behavior is partly determined by his past behavior, however innocuous that behavior was at the time it was performed. In this case, the subject's chance for success was intimately intertwined with his previous implicit decision to play the Guide Line strategy three times, as assigned. Now, under attack, he tried to justify his previous behavior, in a sense, telling himself that he did the right thing, that he would do the same thing over again if offered the choice.

The boomerang effect leads one to interesting possibilities. This finding might be related to the question of how people become more extreme in their attitudes. A committed subject might become more extreme under attack in an attempt to justify his past behavior, since the alternative of abandoning his opinion to agree with the countercommunication is relatively closed. Since the process of self-justification may not be simple, the person might seek out others who are even more extreme as social support for his previous behavior; perhaps even seeking other behaviors to perform that would justify his own. If so, one might turn a moderate into an extremist in a simple but nonobvious manner. First, induce him to perform some behavior consistent with his beliefs, and get him committed to it. Next, attack the attitude in question. We suggest that the person may be more amenable to requests for other extreme behavior, more willing to interact with others holding an extreme opinion on the issue, and end up by becoming more extreme himself. Of course, the effect should depend on a particular combination of degree of commitment and strength of attack. That is, the degree of commitment should be high enough so that the subject can't really change his position, and the attack should be strong enough to arouse the person's defenses (but not so strong that he is forced to abandon his position).

Actually, we know very little about the boomerang effect and when and why it occurs, and the Kiesler–Mathog experiment seemed to offer some good leads. First we thought that we should test the power and generality of the effect. The Kiesler–Mathog experiment was very tightly controlled in order to tease out the effects of number of acts. Extreme control often brings into prominence very weak variables whose effects would be obscured in more ordinary situations. Was our finding of that variety? We decided to test the generality and power of the Kiesler–Mathog finding by doing a field study. In field studies, one loses a great deal of control over the environment of the subjects. In competition with other influences on the person, a given variable must be powerful to have any effect at all. However, we thought that if the interactive effect of commitment and attack were related to the general process whereby people become more extreme in their attitudes, then it must be a rather powerful effect. A field study would be useful.

The following study was carried out at Yale by myself, Roberta Mathog, Phillipa Pool and Richard Howenstine and is not reported elsewhere.

Commitment and the Boomerang Effect: A Field Study

The first consideration in testing the interactive effect of commitment and attack in the field was the implementation of commitment. Should we, for example, translate directly from the Kiesler–Mathog experiment and vary commitment by the number of acts performed by the subject? We decided not, for two reasons. First, varying the number of acts in an uncontrolled setting is not only difficult and awkward, but also invites serious confounding with other important variables, as we discussed in introducing the Kiesler–Mathog experiment. Second, as long as we are testing the power of the effect, we might as well take the opportunity to test its generality to a second method of manipulating commitment.

Briefly, the experiment took the following form. Half of a group of liberal young women were asked to sign a petition in favor of disseminating birth control information in the local high school (pretests showed that almost all of them were in favor of this). The other half of the subjects were not asked to sign. The following day, half of the subjects in each condition found under their apartment doors, a nicely produced leaflet emotionally attacking this position. On the third day, each subject was visited by a girl purporting to be taking a market research survey, jointly sponsored by a number of independent organizations. As part of this survey, the subjects were asked what sorts of action (e.g., contribute money, stuff envelopes) they would be willing to take on behalf of six organizations and whether they wished to be contacted by any of the organizations for volunteer work.

Our hypothesis is an interaction between commitment and attack: Subjects who are both committed and attacked should be more willing to act on their beliefs than either those committed but not attacked or those attacked but not committed. In other words, when a subject is not committed to some consonant behavior, she will be understandably reluctant to volunteer for action on the issue following an attack. When the subject is firmly committed, however, the attack will arouse her defenses, and she will attempt to justify her previous behavior by volunteering for further action.

METHOD

Subjects. Seventy-three young women living in married student housing at Yale University participated and were randomly assigned to conditions. Of these, four refused to sign the petition and were discarded from the analysis, leaving a net sample of 69.

The petition. Half of the subjects were approached in their homes to sign a petition in favor of disseminating birth control information in the public high schools in New Haven, Connecticut. The first experimenter, a young female, introduced herself: "Hello, my name is ______ and I'm on a committee of Yale Wives. May I speak with you for a moment? The Superintendent of Schools is considering a proposition that birth control information be made available in the high schools. We think that this is a good idea so we are trying to collect signatures on a petition to show our support. Would you like to read the petition?"

The mimeographed petition was addressed to the Superintendent and the Board of Education and said, "We, the undersigned Yale Wives, feel that it is both *important* and *necessary* for the protection and education of our youth that *BIRTH CONTROL INFORMATION BE MADE AVAILABLE IN THE HIGH SCHOOLS*." Underneath this statement were three handwritten signatures. After the subject signed the petition, the experimenter thanked her for her interest and left. Signing the petition constituted the committing act.

The Attack. The following day, half of the commitment subjects and half of a similar and randomly selected group (no commitment) received the

the attack on the birth control issue. The attack is reproduced in Figure 4-3. Note that it is professionally printed, the counter-arguments are rather emotionally based, and it is unsigned. A male experimenter delivered the attacks in the late afternoon of each day, sliding it under the apartment door, inside the screen door, or in whatever place was readily available.

birth control information
for teenagers ?

The Board of Education is considering a proposition to make birth control information available in New Haven high schools. We of the Council of Concerned Citizens feel that this is wrong! There are terrible dangers involved which must be made known to the voting public. The following are just a few of the many reasons why birth control information should not be made available in our high schools:

- Information on birth control is TOO PERSONAL to be discussed in coed classes. Rather it should be discussed in the home.
- STUDENTS will be confused since they WON'T UNDERSTAND how birth control information should morally affect their own sexual behavior
- Sexual material presented in a school setting can only lead to PROMISCUITY. As a further result VENEREAL DISEASE would sharply increase among high school students.
- The school system has NO RIGHT to determine when children are mature enough to deal effectively with birth control information. It is NOT THE RESPONSIBILITY OF THE SCHOOL SYSTEM alone to decide a question with such complex moral, legal, and ethical considerations.

BIRTH CONTROL INFORMATION SHOULD NOT BE MADE AVAILABLE IN OUR HIGH SCHOOLS

FIG. 4-3. The leaflet used as the attack on the birth control issue.

The Posttest. On the third day, or as soon thereafter as possible, each subject was posttested. This experimenter, also a young female, said, "Hello, my name is ______, and I'm working for a marketing research agency which has been hired by a number of organizations interested in problems of concern to the New Haven community. We're taking a public opinion survey in order to find out how the public really feels about these issues. I wonder if you'd be willing to help me out. It won't take long. To save your time and ours I'll be asking you questions relating to several issues of community concern. Because of the format of this survey—because there will be several questions on various topics—it is necessary that you hold off any questions or comments until the survey is completed. Pleasc answer all questions as best as you can and please do not ask any questions until the survey is completed. This way we can go faster and it will be a more valid survey." (At this point, the experimenter showed the subject a seven-point Likert scale marked from strongly agree to strongly disagree. The scale was explained to her and she kept it in front of her during questions about attitude items.)

The subject first completed 18 attitude items using the Likert scale. The items concerned water floridation, air pollution, and student unrest. In addition, there were two items indirectly related and one item directly related to the birth control issue. The former were, "The United Nations should distribute birth control information to overpopulated areas in the world," and, "Family planning information should be available to married couples." The question directly related (sixth in the series) was, "Birth control information should be made available in the high schools."

The experimenter then said, "Now that we've finished the public opinion survey as such, we'd like your help on some other questions. In order to get any program rolling, the people with the authority to do so must know that there is support for their proposition. We'd like to get some of your ideas as to how such support can be demonstrated. In general, do you think that people who contribute money to an organization are demonstrating support for that organization? Yes or No?"

After the inevitable affirmative answer, the subject was handed a list of six "organizations." The organizations were described as for or against air pollution,* water fluoridation, and birth control information in the high schools. The subject was asked to which, if any, of the six organizations would she be willing to contribute money. The same procedure was followed for six other methods of demonstrating support: (*a*) joining the group, (*b*) calling people on the telephone to solicit support, (*c*) signing a petition to be sent to the local newspaper, (*d*) signing a petition to be sent to the proper

* Specifically for or against laws requiring industry to install air pollution control devices such as filters or precipitators.

authorities, (*e*) stuffing and addressing envelopes (for propaganda), (*f*) passing out pamphlets on the street corners.

Next the subject was shown a list of nine pamphlets and asked if she would like any sent to her free of charge. Among these were three concerned with birth control, entitled respectively, "The danger of distributing birth control information in the schools," "Eradicate illegitimacy with the pill," and "The importance of educating our youth: birth control information for teenagers." Only the first and third, of course, were specifically related to the petition signed earlier.

The subject was then asked if she would like to be contacted by any of the six organizations (previously described) to volunteer her services. She was given to understand that if she did give her permission, the organization would most certainly contact her and expect her to support them actively in some way. Of course, the experimenter assured her, her name would not be passed on without her explicit permission.

The interview was closed with a question, embedded in a few filler items, asking if the subject had discussed any of the issues recently with anyone.

Methodological Notes. The two female experimenters switched roles regularly so that each was in charge of half of the petitions and half of the posttests (to reduce the possibility that results might be due to any characteristic of a particular experimenter). The experimenter in charge of petitions was also supposed to assign a control subject for each petition signed. This was done by simply observing another woman who happened to be home that day (and therefore, presumably did not work and could be found home another day as well) and jotting down her address. Half of each set was then assigned to the attack condition, using a table of random numbers. This half-list of addresses was given to the second experimenter so that he could distribute the attack the following day. The full list of addresses was given to the posttester, who remained unaware of the condition to which a subject had been assigned.

All work was done during the day so that the husbands would be unlikely to be home. (Note that all actual contact with our female subjects was made by our female experimenters.) To reduce the possibility of suspicion, we asked only one attitude question directly pertaining to the petition (and then embedded among 17 others), and we did not try to ascertain whether the subject recalled signing the petition or if she actually read the attack. The latter two considerations, while reducing suspicion (vis à vis connecting up the separate parts of the experiments as emanating from a single source), no doubt reduced the experimental impact on the subject as well. We cannot be certain, for example, whether a particular subject read or even received the attack, since it might have been blown away by the wind, stolen by a neighborhood child (the apartments are the typical university ones, piled together and overrun by children), or discarded without a glance, as advertising. We can only be certain that the attack was delivered. Consequently, we must consider our results rather conservative.

Results

Attitude. One of the 18 items in the questionnaire given first in the posttest procedure was, "Birth control information should be made available in the high schools." The mean responses to this question are presented in Table 4-1. As the Table shows, there is only one effect of note: for commitment ($F = 15.17$; $df = 1,65$; $p < .001$). Commitment in the guise of signing a petition had a powerful effect on the expression of attitude, leading to a more extreme attitude. The attack appeared to have no effect on this item.

TABLE 4-1

Mean Attitude toward Birth Control Information as a Function of Prior Consonant Commitment and Subsequent Attack[a]

	Commitment	
	Yes Petition Signed	No Petition Not Signed
Attack	1.71[b]	3.29
	(17)	(17)
No attack	1.74	3.31
	(19)	(16)

[a] N's are in parentheses.
[b] The smaller the number, the more one is in favor of disseminating birth control information in the high schools.

There were also two related items: "The United Nations should distribute birth control information to overpopulated areas in the world," and "Family planning information should be available to married couples." Responses to these two items were highly correlated (overall, $r = .65$, $p < .01$), and an analysis of variance was carried out on the summed score. This analysis showed two main effects: Committed subjects were more extreme than uncommitted subjects ($F = 5.07$; $p < .05$), and attacked subjects tended to be slightly more extreme in their attitudinal response than unattacked subjects ($F = 3.93$; $p < .10$). The attitude data are not arrayed quite as expected, but we shall defer discussion until the other relevant data have been presented below.

Volunteering for Further Action. Table 4-2 shows the percentage of subjects in each condition who said that they were willing to be contacted by an organization advocating the dissemination of birth control information, for the purpose of doing volunteer work. One can readily see that these data are quite different than those for the attitude items. The overall interaction is significant ($F = 4.13$; $df = 1,\infty$; $p < .05$). When subjects were not committed, the attack reduced the percentage volunteering (although not significantly). Commitment by itself had little effect: Without attack, 10.5% of the committed subjects were willing to volunteer versus 19% of the uncommitted subjects. Within the commitment conditions, the attack *increased* one's willingness to volunteer (41% vs. 10.5%; CR = 2.21; $p < .05$).

TABLE 4-2

PERCENTAGE OF SUBJECTS IN EACH CONDITION WILLING TO DO VOLUNTEER WORK FOR AN ORGANIZATION ADVOCATING THE DISSEMINATION OF BIRTH CONTROL INFORMATION TO HIGH SCHOOL STUDENTS[a]

	Commitment	
	Yes Petition Signed	No Petition Not Signed
Attack	41% (17)	6% (17)
No attack	10.5% (19)	19% (16)

[a] *N*'s are in parentheses.

Recall that this is a firm measure, requiring an unequivocal behavioral orientation from the subject. That is, it is not a statement of attitude nor a preference, but a firm expectation that if one responds affirmatively, further behavior will be required. The subject was told that the organization would contact her and it presumably would be quite difficult to disengage oneself. This is what Aronson and Carlsmith (1968) refer to as a *behavioroid* measure, about which they say one can be more confident than an attitude measure.

Other Acts. Recall that each subject was asked if she would be willing to volunteer for any of seven actions in favor of the birth control organization: (*a*) contributing money to the group, (*b*) joining the group, (*c*) calling people on the telephone to solicit support, (*d*) signing a petition to be sent to the local newspaper, (*e*) signing a petition to be sent to the proper authorities; (*f*) stuffing and addressing envelopes, (*g*) passing out pamphlets on the street corners. These can be regarded as something midway between the attitude measure and the behavioroid measure discussed above. To voice willingness to act indicates approval of the organization in question, but at that point in the experimental procedure there was no expectation that approval had any other implications. We took as our dependent measure the mean number of the seven possible actions that each subject indicated she was willing to undertake for such an organization. Table 4-3 presents these data.

TABLE 4-3

MEAN NUMBER OF ACTIONS (OF SEVEN) THAT SUBJECTS WERE WILLING TO CARRY OUT FOR THE BIRTH CONTROL ORGANIZATION[a]

	Commitment	
	Yes Petition Signed	No Petition Not Signed
Attack	5.41 (17)	2.41 (17)
No attack	4.74 (19)	3.94 (16)

[a] *N*'s are in parentheses.

These data are quite similarly arrayed as the contact data above. The interaction is significant ($F = 4.09$; $p < .05$). The results may be described in terms of the different effect that the attack had on committed and uncommitted subjects. When uncommitted subjects were attacked, the number of acts for which they were willing to volunteer decreased sharply ($t = 1.94$; $p < .05$). When committed subjects were attacked, the number of acts increased slightly.

We decided to check a little further on the consistency or reliability of the difference between the commitment/no-attack and commitment/attack conditions. There are several ways of going about this. First, we looked at the consistency of the difference across the seven acts. In six of the seven cases, the commitment/attack group was more likely to volunteer than the commitment/no-attack group ($p = .0625$), and in the seventh instance (addressing envelopes) the difference was very small (.71 vs. .74). In short, the difference seems to be reliable in the sense of appearing for each of the contributing acts. A second way of inspecting this difference is in terms of the distributions of total scores. For example, in the commitment/attack condition, 11 of the 17 subjects were willing to do at least six of the seven acts, whereas only five of the 19 subjects in the corresponding commitment/no-attack condition had such extreme scores (68% vs. 26%; CR = 2.65, $p < .01$). In sum, the increase of volunteering of committed subjects under attack seems to be reliable. Of course, the opposite effects hold as well for the uncommitted subjects. For example, uncommitted subjects under attack were less likely to volunteer than the uncommitted subjects not under attack, for *each* of the seven acts, analyzed separately.

Information Seeking. At one point in the posttest, the subject was shown a list of nine titles of pamphlets and asked if she would like to have any of them sent to her at no cost. Three of these were related to the birth control issue: one obviously was in favor of proposed action ("The importance of educating our youth: birth control information for teenagers"), one was against any action ("The dangers of distributing birth control information in the high schools"), and one was relevant but not explicitly for or against information distribution ("Eradicate illegitimacy with the pill"). It is instructive to inspect the percentage of subjects within each condition who asked for each of the pamphlets. These data are shown in Table 4-4.

TABLE 4-4

THE RELATIVE PERCENTAGES OF SUBJECTS IN EACH CONDITION WHO REQUESTED EACH OF THREE PROFFERED PAMPHLETS RELEVANT TO THE ATTITUDE ISSUE: CONSISTENT, INCONSISTENT, AND NEUTRAL

Experimental Conditions		Stance of Pamphlet vis à vis Information Distribution		
		In Favor	Against	Neutral, but Relevant
Commitment	Attack	65%	29%	41%
	No attack	100%	63%	74%
No commitment	Attack	53%	41%	23.5%
	No attack	56%	37.5%	25%

The most interesting thing that the Table shows is the consistency among conditions and across pamphlets. That is, the differences between conditions are about the same, whether the pamphlet was in favor of the distribution of birth control information, against it, or neutral. Regardless of pamphlet, there is little or no difference between the two conditions without commitment. The attack had little effect on the desire to read any of the pamphlets. However, there is a consistent difference between the two commitment conditions for each of the pamphlets. In each case, the committed/attacked subjects were less likely to request a pamphlet, whether it was in favor of information distribution (CR = 2.95, corrected; $p < .01$), against it (CR = 2.11; $p < .05$), or neutral (CR = 1.87; $p < .10$).

One might say that signing the petition made the issues involved more salient and led the committed but unattacked subjects to seek out more information on the issue, both pro and con. Apparently, however, when one is both committed and attacked, the time for leisurely contemplation of the issues is over, and the time for action has arrived. Recall that the committed/attacked subjects were more willing to act on their beliefs, even though they did not care to have any more information about the issue. I should add that the percentages represent the same subjects. For example, all of thc subjects in the commitment/attack condition who requested the pamphlet against their beliefs (29%) also requested the pamphlet in favor of their beliefs (i.e., they are among the 65% in the table). The same thing is true of the commitment/no-attack subjects.

Time Between Attack and Posttest. As mentioned previously, it was not always possible for the posttest to be given on the day immediately following the attack. The experimenter could not always find the subject at home, and the only option was to continue to return to the subject's home day after day until she was home. The actual period between attack and posttest varied between the normal (shall we say, desired) one day and as much as ten days. This variable has not been considered before, and all of the data thus far presented have included all of the subjects, regardless of when the posttest was given. Of the 69 subjects, however, only 46 or 67% were given the posttest with only the one-day interval, evenly distributed among cells. We will only add here that the differences between conditions discussed above are statistically more reliable if one considers only those subjects with the one-day interval between attack and posttest. The effects are not so transitory as to be limited to those subjects, however. The trends are still there for the late subjects although they are understandably weaker (considering both elapsed time and the smaller sample sizes for the statistics, one would expect the effect to weaken over time in this analysis).

The Discrepancy Between Behavior and Attitude. Recall our hypotheses. When subjects were not committed, we expected that, after attack, they would be less likely to volunteer for attitudinally relevant behavior and be less extreme in their attitude. Conversely, when subjects were committed, we expected them to do the opposite following attack: to be more extreme in their attitude and even more willing to volunteer for further behavior for the cause. The data regarding our behavioral measures fit the hypotheses rather nicely. On the other hand, the attitude data were not as expected. For attitudes we found only a main effect for commitment: Committed subjects were more extreme in their attitude than uncommitted subjects, without even a hint of the expected interaction. Why this difference in response between behavior and attitude? We tried to investigate this issue further, insofar as we were able, given the limitations of the data.

In part, the lack of difference in attitude between the two commitment conditions may be due to a ceiling effect. For example, 16 of 19 subjects in the commitment/no-attack condition have scores of 1 or 2 on a seven-point scale. If the attack were to make these subjects more extreme in their attitude, there is little room on the scale to move (zero is not a possibility). Similarly, and expectedly, given the validity of this argument, 16 of 17 of commitment/attack subjects have these extreme scores.

There may also be a small sampling bias that contributes to the commitment main effect for attitude. Recall that four subjects would not sign the petition and, hence, were discarded from the analysis. Such subjects may be against the distribution of birth control information in the schools. There is no such throwing away of subjects in the no-commitment conditions, leading to a slight bias in the analysis of attitude data. To check on this possibility, we inspected the data for the "organization" that was reputedly against information distribution in the posttest. No subjects in either commitment condition were willing to volunteer for *any* behavior connected with this organization, but six subjects in the two no-commitment conditions volunteered for some of this behavior (three in each condition). Indeed of the seven possible behaviors involved, four of these six subjects were willing to volunteer for at least six of the seven actions against the distribution of birth control information (the other scores were 1 and 3). All six had a score of at least 6 on the seven-point attitude measure; the average number of behaviors in favor of distribution that they were willing to perform was 0.5, as opposed to over 4.0 for other subjects; and none of the six was willing to be contacted by the organization espousing the distribution of birth control information. In short, we do have evidence of a slight bias in the attitude data: A few subjects (four, at most) against the issue were discarded from the commitment conditions, while similar subjects (perhaps six) were retained in the no-commitment conditions.

Suppose we simply eliminate these six subjects from our analysis, thus artificially equating the two groups on initial attitude? We tried it, and recomputed our major analysis. Eliminating the six odd subjects from consideration has the same effect on each of our dependent measures; it reduces the overall main effect between the commitment conditions. It makes the means of the two no-commitment conditions closer to the two means of the commitment conditions, regardless of which measure one looks at. As a result, there is little or nothing left in the attitude data, but the predicted interaction that occurred on both sets of behavioral measurements is undisturbed.

It appears that the differences among commitment conditions can be explained with reference to a slight sampling bias in our data. The net result of this means that we obtained the predicted interaction between commitment and attack on all of the behavioral (or behavioroid) measures, but there was little effect of anything on the attitude measures. Given these considerations, one might think that the lack of boomerang effect (on attitude) among the committed/attacked subjects is due to that the fact that there was no room on the attitude scale to move; scores were already extreme. But why no effect of the attack on the uncommitted subjects (on the attitude scale)? I don't know, but one reason might be that the attack was intentionally a weak one, one that we thought beforehand would arouse one's defenses, but still be relatively easy to reject for committed subjects. In this case, it was strong enough so that uncommitted subjects were less willing to participate in attitude relevant behavior but not strong enough to get them to move their mark on the attitude scale from, say, 2 ("agree" on the scale) to 3 ("mildly agree").

It is also noteworthy that the attitude data in the Kiesler–Mathog experiment showed the boomerang effect less clearly than did the data on behavior. (If, indeed, they showed the effect at all). It may be that the phenomenon is more that one simply tries to justify one's current attitude (and previous behavior) rather than that one changes one's attitude. In this view, the subject would not think that he has changed his attitude on the issue; he might instead think the attitude needs acting on or defending with further behavior. If so, it would be mildly ironic since, as we discussed before, this type of extreme behavior should ultimately lead to a more extreme attitude as well. In the present experiment, if we had insisted (or even allowed) that our subjects follow through on the agreed upon behavior of passing out leaflets, contributing money, and so forth, their attitudes would certainly have been more extreme in a very short time, I expect.

Discussion

The Theoretical Relationship between Commitment and Strength of Attack

In both experiments detailed in this chapter, we found an interesting effect of commitment. Under conditions of high commitment, subjects were not only more resistant to attack on their attitudes, but they actually became more extreme, particularly behaviorally, than they were before the attack. In presenting these experiments, we have assumed that a particular process takes place. The committed subject cannot change as a result of the attack. However, the attack threatens the validity of his previous behavior and attitude. We have suggested that, in the process of defending against this threat, the person seeks to justify his previous behavior by (*a*) insisting that he would do the same thing over again if given the opportunity and (*b*) agreeing to commit himself to even more attitudinally related behavior, when requested.

Of course, the boomerang effect has not always been noted in commitment experiments. In both the Kiesler–Sakumura, and the Kiesler, Pallak, and Kanouse experiments, committed subjects were simply more resistant to the attack. They did not become more extreme following the attack. When, then, are we to expect the simple resistance phenomenon and when an intensification of attitude and behavior? As we briefly mentioned before in passing, it should depend on a particular combination of degree of commitment and the strength of the attack. The attack must be strong enough to arouse one's defenses, but weak enough (relative to the level of commitment) that one can eventually dispense with it and reject it. With an extremely strong attack we assume that one will eventually give in and change one's opinions. With an extremely weak attack, perhaps one would not attend to it all, rejecting it easily as unworthy of serious attention. The logical implication of this argument is a family of curves, representing the complex interaction between degree of commitment and the strength of attack. One possible set of these curves is represented in Figure 4-4.

Consider the effects of the different levels of commitment separately. The Figure indicates that when one has only a very low level of commitment to some consonant behavior, then even a relatively weak attack would probably produce some change in associated attitudes. Further, for this low commitment, an increase in the strength of attack leads to a corresponding increase in the effect on the individual. For moderate commitment the general shape of the curve is similar, but shows less change for any level of strength of attack. We have indicated, however, that the boomerang effect will occur for subjects moderately committed when the attack is very weak. As mentioned, this combination should arouse one's defenses (leading one to try to justify his previous behavior to himself), but the attack is still relatively weak enough to be eventually rejected. Under high commitment, the shape of the curve is somewhat different. This is due primarily to the presumed peculiar situation of extremely high commitment and a very weak attack. With this combination, we are hypothesizing that the attack is not powerful enough to even arouse one's defenses, and the subject would simply reject the attack forthwith and without serious consideration. Consequently, the curve shows that a weak attack will have little or no effect on a highly committed individual. However, as we increase the power of the attack on the highly committed person, we began to arouse his defenses. He responds negatively to this, and Figure 4-4 shows the boomerang effect for the combination of high commitment and a moderate attack. The highly committed subject under a moderately powerful attack may be considered as in the same psychological state (with similar results) as the moderately committed person under a weak attack.

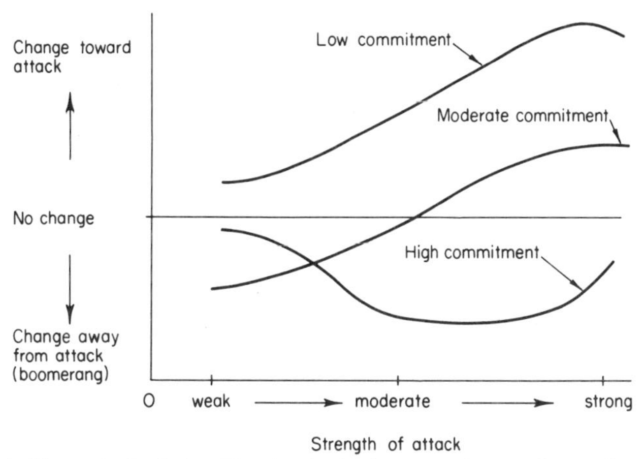

FIG. 4-4. Theoretical relationship of attitude change to degree of commitment to consonant behavior and the strength of attack on an attitudinal position.

Consider, for example, the results of the Kiesler–Sakumura experiment and those in our last experiment (Kiesler, Mathog, Pool, and Howenstine). I would think that the translation of commitment was approximately the same for those two experiments. In one case, high commitment subjects recorded a public speech; in the other, they signed a public petition. Psychologically, these are probably quite similar. For the sake of exposition, let's say that in both cases, we have low and moderate levels of commitment. The difference in results then comes from the difference in the strength of the two attacks. In the Kiesler–Sakumura study, subjects read a nicely printed communication handed to them by a (junior) psychologist in a university sponsored event as a semiregular part of their psychology course (that is, it was required that they participate in experiments). Let's call this a moderately powerful attack; several things lead the subject to take the counter-communication seriously; hence, the results represented in Figure 4-4. Under moderate attack, the moderately committed subjects change not at all, and the subjects under low commitment change their attitudes in the direction advocated in the counter-communication.

One could argue that the attack in the Kiesler *et al.* experiment is much weaker. An anonymous and emotionally based flyer was stuck under their door. This does happen occasionally, and such things do not require much serious attention (as would the same thing delivered and read within an experiment in the laboratory). The Kiesler *et al.* results are represented in Figure 4-4 under low and moderate commitment for a *weak* attack. The graph shows that under weak attack, the low commitment subjects should show some change toward the attack and the moderately committed subjects should boomerang.

Of course, I don't mean that the results of these experiments were derived from implications of the figure and therefore support its theoretical representation. Quite the opposite. Considering the results led us to pose the relationships in the figure. The results are consistent with the figure, as well they must be. However, the implications of the interactive effects of commitment and attack deserve separate test.

The Escalation of Commitment

There is an interesting implication of the Kiesler *et al.* experiment. That is, when you attack a committed person and your attack is of inadequate strength, you drive him to even more extreme behaviors in defense of his previous commitment. His commitment escalates,* in a sense, because the number of acts consistent with his belief increases. In addition, as a result of these other behaviors, the person is likely to encounter information and other people that very well might lead him to an even more extreme attitude, even more behavior, and so forth. There is a moral. Suppose you are considering trying to convince bigots to be more liberal. In discussing one set of possible arguments, you say, "Let's try it, *it can't hurt.*" The present data suggest quite the opposite. It damned well *can* hurt, because it might send your hypothetical subject scrambling in an even more extreme fashion than he was before.

In that sense, the escalation of commitment depends upon a particular combination of degree of commitment and strength of attack. It is important to emphasize that it is the *degree* of commitment that is critical, not commitment *per se*. Consider, for example, the difference in results for the one-act and three-act conditions in the Kiesler–Mathog experiment. If one views commitment as a yes-or-no, black-or-white variable, then subjects in both of these conditions were committed (and subjects in the zero-act group were uncommitted). But the large difference in results in that experiment does not appear between committed and uncommitted subjects, but rather between a low and moderate level of commitment. In short, thinking of commitment

* I am indebted to David Kanouse for suggesting the phrase.

as a dichotomous variable would not do adequate justice to those data, much as we suggested in Chapter II.

The attack was necessary also. The attack provided the emotional impetus, the motivation, as it were, to change. Commitment in isolation had little effect. One can, however, consider the term "attack" very broadly. Consider, for example, an experiment by Marlowe, Frager, and Nuttall (1965). Liberal Harvard undergraduates were asked their opinions of Afro-Americans. They responded, of course, very favorably. Their opinions are now open and public, and we might consider this a committing act of sorts. All subjects were then told that their attitudes were too liberal to take part in an attitude survey for which they would have been paid either $1.50 or $20.00. In the terms of Marlowe, Frager, and Nuttall, subjects suffered for their beliefs, but some suffered more than others. Is it stretching it too far to consider this suffering as an indirect attack on belief? Perhaps not.

In a second and unconnected interview, subjects were asked to volunteer as unpaid guides to show Harvard to African Negro students. The dependent variable was the percentage of students who volunteered, as a function of previous loss. Of the students who lost only $1.50 as a result of holding too liberal an attitude, 43% volunteered as guides. Of those suffering $20.00 worth, 77% volunteered. Our analysis would have to consider commitment as identical for the two conditions but the attack of differential strength. Losing $20.00 because of belief has stronger negative implications for belief than does losing only $1.50. The similarity in effect between this experiment and the two commitment conditions in Kiesler *et al.* is striking. I am not as strongly urging the reader to accept this explanation of the Marlowe *et al.* experiment* as to consider the term "attack" in a very broad sense.

A Concluding Note on Attitudes and Behavior

In both of the experiments presented in this chapter, the results were much clearer for behavior than they were for the subjects' attitudes. The obvious question is, Are the conclusions here to be limited only to self-justifying behavior, or is there a similar process for attitudes? Can we get the boomerang effect with attitudes as well as behavior? The answer is yes, we can, as the three experiments detailed in the following chapter will attest.

* Marlowe *et al.* explain their data in terms of dissonance theory, positing that greater suffering for one's belief should produce larger amounts of dissonance. This explanation, of course, is not precluded by the present analysis.

V

COMMITMENT AND FOREWARNING

The commitment model is also applicable to situations in which the individual is forewarned of an impending attack on his beliefs. In the present chapter, we consider three original experiments on this topic and show how these three experiments suggest a resolution between apparently conflicting views of the effects of forewarning. Proper introduction requires a short review of other data on this issue.

There have been two main findings and concomitant theories on the effects of forewarning of attack. Some studies show that forewarning a person of an impending attack on his beliefs either nullifies the attack or produces a boomerang effect. For example, Kiesler and Kiesler (1964) had subjects read a communication which, for two groups, contained a footnote stating that the article was designed to make them change their opinions. For one of these groups, the footnote appeared on the first page of the article; for the second, the same footnote appeared at the end of the article (in addition, a third group had no footnote, and a fourth, neither footnote nor article). In each case, the article was counter-attitudinal; it represented an attack on their current beliefs.

When the footnote appeared on the first page, we can consider the subjects *forewarned*. Several things drew their attention to the footnote, and it is likely that they read it before beginning the article. Thus, prior to reading the article, these subjects knew that the article advocated an opinion contrary to their own and that it was supposed to induce them to change this opinion. The second group of subjects, which Kiesler and Kiesler called the *after-*

warned subjects, read at least the first page (of the page-and-a-half article) before stumbling onto the footnote. Considering the two additional control conditions (no footnote and no attack, respectively), this study represents a reasonable test of the effects of forewarning on resistance to subsequent attack. The results showed that subjects who read the footnote at the beginning of the article, that is, those forewarned of attack, were less influenced by the communication than subjects who either read the footnote at the end of the article or did not read the footnote at all. Indeed, there was a suggestion of a boomerang effect. That is, there was a tendency for forewarned subjects to adopt even more extreme attitudes following attack than they had held prior to it (compared to the condition receiving neither the attack nor the footnote: $t = 1.54$; $df = 87$). This resistance (or boomerang) effect has been found in a number of studies (e.g., Ewing, 1942; Allyn & Festinger, 1961; Husek, 1965; Freedman & Sears, 1965). This combined set of studies constitutes one-half of the empirical picture of forewarning.

McGuire (e.g., McGuire & Millman, 1965) has suggested quite a different model of forewarning and its effects. McGuire argues for the opposite effect: that when forewarned, the subject will tend to abandon his attitudinal position and take up (at least partly) the position to be advocated in the impending attack. McGuire and Millman say that,

> People tend to be anxious about their ability to resist social pressure; . . . hence when told in advance that certain beliefs that he happens to accept will be exposed to skillful persuasive attacks, the person worries that he will succumb to the arguments and appear gullible. An elegant self-esteem preserving (and face-saving) maneuver in this situation is for the person to decide, before the attack comes, that he did not really hold the target belief in the first place [p. 471].

In this view, to be convinced by a counter-communication is embarrassing and a blow to one's self-esteem. The forewarning implies that the attack will be impeccable and devastating, and the subject will undoubtedly have a new opinion after reading the counter-communication. To avoid the negative implications of appearing gullible, he adopts the new opinion (or what he thinks it will be) *before* the attack, thus effectively dealing with the demands of reality (i.e., the attack) and his own self-view at the same time. In short, this process is a distortion of one's beliefs to oneself so that one can both handle the attack and preserve one's self-esteem.

McGuire suggests several limiting conditions for the usefulness of anticipatory lowering of beliefs as a device for preserving one's self-esteem. One limitation is the type of issue. When the issue is an emotional, unverifiable one, a matter of taste perhaps, then being persuaded has clearer implications for one's self-esteem than when the issue is a dry technical one, a matter of objective, verifiable fact. In McGuire's view, being persuaded on technical issues reflects objectivity and openness to well-documented argumentation. If one were resistant to persuasion on verifiable issues, it would not be a boon to one's self-esteem, since it would only imply close-mindedness. Thus, anticipatory belief change is not expected to occur for technical issues. McGuire and Millman tested this hypothesis by warning subjects of an impending attack on issues that were either *emotional* or *technical.* As they had predicted, forewarned subjects showed anticipatory belief change on the so-called emotional issues but not on the technical ones.

McGuire proposes a second limitation on his hypothesis: that the subject's initial belief should be relatively ambiguous. The person must distort his own opinion to himself, and if that opinion is not ambiguous, distortion is difficult. Without ambiguity, then, it would be difficult to employ the face-saving strategy of anticipatory belief change. Whereas McGuire requires ambiguous beliefs, most (but not all) of the studies showing a resistance effect for forewarning have used topics that were relatively important.*

In short, we have both an empirical and a theoretical conflict. It is clear that under some conditions, unspecified, forewarning a subject of an impending attack on his beliefs either nullifies the effect of the attack or causes subjects to react negatively and become even more extreme than before. On the other hand, the data of McGuire and Millman clearly show (with an accompanying explanation) the opposite effect: Their subjects treated the forewarning as an attack in itself, one might say, and changed their opinions accordingly.

There are several possible explanations for this empirical discrepancy. In fact, it is not necessary for the two sets of data to be related in a straightforward way. For example, the McGuire theory deals most specifically with the effects of forewarning,† whereas the opposing set of data largely confounds forewarning and attack. Kiesler and Kiesler, for instance, did not try to test the effect of forewarning by itself. They were interested in the combined effects of forewarning and attack, and so they did not separate them.

Not surprisingly, however, this conflict in data (indeed, if you are willing even to accept it as a conflict) set off a train of thought in us that ended up with one particular variable in mind: commitment.

The commitment findings detailed in the last chapter can be applied to the

* I imply, of course, that when a person thinks an issue important, his opinion on the topic tends to be well formed and unambiguous.

† Actually to be precise, McGuire says that emotional and technical issues should have the same effect when forewarning and attack are considered together. It is just that for emotional issues, the major part of the total change is directly due to the forewarning, whereas for technical issues, it is a consequence of the attack.

study of forewarning with but two simple assumptions. First, we must assume that in previous research on forewarning, the degree of commitment varied from study to study. Secondly, we must assume that a forewarning can be considered as an attack of sorts. The first assumption is obviously plausible, at least in isolation. The second seems reasonable enough. A forewarning is an attack of sorts. When forewarned, the subject knows, for example, that there are others who do not agree with him on the issue (which may or may not have occurred to him before). Further, he knows that he shall be hearing from these folks shortly.

Recall our previous complicated discussion of the interactive effects of degree of commitment and the strength of attack on one's attitude. There we said that when the attack is extremely powerful or previous commitment is very low, the subject will abandon his attitudinal position and adopt the advocated opinion. However, when, relative to the level of commitment, the attack is strong enough to arouse one's defenses but weak enough to be successfully dealt with eventually, the boomerang effect occurs. Following this special combination of commitment and attack, the subject will show even more extreme attitudes than he did prior to the attack.

Apply this reasoning now to the findings on forewarning. The effects are similar. Under some conditions, the person responds negatively to the forewarning; under other conditions he responds positively. Could not then the difference between experiments reflect a corresponding difference in commitment?

Why not? If the person is mildly committed and the forewarning represents only a weak-to-moderate attack, then we expect the subject to change his opinion in the direction advocated in the attack (that is, implied in the forewarning). With greater commitment, however, and the same strength of attack, the person's defenses should be aroused and he should respond negatively to the attack; he should boomerang. In short, our commitment notions might easily be applied to the data on forewarning. If we are correct, research on this issue would help clarify apparently conflicting data on forewarning.

The following three experiments, by James M. Jones and myself, explore the issues of the interactive effects of commitment and forewarning of attack. The experiments have not been published elsewhere. In the first experiment, we focus on the differences of topic and issue that McGuire has written about. The results of this experiment led to the following two, in which we specifically manipulated degree of commitment.

The Interactive Effects of Commitment and Forwarning: Three Experiments

Experiment I

In this experiment, we tried to clarify the distinction that McGuire has made between emotional and technical issues. Recall that the unique aspect of McGuire's self-esteem theory is the prediction of a different effect of forewarning for emotional and technical issues. At this point, we accepted the distinction, but wondered what the psychological variable underlying the distinction was. We reasoned that one distinctive characteristic of emotional issues is that subjects feel their opinions are as valid as those of any expert ("I don't know anything about art, but I know what I like"). For technical issues, on the other hand, objective facts exist which potentially make one opinion more tenable than another. For emotional issues, there is no "right answer" in a sense; one person's guess or opinion is as good as any other's. For technical issues, there is a right answer; the issue can be resolved, and expertise is the critical factor.

In Campbell's terms, we tried to triangulate the emotional–technical distinction by translating it in a different way than McGuire. If successful, we would not only give some support for the McGuire model of forewarning, but we would also have a deeper understanding of the critical input for the theory: the distinction between emotional and technical issues. Parenthetically, we might add that we were not successful, but the experiment is important in that clear, but unexpected, side effects gave us some insight into the process of forewarning and led to Experiments II and III.

In Experiment I, we manipulated the extent to which a forthcoming communication, which disagreed with the subjects' opinions, was based on *complete*, incontrovertible evidence or simply *partial*, preliminary evidence. This was our translation of McGuire's technical and emotional concepts, respectively. Our predictions followed McGuire's reasoning. When communications are based on partial information, anticipatory lowering of belief should occur. With partial information, as in emotional issues, it would be damaging to one's self-esteem to be convinced later, so one presumably would distort his opinion immediately after the forewarning. Of course, when communications are based on complete evidence, no anticipatory lowering of belief should occur.

The experiment essentially replicates the McGuire and Millman experiment, except that the variable we thought to underlie the emotional–technical distinction was experimentally manipulated.

Method. Seventy-six male and female undergraduates at the University of Bridgeport received questionnaire booklets that were allegedly part of a student opinion survey. In this and following studies, subjects were tested in their regular classrooms in groups of about 20. The booklets contained all of the dependent measures and experimental manipulations and were constructed as follows.

1. The first pages indicated that a special committee of (fictitious) scholars had been investigating the problem of overcrowded colleges in the United States for three years. The introduction went on to say that the remainder of the booklet would include statements of the committee's proposed remedies for this problem and would provide an opportunity for students to indicate their reactions to these proposals.

There were four of these remedies, each one contrary to the average subject's opinion on the issue. Each subject was forewarned on two of them, which two varying from subject to subject. Independently of this, two of the proposals were presumably based on complete information, and two were based on partial information. The introduction to the proposal based on complete information read,

> As stated previously, some of the proposals were based on an exhaustive survey and data collection. All possible sources of information were questioned, all relevant records were studied, and where possible comparisons with existing programs were made. These data have provided very firm support for many of the proposals made by the Committee. An example of a proposal which has the ample support of the data is that . . .

The introduction to the proposal based on partial information read,

> An alternative means of arriving at some of the proposals was essentially an informal survey of a few students. The information upon which these proposals were based was obtained from casual conversations, observations and some anecdotal evidence. Also, some of the proposals were based on some impressions and intuitive ideas which seem, to the committee, to be viable means of resolving the problem. Although many of these proposals do not have direct evidence to support them, the members of the committee feel they warrant serious consideration. An example of such a proposal, which you will read later, is that . . .

2. All subjects then read examples of two of the four proposals they presumably were to read later in the booklet. These examples constituted the forewarning; they stated what the proposed remedy was (i.e., the position to be advocated in the communication to follow), without documentation. One of the examples was said to be based on complete information; the other, on partial information (see above).

3. Following the two forewarning statements, half of the subjects completed a questionnaire containing the dependent measures, the other half answered a filler set of items, unrelated to the dependent measures.

4. All subjects read the four proposals, that is, the four communications, and then answered the set of questions containing the dependent attitude measures.* Two of the proposals were said to be based on partial information, and two, on complete information. Naturally, this tallied with what subjects had been told on the forewarning.

5. Lastly, subjects were asked to state their opinions of the committee's purpose in administering the questionnaire, to evaluate the possible effectiveness of the proposals, and to make general comments about the questionnaire and the committee. Of course, these items helped us to determine whether subjects were suspicious in any way and if they generally accepted the experimental guise. When they were completed, the experiment was terminated, the deceptions and reasons for them were fully explained, and the nature and purpose of the experiment were outlined.

Proposals. Each proposed remedy (that is, each communication) was about one full typewritten page. Each mentioned arguments for the inadequacy of the present educational system and stressed the ways in which the proposal would contribute to speeding up the educational process. Presumably, the major aim of the committee was to reduce the BA degree to a three-year, rather than a four-year, program; and the specific proposals were directed at ways in which this aim could be achieved. The four proposals were (*a*) a policy of supervised and compulsory library study (three hours per day) should be instituted in colleges and universities across the country, (*b*) colleges and universities should institute a program whereby all upperclass students would be required to tutor beginning students for two hours per day, (*c*) all dating during the week should be eliminated, and (*d*) colleges and universities should raise the minimum course requirement to 21 hours per semester (as opposed to the usual 15 or so). Needless to say, the students did not regard the proposals enthusiastically.

* No-attack subjects filled out the dependent measures both before and after reading the committee's proposals, but only their first scores were analyzed. Attack subjects filled out the dependent measures only after they had read the proposals. The attack messages did produce opinion change but only if subjects had not been forewarned and if the proposals were based on partial rather than complete information. The attack by information interaction (within non-forewarned topics) was significant ($F = 4.39$; $df = 1{,}160$; $p < .05$). Since the attack messages had minimal impact in this study, they were excluded from the subsequent two studies and will not be discussed further. They are not critical to the line of thought to be developed since the issues under discussion concern forewarning rather than the effect of attack itself.

Dependent Measures. Each subject was asked two questions about each proposal. One of the questions, the extreme form, simply restated the conclusion of the committee. The other question was stated in a much milder way (e.g., "Students should spend more time in the library"). Subjects responded to these statements, eight in all, on 13-point, a priori rating scales labeled at the end points with "Strongly Agree" (13) and "Strongly Disagree" (1).

Experimental Design. The three independent variables (forewarning, attack, type of information) were combined into a 2 × 2 × 2 factorial design. Topics were counterbalanced across conditions. This allowed us to look at main effects for proposals and their interactive effects with independent variables; however, we had not expected such interactions at the outset of the experiment. A control group filled out the questionnaire containing the dependent measures but did not read the intervening experimental manipulations in the booklet. This group was included to determine what effect merely being in the experiment might have on subjects' opinions.

Results. Two significant effects were found. The first effect was a main effect for topics and consisted of greater agreement with the tutoring and library proposals than with the dating and hours proposals. A contrast involving one degree of freedom was highly significant ($F = 12.88$; $df = 1{,}160$; $p < .001$) for this effect.

The second effect was a topic-by-forewarning interaction (within complete information only), and its form is shown in Figure 5-1. When forewarned, subjects agreed more with the tutoring and library proposals than when not forewarned ($t = 2.50$; $df = 94$; $p < .02$). However, for the other two proposals, dating and hours, forewarned subjects agreed less than nonforewarned subjects ($t = 6.53$; $df = 94$; $p < .001$).* A contrast for this overall interaction was highly significant ($F = 8.65$; $df = 1{,}160$; $p < .01$). Mean opinion scores for the control subjects were very similar to scores for nonforewarned subjects. Merely being in the experiment had little effect on subjects' opinions.

When subjects had only partial information, there was no significant topic-by-forewarning interaction. However, the complete information conditions might simply be viewed as a more skillful attack on the subjects' beliefs. The more effective subjects expect the attack to be, the more likely they should be to use the anticipatory belief change to preserve self-esteem. Also, the more skillful the expected communication, the more the subjects'

* Of course, since each subject had an attitude score on each of the four topics we technically should not speak of forewarned subjects, but rather, of those topics on which the subject was forewarned. We adopted the former style for simplicity of exposition.

defenses would be aroused. Thus, in this case at least, the presence of complete information in the expected attack magnified the effects, both boomerang and anticipatory lowering of belief.

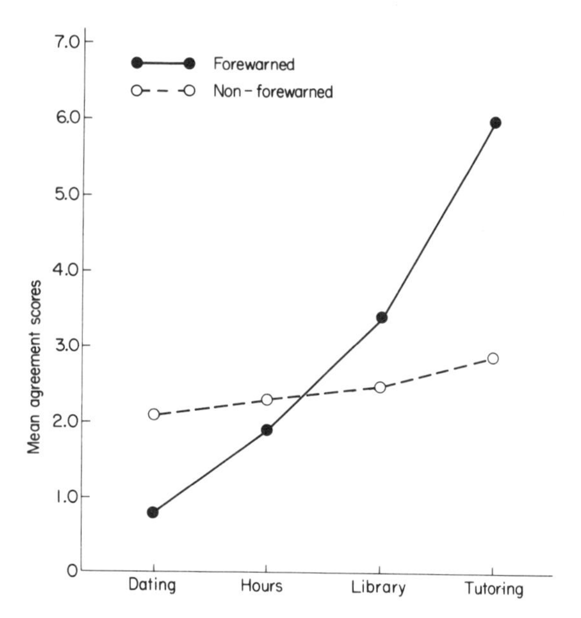

FIG. 5-1. Mean agreement with proposals as a function of forewarning. The larger the score, the greater the agreement.

Discussion. We were apparently wrong in our understanding of McGuire's emotional–technical distinction. We had thought that an emotional issue might correspond to partial information, and a technical issue, to complete information. As far as one can draw a conclusion from this experiment, this is incorrect. We did not obtain the expected effects for partial and complete information.

We had not been totally satisfied with McGuire's distinction, primarily because it depends on a classification of topics. We had hoped to bring some light to this area by demonstrating what the underlying psychological variable was. We ended up, however, with a similar level of explanation for our experiment: The results depended on topic. Consequently, we returned to our initial level of questioning. What produced these effects? What is the psychological variable underlying them?

Subjects did have more extreme opinions on the topics which produced the boomerang effect (dating and hours) and, in general, saw greater utility in the library and tutoring issues. Extremeness of opinion and harsh behavioral consequences of accepting the contrary position might be important variables in determining which of the two effects would occur. Perhaps, the more extreme subjects' opinions are, the more likely that forewarning would produce increased resistance to counter-arguments. Similarly, the more negative the consequences of accepting a contrary position, the more likely that the forewarning would arouse the subjects' defenses. For example, if subjects agreed to give up all dating during the week, a pleasurable part of their social lives would be lost. However, agreement to spend more time in the library has academic advantages that might offset the negative consequences associated with loss of free time. As the consequences of accepting the contrary position become less negative, the likelihood of using anticipatory belief change as a face-saving device might increase.

In some ways, this line of reasoning sounds similar to that proposed in Chapter IV and the first part of this chapter about the interactive effects of degree of commitment and the strength of the attack. The topic differences in Experiment I led us to consider whether or not the underlying variable might be one of previous commitment. It is not unreasonable to suppose that the two topics about which subjects held extreme attitudes, might also be associated with previous committing behaviors. In this view, subjects would be more committed on the dating and hours questions. The moderate attack implied in the forewarning would presumably arouse subjects' defenses, and in the process lead the subjects to have even more extreme attitudes than before, much the same process as proposed for the committed subjects in the Kiesler *et al.* experiment described in the last chapter. On the other two issues (library and tutoring), the level of commitment to previous behavior would not be sufficient to withstand the attack implied (and, to some extent, explicit) in the forewarning.

This chain of thought led us to try to manipulate commitment directly and vary forewarning independently. In both of the studies to follow, commitment and forewarning were manipulated orthogonally in a 2×2 factorial design. We predict that forewarning will produce opinion change for uncommitted subjects, but that subjects who have been experimentally committed to their beliefs will not change after forewarning. Assuming the proper combination of commitment and attack, committed subjects should become attitudinally more extreme following forewarning.

Experiment II

Restated, the purpose of this experiment was to reproduce the substance of the topic-by-forewarning interaction found in Experiment I by substituting the psychological variable of commitment for topic difference. If our analysis of the mechanism underlying those results is correct we should be able to reproduce both the anticipatory change and the reactance, the boomerang, for one topic. Therefore, in this experiment, we used essentially the same cover story but only one of the topics, i.e., the tutoring proposal.

Method. The general procedure was the same as for the previous experiment. Seventy-six male and female undergraduates received questionnaire booklets (in class) containing all of the experimental manipulations and dependent measures. The booklets were constructed as follows.

1. Subjects first responded to a set of questions, among which were two questions about the target belief (the tutoring proposal), and one question on reducing the BA degree from a four- to a three-year program. This both gave us a pretest and allowed the commitment manipulation, as follows.

2. After completing the questionnaire, subjects were requested to turn back to question #5 (the target question) and put their initials next to it. Each subject was informed that he would be asked later to list the reasons why he marked that particular item as he did. Half of the subjects were instructed that they had been randomly selected to present those arguments publicly before the class (the committed subjects), while the other half learned that they had not been selected to do so (non-committed). This information was given in the booklet by means of a statement: "you (have/have not) been selected . . . ," with the appropriate verb crossed out by hand. To us, this method seemed better than having the whole statement duplicated since it left it unclear exactly how many students were selected for public presentation. Also, in the instruction to return to item #5, the number "five" was handwritten, thus leading subjects to think that others would be listing reasons but not about the same item. All subjects expected to list reasons for their belief and each subject initialed the target item. Consequently, committed and non-committed subjects were probably equally familiar with the item and the issue was equally salient between conditions.

3. Cross-indexed with commitment, half of the subjects read in their booklets that they would later read a communication advocating the tutoring proposal (a position contrary to their beliefs). The other half was told that they would read a communication but were given no substantive information about it. Information in both cases was printed in the booklet, but the referral to the target item and the commitment manipulation were handwritten. Thus, the subjects should conclude that the matching up of their item and the communication on the same topic must be a coincidence and that few, if any, others were in the same position.

4. All subjects then filled out a different questionnaire, which also contained the two tutoring questions and the BA question. As dependent measures, we computed the amount of change for each of these three items. After subjects had completed all questions and had handed in their booklets,

the true nature of the experiment was revealed and discussed in class. Of course, all deceptions, and the need for them, were fully explained and the subjects were sworn to secrecy.

Results. A composite change score was obtained for each subject by summing his change scores across the three dependent measures. When subjects changed their opinions toward those to be advocated in the communication, the change score was computed as positive. When subjects changed in the opposite direction, it was regarded as negative.

The variances of the change scores for the two commitment conditions were significantly smaller than the variances in the two non-commitment conditions. The theoretical significance of this will be treated a little later. Although the pattern of means was as predicted, the severe heterogeneity of variance precluded using the analysis of variance. Consequently, the proportion of subjects whose composite change score was positive was computed for each condition. These proportions were transformed to arcsines (Winer, 1962), and the analysis of variance was then carried out on the transformed scores (see Gilson & Abelson, 1965).

Figure 5-2 shows the percentage of subjects in each condition whose composite change score was positive. The predicted interaction is significant ($F = 3.89$; $df = 1, \infty$; $p < .05$). When committed to their beliefs, significantly fewer forewarned subjects showed positive change than non-forewarned subjects (CR = 1.75; $p < .045$, one-tailed test). When not committed, forewarned subjects showed positive change more frequently than non-forewarned subjects, but the difference is not statistically significant.

This pattern of results is the same for each of the dependent measures. An analysis of transformed proportions for each of the three measures showed a clear interaction for the BA and weak tutoring questions ($F = 3.50$ and 2.83, respectively; $df = 1, \infty$; $p < .10$ for each) but not for the strong form of the question.

Although subjects were specifically committed via the strong form of the tutoring question, one might expect that their reactions to the BA and the weak tutoring questions would be essentially the same as their reaction to the question specific to commitment. However, the predicted results were obtained for the BA and the weak form, but no differences were observed for the strong form. Part of the problem seems to be that the strong form of the question was almost impervious to change: 67% of the subjects showed no change on the strong form (and the other 33% could be due to simple regression effects).

In sum, our predictions were supported, but we are a little unsure about firm conclusions because of the lack of change on the item specific to commitment. Just to be on the safe side, we carried out a third experiment. In this case, the belief specific to the commitment manipulation was extreme also, but the consequences of accepting the contrary position were not so negative as to preclude any change at all.

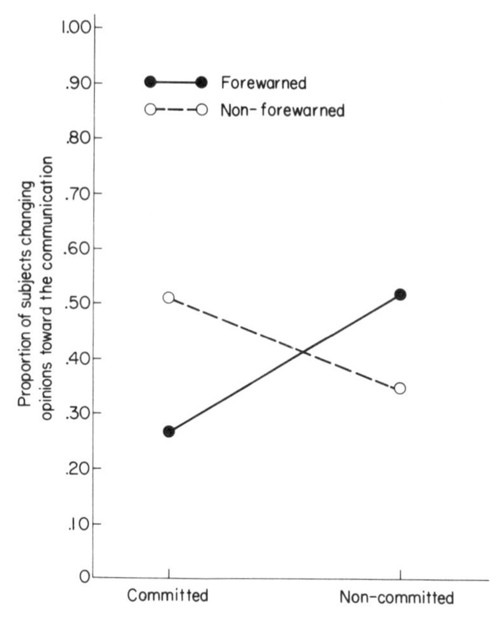

FIG. 5-2. Proportion of subjects changing their opinions toward the expected communication on the composite change score. The number of subjects upon which each proportion is based is 19.

EXPERIMENT III

Method. The procedure for this experiment was essentially the same as for the previous one. Subjects were again male and female undergraduates at the University of Bridgeport, and all manipulations were contained in booklets. The belief by means of which commitment was manipulated was, "Students should have a wider role in determining university policy," a hot issue for most undergraduates. The anticipated counter-communication was to be a recorded speech by a sociology professor from the University of Bridgeport. A tape recorder was prominently displayed while subjects were filling out the questionnaire.

As a further methodological refinement in this experiment, non-committed subjects actually received the same manipulation but about a different topic, as opposed to not being committed at all as in the last experiment. That is, all subjects anticipated having to speak in front of the class, but only half of them expected to speak on the experimental issue. Similarly, non-forewarned subjects also expected to hear a speech but were told that it concerned a different issue. Whatever effects that expecting to speak in front of the class and hearing a speech might arouse can be effectively ruled out in this case since all subjects behaved under those conditions.

Again, subjects filled out a set of questions before and after the manipulations, and in each instance, items on student involvement were included.

The amount of change on these items constituted the dependent measure.

Results. Again, the variances of the change scores were significantly smaller for the commitment conditions than for the non-commitment conditions. Consequently, the same statistical analysis of transformed proportions used in Experiment II was also used here. Figure 5-3 shows the pattern of these results. The predicted interaction was marginally significant ($F = 2.80$; $df = 1, \infty$; $p < .10$). When not committed, forewarned subjects more frequently changed their opinions in the direction to be advocated in the communication than did non-forewarned subjects (CR $= 1.83$; $p < .05$, one-tailed). When previously committed, forewarned subjects changed less frequently than did non-forewarned subjects, but this difference is not statistically significant.

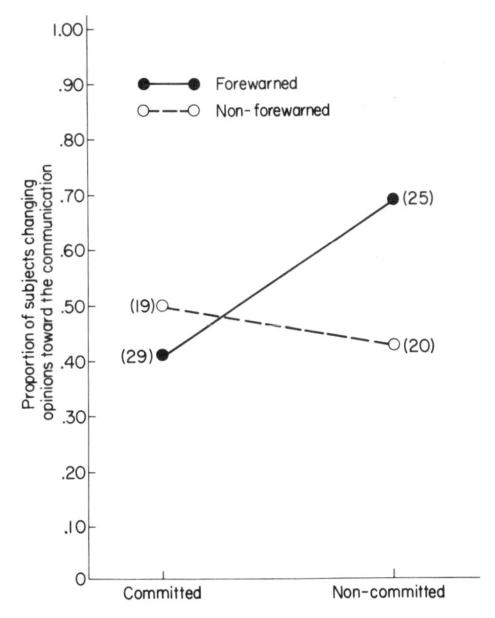

FIG. 5-3. Proportion of subjects changing their opinions toward the expected communication on the student involvement question. The number of subjects upon which each proportion is based is given in parentheses.

As a baseline for change scores in the absence of any experimental manipulations, a control group of 21 subjects filled out all of the questions, but received none of the intervening manipulations. The proportion of these subjects changing toward the communicator's position is .28 (although the mean change for these subjects is zero). This proportion is significantly smaller than the proportion of forewarned, but uncommitted, subjects changing in this direction (CR $= 3.00$; $p < .01$) but not significantly different from the proportion of positive changes for any of the other experimental groups.

Discussion

The pattern of results in all three experiments is strikingly uniform. If, as we reasoned, the dating and hours topics represented greater prior commitment than the tutoring and library topics, then we obtained an interaction between commitment and forewarning in each experiment. When subjects were not committed, then a forewarning of an impending attack led them to abandon their beliefs (anticipatory lowering of belief, in McGuire's terms). The opposite result occurred for committed subjects. Following forewarning, committed subjects became even more attitudinally extreme than before. Of course, the individual comparisons were not all significant: The difference between commitment conditions was significant in Experiment II but not in Experiment III; the difference between uncommitted subjects was significant in Experiment III but not in Experiment II. This type of ambiguity is disconcerting and led us to follow up these individual comparisons a little.

Since Experiment III was a conceptual replication of Experiment II, we may legitimately look at them together. Therefore, an analysis of transformed proportions was performed on the combined data for Experiments II and III. This is not a terribly sophisticated analysis, but it is not an unreasonable one either. When combined, the commitment-by-forewarning interaction is highly significant, of course ($F = 6.71$; $df = 1, \infty$; $p < .01$), but it is the individual comparisons that we are after in this analysis. When committed, forewarned subjects changed significantly less than non-forewarned subjects (CR $= 2.38$; $p < .01$, one-tailed). When not committed, forewarned subjects changed significantly more than non-forewarned subjects (CR $= 1.72$; $p < .05$, one-tailed). In short, it seems reasonable to conclude that both forewarning effects are reliable (although, in this case, the data for the committed subjects are somewhat clearer).

On the basis of these experiments, one might suggest that the topics used by previous investigators have differed along the dimension of commitment. For example, the topic used by Allyn and Festinger (1961) was that teenagers are a menace on the roads and should be strictly controlled by effective new laws. For their subjects, high-school teenagers, accepting these arguments would have had immediate, unpleasant consequences. McGuire and Millman (1965), on the other hand, used topics that were not personally involving (e.g., the high probability of a communist takeover in Latin America). Differences in topics used by these investigators could have accounted for their different results.

McGuire would agree, of course, but would perhaps suggest that these differences are along the emotional–technical dimension rather than pertaining to commitment.* We note that self-esteem theory does predict that overall attitude change (following attack) should not differ for forewarned and nonforewarned subjects. The forewarned subjects presumably change (mostly) prior to the receipt of the communication, whereas subjects not forewarned change (mostly) as the result of hearing the communication. But the change in each case should be the same. Other investigators (Kiesler and Kiesler, Allyn and Festinger, Experiment I) have found overall change, following attack, to be less for forewarned subjects than for subjects not forewarned. The results of the present experiments suggest that the experimental finding that forewarning produces greater resistance is due, in part, to the immediate effect of forewarning on subjects' attitudes.

These data do not sound the death knell for self-esteem theory. Quite the opposite. Self-esteem theory predicts that under some conditions, at least, forewarned subjects will abandon their opinions. For two topics in Experiment I and for uncommitted subjects in Experiments II and III, forewarning did indeed have this effect. McGuire and Millman even anticipate the effect of commitment. They say that, "If he (the subject) is already clear in his own mind (and especially if he is publicly committed) to an initial stand on the issue prior to forewarning of attack, it would hardly be feasible to employ this face-saving anticipating lowering strategy [p. 472]." We accept the parenthetical reference to public commitment, and simply add that it not only nullifies the anticipatory lowering of belief, but can lead to an intensification of belief. We would have to take issue with the phrase "clear in his

* We run the risk here of being thought (with some justification) overly eager to pose issues. There is no necessary reason why other experiments must have reference to either the emotional–technical distinction or commitment. Empirical discrepancies among experiments on forewarning led us to consider the possible interactive effects of commitment and forewarning, which in turn produced the three experiments described here. They show that commitment does help to determine the effects of forewarning, but they in no way exclude from consideration possible effects on forewarning of other variables, such as self-esteem, dissonance (Cohen, 1962), vigilance (Janis, 1962), or what-have-you. Any number of separate variables could interact with forewarning, much as we suggested at the beginning of the chapter. Commitment is only one of these.

own mind." In our second and third experiments, subjects' beliefs were clear in their minds since their initial opinions were extreme and they had expressed them less than 20 minutes earlier in the pretest. In the third experiment, this was especially true since the opinion used (students should have a wider role in determining university policy) was a pressing campus issue at the time the experiment was conducted. Thus, when subjects read the forewarning statement, it seems highly unlikely that initial opinions were unclear in their minds. In both experiments, uncommitted subjects did change their opinions following forewarning. Perhaps then, this change should not be attributed to a self-esteem preserving strategy.

Another possibility is to view forewarning as a mildly persuasive communication. This interpretation suggests that, in the absence of firm commitment, forewarning will have a persuasive impact on subjects' beliefs. This notion is consistent with the findings of McGuire and Millman (1965), Papageorgis (1967), Freedman and Sears (1965), and Allyn and Festinger (1961). However, as we have suggested, the effect of this mildly persuasive communication should depend on previous commitment. In some cases it will have no effect, in others it will produce some change, and in yet others, the subject's beliefs will become more extreme.

We hasten to add that we have been discussing McGuire's ideas, but we have not tested his theory. The unique aspect of the self-esteem theory is that forewarning produces anticipatory change for emotional issues but not for technical ones. This hypothesis was not directly tested in any of our experiments. Experiment I was designed to test one interpretation of it, but the results did not warrant any conclusion about the issue distinction. Indeed, as we suggested earlier, this probably only means that our interpretation was incorrect and does not reflect on the hypothesis itself. McGuire says his effect occurs for emotional issues but that commitment nullifies it. The topics used in Experiments II and III could easily be regarded as emotional; we found anticipatory lowering of belief, and commitment did, at minimum, nullify the effect.

In the third experiment, subjects were also asked how important each of their opinions were to them. For forewarned subjects, the more important their opinions on the student involvement issue, the less frequently they changed. Overall, the proportion of subjects changing their opinions toward the communicator was smaller for subjects above the median on the importance questions than for subjects below the median: 44% vs. 68% (CR = 1.82, $p < .07$). We add that committed subjects changed less frequently than uncommitted subjects, whether they were above or below the median on the importance question (CR = 2.19, $p < .05$). Thus, the effect of the experimentally induced commitment was independent of the (uncontrolled) importance of the issue to the subject. It is interesting to speculate precisely what the importance question was measuring. It may be, for example, that when the subject stated that his opinion was very important to him, he was merely informing us of previous, extra-experimental commitments on his part. This has interesting implications, if true. Since the two sources of commitment acted independently, we would conclude that they were additive in nature, much as we were speculating previously with reference to the number of acts in the last chapter. We don't have the evidence to say one way or the other. "Importance" could be a measure of any one of several variables with implications for attitude change.

The relationship between commitment and forewarning discussed here bears resemblance to other theoretical views (e.g., Sears, Freedman, & O'Connor, 1964; Freedman & Sears, 1965; Apsler & Sears, 1968). Katz and Feldman (1962) showed that the effects of the televised debates during the 1960 presidential election campaign "resulted primarily in a strengthening of commitment to one's party and candidate [p. 208]," that is, a boomerang effect. Sears and his colleagues reasoned that this polarizing effect of a debate on strong partisans may result in part from defensive processes activated by anticipation of the debate and not solely from exposure to the debate itself. In an experiment designed to test this notion, subjects were either committed or not committed to a jury verdict they had made, and subsequently led to believe they would hear two speeches, arguing respectively for acquittal and conviction. These speeches were either part of a debate, or simply two independent speeches. Sears, *et al.* found that, when subjects anticipated hearing a debate, the committed subjects showed less opinion change and a significantly smaller variance among their opinions. However, when subjects were not committed to their verdicts, anticipating the debate produced greater opinion change and significantly larger variances among opinions.

If anticipated debate is similar to our forewarning conditions, the parallel is rather clear. When subjects anticipate hearing a forthcoming persuasive communication, whether part of a debate or not, committed subjects will show less opinion change than uncommitted subjects. In the present experiments, the variances for the committed but forewarned subjects were also smaller than those subjects uncommitted but forewarned.

Conclusions

These three experiments suggest that ideas about commitment may be usefully applied to the study of forewarning. The response to forewarning of attack was critically determined by the degree of previous commitment. When commitment was very low, one responded to the forewarning by partially abandoning one's attitudinal position. That is, the forewarning appeared to have the effect of a mild attack on the subject's attitude. The response to forewarning of attack was reversed for committed subjects. When committed, subjects became even more extreme in their opinions following forewarning than they were previously.

Superficially, these results are similar to those presented in the last chapter concerning the effects of actual attack and commitment. To fit the two batches of data together demands that we assume that a forewarning of attack is still an attack of sorts, though a relatively weak one. Recall that our explanation of the attack data implied that a boomerang effect (an intensification of attitude) follows a particular combination of strength of attack and degree of prior commitment. The attack must be strong enough to arouse one's defenses but weak enough to be overcome eventually.

A proper test of this combination hypothesis would demand that we be able to specify in advance the particular strength of attack and the particular degree of commitment necessary to produce the effect. At the present time our measurements of both variables are inadequate for the task. We now have only an ordinal measure of commitment. We can specify the level of commitment in advance, but only in the weak sense of being more or less commitment than produced by some other set of conditions. In addition, it is not yet clear that we can effectively scale the strength of attack, even in the weak ordinal sense, without a great deal of effort beforehand (and using a different group of subjects). Given these inadequacies of measurement, a parametric study suggests itself: an experiment with a number of different levels of commitment and a number of different levels of strength of attack. Such a study would allow us to clarify several ambiguities now existing and, in addition, would suggest the theoretical refinements necessary for more precise prediction. It has not yet been done, however.

Nonetheless, the two experiments in the last chapter and the three experiments described here all produced the same interaction. The theory of the interactive effects of commitment and attack deserves consideration on this basis alone. Further elaboration demands a more precise independent measurement of commitment, and a deeper understanding of the process involved when one is committed to some behavior. The next chapter considers the latter question.

VI

UNDERLYING VARIABLES

A unique aspect of the manipulations in our studies is that, by itself, commitment produces no attitude change. Instead, it determines one's reactions to subsequent events. The evidence from these studies suggests that commitment alone is not motivating. One may ask, what then mediates the resistance to change observed in these studies? We have suggested several possibilities in Chapters II and III but have not yet tried to sort among the alternatives. The following experiment, by Jerry R. Salancik and myself, approaches the question experimentally.

Behavioral Commitment and Retention of Consistent and Inconsistent Attitude Word-Pairs: An Experiment

One possibility is that commitment makes salient to the individual those cognitions related to his attitudes. Should this occur, one could expect greater resistance to counter-communications for two (not mutually exclusive) reasons: (*a*) The availability of salient cognitions allows the committed person to refute or avoid attacks on his beliefs more easily; (*b*) A less active process suggests that the salient cognitions organize in a consistent manner to codify one's beliefs such that inconsistent information (coming from an attack) is not easily assimilated by the committed individual. Several studies on the learning and forgetting of counter-attitudinal material suggest this second possibility.

Fitzgerald and Ausubel (1963; also, Fitzgerald, 1962; Ausubel, 1963) argued that the forgetting of material contrary to beliefs is due to lack of an adequate organization of cognitions which would facilitate stable incorporation of the inconsistent material. High-school students who studied an organizing principle prior to learning the southern point of view about the Civil War remembered more of the material than did a control group who studied a purely descriptive passage (Fitzgerald, 1962). However, the effect dissipated when initial attitude was controlled for. Kleck and Wheaton (1967) observed that closed-minded individuals (Rokeach, 1960) recalled less opinion-inconsistent than opinion-consistent information, while open-minded subjects recalled slightly more inconsistent information. Kleck and Wheaton also attempted to study the effect of commitment on memory of consistent and inconsistent information and found no differences. They suggested the manipulation was weak, merely requiring high schoolers to verbalize their opinions on popular music and a minimum driving age before a well-dressed college student.

To gather evidence on the cognitive saliency effect of commitment, individuals in the present study were asked to record a speech and then to learn pairs of words which were either consistent, inconsistent, or irrelevant to the speech. The speech was designed to be consistent with subject's attitude. The taping had implications and consequences for the future which were either personally binding (committing) on the individual or not.

The underlying model for this experiment postulates two processes. First, the speech is a stimulus for determining what cognitive elements become salient for the individual. Presumably, the speech stimulates thoughts consistent with it and with the individual's attitude. Second, the binding act for committed subjects organizes cognition into a network of related thoughts. Such an organized pattern of cognitions should provide effective mediators for retention of certain paired associates in the same way that natural language mediators do (Adams, 1967). Commitment should thus facilitate retention of consistent word-pairs while interfering with retention of inconsistent and irrelevant word-pairs. Uncommitted people should not retain consistent word-pairs as easily as committed people since they will not have the salient cognitions readily available for mediation.

METHOD

Twenty-six nursing students at Yale University were privately contacted for participation in a study of "Public Speaking Behavior." Upon arrival, they filled out a questionnaire asking if they ever did any public speaking and determining their opinions on a number of issues, including civilian review boards. After filling out the questionnaire, the subjects were asked to tape a speech; at that time, the pretest was justified by telling them that their attitudes could affect their recordings.

Procedure. The experimenter said he worked for an organization studying factors contributing to effective public speaking. In this regard, he outlined a series of studies planned for the next few months on memory, listening capacity, voice projection, and delivery strategies. Before any studies could begin, however, someone was needed to tape a speech. Each subject was asked if she would help out. All subjects agreed to do so although they did not know what the speech was about.

It was explained that the taped speech would be used in a later study to compare delivery strategies for their persuasive effectiveness. The subject was told other people had recorded speeches where they pretended to be either excited, annoyed, emotional, or cool and intellectual about the issue. The experimenter said that the present need, however, was for someone to simply sit down and read a speech into a tape recorder, without pretending to be anyone but oneself.

The subject agreed to tape the speech. The experimenter described the consequences of doing so; he showed the nurses a chart from an earlier study illustrating the persuasive effect of the different delivery strategies. The effect of one strategy was pointed out: "This is the strategy where someone simply sat down and read the speech. As you can see, it was pretty effective." The chart indicated that over 60% of those hearing this delivery were persuaded.

Subjects were told the tape would be heard by nursing and medical students in future studies. Subjects read the speech to themselves, after which the commitment manipulation was attempted by varying the public nature of the subject's tape. The experimenter explained the subject's voice could (high commitment) or could not (low commitment) be recognized by friends who might be in later studies.

All subjects were then asked if they were sure they didn't mind making the tape:

> I can't myself feel comfortable asking you to put your voice on this tape if the speech itself—the way it is written, what it says and the way it goes about it—if the speech is very objectionable to you and if it would make you feel uncomfortable to put your voice on this tape. If it is very objectionable, maybe we could re-write it to make it less objectionable.

All subjects readily agreed to go ahead, although some freely admitted they might not agree with the speech completely.* The intention of asking this

* Verbatim responses were recorded. There was no difference between the two groups' statements about agreement with the speech.

was to make the subject feel that she was freely agreeing to do something which had consequences for the future. The subject then read the speech aloud once and then read it into the tape recorder.

The speech was presented as a December 12, 1966, editorial given by a Buffalo, New York, television station, promoting the establishment of a civilian review board in Buffalo. The speech indeed was written as a five-minute editorial in a low-keyed, journalistic style of attributing every fact and opinion carefully (e.g., "The President's crime commission concluded in a 228-page report . . ."). It was written in an attempt to carry the reader through an argument which presented the policeman as a potent force in causing discord in ghetto areas. A mutual dislike between the police and the ghetto was illustrated, and it was stressed that a civilian complaint review board was needed to ease tensions by providing a place for ghetto residents to air complaints.

Commitment Manipulation. Subjects in the high commitment condition were told that a special microphone was being used to make their voices more recognizable. The microphone was "a handsome $250 studio mike" and had "the special property of picking up a voice with a minimum of background noise and machine noise, both of which distort recognition of one's voice." High commitment subjects were also told that their tape would be put through a spectrograph analysis and the noise generated by the machine taken out so that "if we took your tape and you, and had a friend of yours listen to both, they couldn't tell the difference." Committed subjects also read their names, addresses, and ages into the tape before the speech.

Low commitment subjects were presented with a cheap microphone made from a plastic skin-lotion bottle. This microphone, they were told, would distort their voices even more than a tape recorder usually does. Further, they were pointedly instructed not to give their names, as it was explained, "We do all this obviously because we don't want people around here who might know you to recognize you on this tape." The spectrograph machine was mentioned as having the effect of further distorting the subject's voice without destroying the content. Samples of the tape were played back to each subject.

When the taping ended, the experimenter paused and solicitously explained that another area he was interested in was what makes for an effective speech itself. One way of going about this was to see what is remembered from a speech. So, to try to get a feel for this, they would do a learning task.

Paired Associate Learning. This phase of the experiment consisted of three learning trials on a standard memory drum and one free recall period. Each trial consisted of an exposure period, a counting period, and cued-recall period. Following the exposure and counting period, the experimenter held up the stimulus word in each of the 15 pairs on a 3 × 5 index card. The subject tried to recall the appropriate response.

The first trial allowed a two-second exposure to each pair and a two-second interpair interval. After exposure to all 15 pairs, the subject was asked to count backwards by three's for 15 seconds. The experimenter held up a starting number and stopped the subject after 15 seconds. The second trial also gave the two-second exposure and interpair interval but followed by a 10-second counting period. The third trial increased exposure to four seconds with no counting period. The sequences of exposure and counting were selected on the basis of pretests which indicated the task was sufficiently difficult to permit effects on retention. Counting served to interfere with recall.

Following the three learning trials, the experimenter had the subject count for 30 seconds, during which some forgetting and interference were expected to occur. Subjects were then asked to recall as many of the words as they could on both the stimulus and the response sides, in any order the words came. This was the free recall session.

The word-pair list was always presented in the same order. It contained five pairs that were inconsistent with the recorded speech, five pairs that were consistent, and five pairs that were irrelevant to the communication. The consistent and inconsistent pairs were selected from hundreds generated under advice of others.* Consistent pairs were selected so that when the two words were put together they would suggest a relationship which was unfavorable to the police, favorable to civilians, or both. Inconsistent pairs attempted to achieve the opposite. In the sense intended here, the pair Trust–Bullet, for instance, would represent two inconsistent concepts. This pair should be particularly inconsistent for subjects who believed civilians should be safeguarded against police harassment. That is, if one maintains that there is conflict between ghetto resident and the police and sympathizes with the ghetto resident, then the pair of words, Blow–Frisk, have a compelling connection between them, as do Harass–Swagger. On the other hand, Home–Violence would seem to fit together only from the point of view of the police, or their supporters. A list of the pairs and their order of presentation appears in Table 6-1.

A posttest was given under the guise that, since this was still an early stage of the research, information evaluating the speech would be helpful. The

* The validity of the classification of the pairs depended upon the outcome of the experiment since there were no independent data confirming the a priori selection. The selection process enabled reducing over 100 pairs to 20 for pretesting. The final 15 were selected from these 20.

posttest was presented as the questionnaire later subjects would use to compare the speech the subject taped with another. Subjects were asked to evaluate the effectiveness only of the speech which they knew about. Opinion questions were also asked.

TABLE 6-1

PRESENTATION ORDER OF CONSISTENT, INCONSISTENT, AND IRRELEVANT WORD-PAIRS

Pair	Category
Victim–Critic	Consistent
Crusade–Wire	Irrelevant
Defiance–Damage	Inconsistent
Complaint–Threat	Consistent
Campaign–Opposition	Irrelevant
Safety–Hate	Inconsistent
Route–Action	Irrelevant
Blow–Frisk	Consistent
Trust–Bullet	Inconsistent
Victory–Challenge	Irrelevant
Harass–Swagger	Consistent
Bitter–Protection	Inconsistent
Returns–Primary	Irrelevant
Objection–Gun	Consistent
Home–Violence	Inconsistent

Summary of Procedure. Nursing students taped a speech, consistent with their opinions of civilian review boards, which would later be used to persuade other nurses and medical students, some of whom they might know. High commitment subjects were led to believe that they could be recognized and identified while low commitment subjects presumably thought they could not. All subjects were given three trials to learn pairs of words which were either consistent, inconsistent, or irrelevant to the position advocated in the speech. Following the three learning trials was a 30-second counting period, after which the nurses recalled in any order all of the words they could. It was expected that high commitment subjects would retain more consistent pairs and fewer inconsistent and irrelevant pairs than low commitment subjects.

RESULTS

Manipulation of Commitment. Although there is no simple check on the effectiveness of the manipulation of commitment independent of the recall data, subjects were asked to indicate on a 10-point scale (*a*) how much they would change the speech to make it better and (*b*) how much they would change it to make it more reasonable. Low commitment subjects expressed more desire to change the speech for the better than high commitment subjects (7.77 vs. 5.08; $F = 9.99$; $p < .01$). They also thought the speech could be changed to make it more reasonable (5.54 vs. 3.39; $F = 3.38$; $p < .10$). One can only suggest these responses as measures of the propensity to change without drawing literal parallels to measures of resistance to attack in our previous research.

While affecting propensity to change the speech, the manipulation did not affect evaluations of the speech's effectiveness. The two groups did not differ in measures of the effectiveness of the speech (*a*) to interest an audience, (*b*) to motivate an audience to accept the conclusions, or (*c*) to arouse curiosity in the issue. Nor did commitment affect answers to a direct question asking how much each subject agreed with the conclusion of the speech. All *F*-ratios were less than 1.

Attitudes. Two questions were asked to estimate attitudes toward civilian review boards: How strongly would you support a civilian review board in your city? and Do you agree or disagree that police conduct should be reviewed by citizens? The two questions were averaged for analyses. The pretest showed high commitment subjects were slightly, but unreliably, more favorable (6.42 vs. 5.15; $F = 1.60$).

Evidence from previous studies indicated that the commitment manipulation used in the present study should not by itself change attitudes (Kiesler & Sakumura, 1966; Kiesler, Pallak, & Kanouse, 1968). The present data are consistent with this expectation (mean change over the pretest score: .84 vs. .12; $F < 1$).

Learning. Differential learning of word-pairs would fit with the postulated effect of commitment on the reception of consistent and inconsistent information. However, two factors might mitigate clear differences in learning. First, the present study was conducted without controlling many sources of variance in paired associate learning, such as order of exposure, recall presentation order, and number of presentations. Learning differences could conceivably be held down by these other sources of variance. More importantly, with only three learning trials, one would not expect near perfect learning in either condition. Hence, this experiment represents a very conservative test of learning differences.

Analyses were made of the pairs recalled for Trial 2 and Trial 3. Too few pairs were correctly recalled on Trial 1 to analyze. In Trial 2, which allowed a two-second exposure, there are no differences in total number of pairs recalled by the two groups. Both groups correctly recalled about five pairs.

There is, however, a slight tendency for the low commitment subjects to have correctly recalled fewer consistent pairs than the high commitment subjects (1.23 vs. 1.69; $F = 1.27$). Over both groups, irrelevant pairs were learned more easily than either consistent or inconsistent pairs (see Figure 6-1).

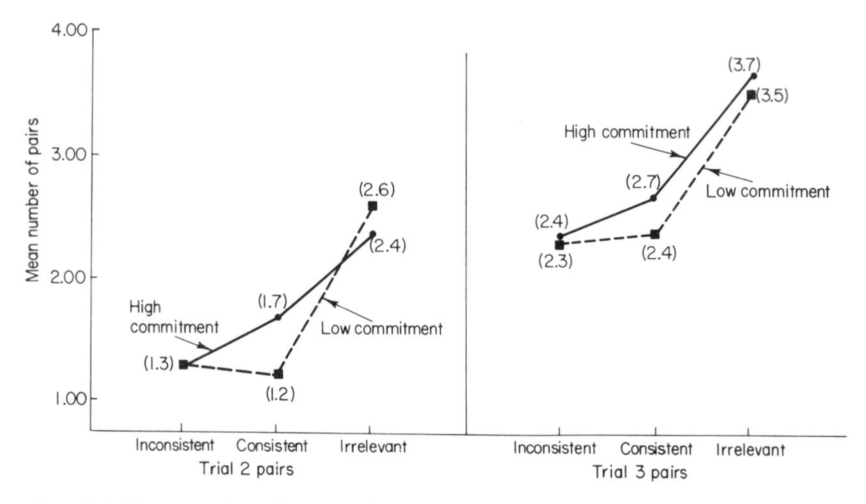

FIG. 6-1. Mean number of word-pairs of each category recalled correctly during cued recall in Trials 2 and 3.

By Trial 3, when subjects were allowed a four-second exposure, there are no differences between the two groups. Both groups correctly recalled about eight pairs. To further explore whether there were any differences in learning, an index was computed on the basis of the pairs in each category which were recalled on both Trial 2 and Trial 3. Pairs recalled on both trials might presumably reflect a more reliable estimate of learning. To test whether high commitment subjects learned more consistent than inconsistent pairs, an index was prepared by subtracting inconsistent from consistent pairs and dividing by the total number of pairs recalled. The mean proportion for the high commitment subjects was .115, and for the low commitment subjects, .075 ($F < 1$). The data from Trial 2 and Trial 3 indicate that there were no initial learning differences between the high commitment and low commitment groups.

Recall. Figure 6-2 indicates the effect of commitment on recall of consistent and inconsistent pairs. After the three learning trials, subjects were asked to count backwards by three's for 30 seconds and then to recall in any order as many stimulus and response words as they could. No instructions were given to recall the words in pairs. However, since the words should have been easier to recall if they were organized in some meaningful fashion, it was expected that all subjects would recall some of the words in pairs.* Further, high commitment subjects should recall more consistent than inconsistent or irrelevant pairs compared to the low commitment subjects.

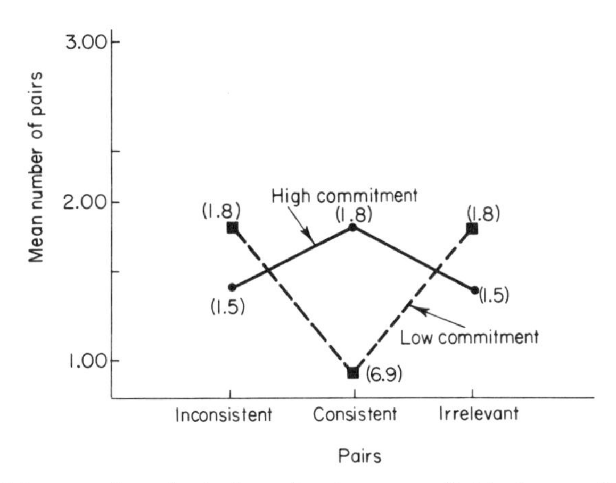

FIG. 6-2. Mean number of pairs in each category recalled in free recall session.

First, it should be noted, there was no overall difference, between the two groups, in the number of pairs they recalled. Rather, it was the pattern of pairs that distinguished the high commitment subjects from the low commitment subjects, that is, the interaction. The overall interaction was significant ($F = 3.59$; $df = 2{,}48$; $p < .05$). Furthermore, the interaction involving only consistent and inconsistent pairs was also significant ($F = 5.07$; $df = 1{,}48$; $p < .05$). High commitment subjects retained more consistent pairs (1.85) than inconsistent pairs (1.46), whereas the low commitment subjects retained fewer consistent than inconsistent pairs (0.92 and 1.85, respectively).

To explore the source of these differences another analysis was made in an attempt to control for original learning of the pairs. For each category the ratio was computed of those pairs which were retained on the free recall period to those pairs in that category which were learned on Trial 2 or Trial 3, or both. This ratio was computed for each subject and represents the proportion of those pairs in that category which were retained once learned. Figure

* The words recalled by the subject were recorded in sequence. A pair is any two adjacent words which belonged to the same pair in the three learning trials. An analysis of words alone parallels that for pairs. High commitment subjects recall significantly more consistent and fewer inconsistent pairs than low commitment subjects. An analysis of unpaired words (words $- 2 \times$ pairs $=$ unpaired words) showed no differences between either the groups or the type of words they retained.

6-3 illustrates the average ratios for the high and low commitment groups. For the high commitment subjects an average of .421 of the inconsistent pairs were retained. The average for low commitment subjects was .705. The average difference of .28 is reliable ($F = 4.64$; $df = 1{,}24$; $p < .05$).

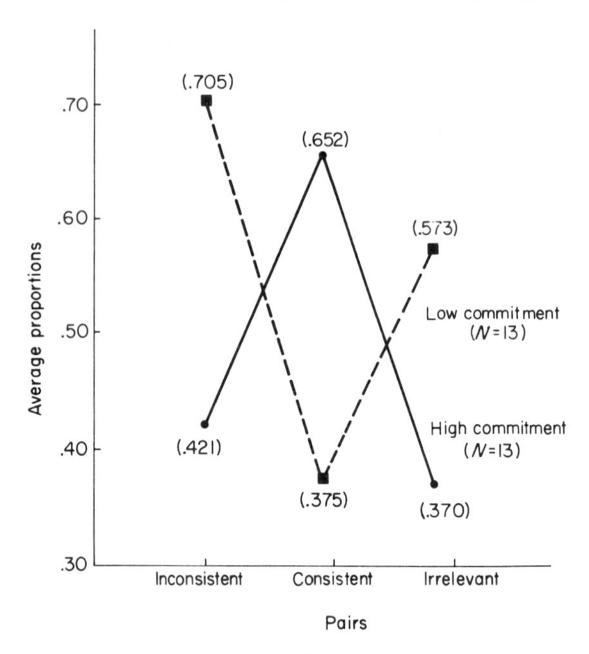

FIG. 6-3. Average ratios of pairs recalled in free recall/pairs recalled in cued recall on Trial 2 and/or Trial 3 for each category.

High commitment subjects retained a greater proportion of the consistent pairs than the low commitment subjects (.652 vs. .375; $F = 3.13$; $df = 1{,}24$; $p < .10$). They also recalled a lower proportion of the irrelevant pairs, but the effect is unreliable (.370 vs. .573; $F = 2.55$; $df = 1.24$; n.s.). The interaction prediction still obtains. For each subject the proportion of inconsistent pairs was subtracted from the proportion of consistent pairs which were retained on the free recall period. For high commitment subjects the average index is .231 and for low commitment subjects $-.330$ ($F = 13.50$; $p < .001$). To control for initial attitudes, a covariance analysis was performed on this index, with the pretest question on support for civilian review boards as a covariate. This question showed the strongest initial difference between the groups. High commitment subjects still retain more consistent and fewer inconsistent pairs than the low commitment subjects ($F = 10.05$; $df = 1{,}23$; $p < .01$).

From the above analyses it is clear that the high commitment subjects forgot the pairs which were inconsistent with the speech they taped more easily than did the low commitment subjects. On the other hand, the low commitment subjects forgot the pairs which were consistent with the speech more easily than the high commitment subjects. There was a tendency for the high commitment subjects to retain fewer irrelevant pairs, but the effect is neither strong nor reliable.

Discussion

Unlike many previous studies of the effect of attitudes on learning and recall, the differential retention observed in the present study cannot be explained as a function of prior familiarity with consistent and inconsistent information due to differences in initial attitudes. (See Weiner, 1966, for criticism of earlier literature on this point.) Except for sampling error the two experimental groups did not differ in their initial attitudes or, presumably, in their experience with the words used in the learning task or the information contained in the speech. Further, when initial attitude was controlled by covariance, the high commitment subjects still retained a significantly greater proportion of consistent pairs and a lesser proportion of inconsistent and irrelevant pairs.

Generally, many methodological difficulties facing interpretations of verbal learning experiments were ruled out by the unique interaction in the data. For example, order effects, while strong, were constant for the two commitment conditions and balanced among the pairs. Thus, while order effects presumably contributed to the overall level of recall within each condition, they do not provide us with a reasonable explanation of the differences between conditions.

The present experiment further cannot easily be explained by assuming differential arousal between the two commitment conditions. An assumption of differential arousal would not necessarily provide a description for the unique interaction observed in the data. Arousal might suggest an overall difference in learning, of which there was none. Further, a rudimentary measure of arousal (the length of time to tape the speech) did not distinguish the commitment groups.

Another possible explanation of the data is bias due to the experimenter differentially cueing subjects about what to learn. Since the experimenter held up the stimulus words for the subject to recall the appropriate response word, he had the opportunity to systematically vary the exposure to each pair during the cued recall phase of the three learning trials. However, such an interpretation would argue for differential learning, of which there was none. The effect of commitment on consistent and inconsistent pairs occurred only during the free recall period when the experimenter did nothing but record the words generated by the subjects.

To describe the data in this experiment, one can postulate that behaviors which bind an individual to his beliefs also affect the organization and salience of cognitions relevant to those beliefs. We have emphasized commitment as a process involving a behavioral act. As discussed in Chapters II and III, this psychological process involves memory of past behavioral acts which are more or less difficult to deny or distort when later faced with an inconsistent communication. Another possibility suggested by the present experiment is that cognitions relevant to one's beliefs are more salient when one is committed to those beliefs. That is, the committed person is more likely to think about things related to his belief and perhaps even see more things as related to this belief.

Besides this notion of the cognitive effect of commitment, a number of assumptions are needed to describe the psychological process in the present experiment.

1. The word-pairs elicit associations which relate the two words in the pair for an individual. The *consistent* words in this experiment were constructed to be consistent with a speech describing the police as hostile to ghetto residents in both attitude and manner. Ghetto residents, on the other hand, were described as both the protagonists and the underdogs in a continual discord with the police. *Inconsistent* word-pairs link words which are favorable to the police with words which are unfavorable to the police (Trust–Bullet) or with words incompatible with the function of the police (Safety–Hate).

2. Commitment makes certain cognitions salient: those which are related to the position expressed in the speech and the individual's own attitude. These salient cognitions can have two effects. They can facilitate associations between the words in a pair, and they can provide mediators for linking the associated word-pairs with an individual's cluster of cognitions.

3. Associations or mediators which are consistent with the cognitions made salient by commitment facilitate retention of the word-pair. Inconsistent associations or mediators interfere with retention of the word-pair.

These three assumptions provide a plausible interpretation for the observation that high commitment subjects retained more consistent word-pairs than inconsistent. Other assumptions have to be added to describe why low commitment subjects retain more inconsistent than consistent word-pairs. If salient cognitions are not as readily available for the low commitment subjects as they are for the high commitment subjects, one might expect that the easiest and the most striking pairs be retained best. From the data in Trial 2 and Trial 3 (Figure 6-1) it appears the most difficult pairs for all subjects to learn were the inconsistent ones, while the easiest pairs were the irrelevant ones. Further, the inconsistent pairs are also the most striking in terms of the incongruity of the concepts paired. One should thus find that, if fewer cognitive organizational effects are operating in the low commitment condition, subjects should retain best the inconsistent and irrelevant pairs.

CONCLUSIONS

This experiment suggests two possibilities for the underlying process mediating the effects of commitment. It appears that commitment affects either the *salience* of cognitions (thoughts, previous behaviors, etc.) consistent with the behavior performed or the *organization* of these cognitions into a consistent whole. The design of the experiment does not allow us to differentiate between these two alternative processes, but it appears that one or the other is at work in our experiments. But whether affecting the salience or organization of cognitions, greater commitment would make it more difficult to deny or distort one's previous behavior under attack, without necessarily affecting one's attitude at the time of action.

Of course, the two processes are not mutually exclusive and it is possible, perhaps likely, that commitment manipulations affect both salience and organization of one's relevant cognitions. Clearly, the next step is an experiment which attempts to assess the two processes independently within one design. As yet, however, the study of the organization of cognitions (or even the connection between two of them) has not progressed to the point where greater or lesser organization is a reliable dependent variable. Salancik and I spent some time on this problem studying the organization of cognitions about the Vietnam war. Various techniques (e.g., pattern analysis and factor analysis) yield reasonable (but somewhat fuzzy) pictures of the way subjects' attitudes and thoughts about the war hung together. However, with none of the techniques were we able to detect or devise (depending on technique) reliable changes in pattern. One of the difficulties, which surprised us, was that subjects' attitudes about various aspects and implications of the war were not highly organized to begin with, making the study of change of pattern well nigh impossible (recall the discussion in Chapter I concerning the reliability of pretest and change scores). At any rate, the definitive experiment on this issue has yet to be done.

Finally, salience and organization of cognitions do not exhaust the possible variables affected by our commitment manipulations. We have suggested others previously and will return to the problem again in this monograph.

VII

COMMITMENT TO FUTURE INTERACTION WITH OTHERS

In the research discussed thus far, subjects committed themselves to some specific behavior with clear attitudinal implications. In each case, they chose to carry out a behavioral request, and, by experimental design, the behavior became important in reacting to subsequent events. In the Kiesler–Sakumura experiment, the contingencies for the original behavior determined one's acceptance of a subsequent attack on one's belief. The less one was paid for the original behavior, the greater was the resistance to the attack.

With but a little effort, this view of commitment can be extended to the study of interpersonal interaction. The particular variable we have studied is the anticipation of future interaction with others. In the basic paradigm we have used, some subjects expect to be interacting with others, in a group say, for some time, and other subjects expect the interaction to terminate soon. We then determine the effects of anticipation of future interaction upon the acceptance of influence attempts and reactions to the others' behavior. This chapter presents some of this research.

Where does commitment come in? Is the commitment model related to the study of anticipation of future interaction? I think it is, but a direct analogy has never been explicitly drawn. Let me try to show how commitment to future interaction might be psychologically equivalent to commitment to some specific behavior.

Perhaps the critical element for connecting the two types of commitment is the matter of choice. Recall, for example, our discussion of the first experiment in Chapter IV. There we argued that the person who elected to play the Guide Line strategy three times was more responsible for the position he was in than the person who only elected to play that strategy once. The greater volition implied by the repetitive selection of the strategy produced greater commitment. In this view, we could have alternatively had all subjects play the strategy once and varied the degree to which they felt they were free to do so. The Kiesler–Sakumura experiment is also applicable. In general, with lesser amounts of pressure to perform a specific behavior, the person is more committed to the behavior. Lesser amounts of money in the Kiesler–Sakumura experiment led to greater commitment. Commitment meant that the subjects could not distort or deny their previous behavior and, hence, led them to be more resistant to the attack which ensued.

Implied choice (or minimal pressure to comply) is also involved in the study of the anticipation of future interaction with others. The person chooses (or thinks he has) to continue the interaction over a period of time. When the subject responds affirmatively to the question, Can you return for three more hour sessions with this same group?, the affirmation is an act, a piece of behavior, and we may legitimately discuss the degree to which the subject is committed to it. We might, for example, set up an experimental setting in which all subjects agreed to return for three sessions in the future. We could then manipulate other aspects related to the agreement, and have them theoretically related to commitment. We could vary whether the agreement was public or not, or how much money the subject was offered to acquiesce.

In a different vein, we could vary the probability that the subject could change to a different group later if he wished, directly varying the degree to which he could undo his behavior of agreement. Or we could do it wholesale and vary simply whether the person was committed to future interaction or not, without regard for degree of commitment. In each case, some subjects would be more committed to future interaction than others.

We can rephrase the discussion and make the analogy with our previous research more explicit. What is the person committed to? He *chooses* (a behavior) to engage in a certain amount of future interaction with the group (which involves more behavior). We can think of these as two behaviors for analytical purposes. Depending on our manipulation, we could vary the degree of commitment to either the choice or the future behavior (although they are not completely independent). With regard to choice, subjects might expect the same amount of future interaction, but some might (experimentally) freely choose to engage themselves whereas others could be forced to do so. The former would be more committed. On the other hand, we could manipulate commitment to the second behavior (the future interaction itself) directly by varying the probability that the individual could withdraw from the group if he wished. In a sense, these people could be differentially bound to the future interaction. However, choosing to join the group and the probability of continuing the interaction are not independent. In fact, they are closely related. The behavior of joining the group is more easily distorted or reinterpreted when it has no future implications. With only a small probability of continuing the interaction, one is less committed to the act of joining, because one can easily reinterpret the act. By the same token, the amount (or content) of the future interaction to which one is bound also affects the degree of commitment to the initial behavior. It would be more difficult to reinterpret the original choice (by possibly saying, for example, "I wasn't really interested, but I had nothing else to do that hour.") if one is committed to three hours of future interaction rather than the one hour typical of laboratory studies.

There are striking similarities between committing oneself to some specific behavior and electing to interact with a group over a certain period. Therefore, to introduce our group data, I have elected to present the theoretical analogy stressing the act of choosing to join the group. However, the reader may be able to think of alternative considerations and find the ambiguity curious. I agree that the issues and the problems of translation are not as simple as perhaps I have made them sound. In fact, our studies of behavioral commitment and commitment to future interaction have led relatively independent lives, coming together only for metaphorical reunions like the current one. The purpose of the present chapter is to try to sketch the lines of contact more vividly between the two bodies of data. I find intriguing the possibility that two such diverse batches of data might be handled by the same theoretical underpinnings and beg the reader's indulgence until I have completed my exploratory case. We shall return to these issues later in the chapter.

Intra-Group and Extra-Group Communication

Commitment to future interaction with others has implications for subsequent events that may occur in the group. Suppose the person later receives a counter-communication arguing against one of his beliefs. If this belief is somehow related to his membership in the group, then his commitment to the group (for this is how we will use the phrase, although it is not altogether correct) will affect how he reacts to this influence attempt. There are two obvious varieties of group settings involving communications.

In the first case, suppose that the subject is committed to future interaction with group A, which has specifiable norms and/or attitudes with which presumably the subject agrees (or he probably would not have agreed to continue the interaction). Later, these attitudes are attacked by group B or any outside source, including the traditional unnamed source in communication studies.

One's reaction to an extra-group attack on belief should be fairly obvious. When the attitude is relevant to membership in the group or continued interaction with the group, then greater commitment to the group should produce greater resistance to attack. Before the subject could accept the attack completely and change his opinion, he would have to repudiate the group, since a changed opinion and continued membership would be very uncomfortable for him. The more committed he is to future interaction, the more difficult it should be to reject the group. Rejecting the group and having chosen to join it would be inconsistent.

In sum, the greater the commitment to the group, the greater the resistance to attack from an outside source. This hypothesis has never been directly tested, to my knowledge. Related hypotheses have been tested—a number of them. For example, the greater the valuation of group membership, the greater the resistance to outside attack (Kelley & Volkart, 1952), and the greater the salience of group membership, the greater the resistance to outside attack (Kelley, 1955). Both valuation of group membership and salience of membership are closely related to the commitment hypothesis, but neither the Kelley and Volkart nor the Kelley experiment could be considered a direct test of it. Of course, the commitment hypothesis might be severely limited by a number of variables such as attraction to the group, centrality of the attacked attitude to the group's well-being and locomotion, and idiosyncrasy credit (Hollander, 1958). That is, under some conditions, the effects of these variables might be expected to swamp or obscure effects of commitment.

In addition to extra-group attack, the second variety of communication setting is obviously intra-group attack: attack on one's belief from inside the group. Translated, this simply means that the individual is committed to a group with which he disagrees on some relatively important issues. In this case also, resolution of an uncomfortable situation is connected with dissolving one's relationship with the group. But the implications for change are the opposite of what we expected when the attack was from outside the group.

With extra-group attack, greater commitment to the group leads to greater resistance to attack. With intra-group attack, greater commitment to the group should lead to greater attitude change, that is, less resistance to the attack. To resist the attack from within the group would necessitate rejecting the group. To the extent one cannot reject the group or would find it difficult to do so, one must deal with the attack seriously. As I have suggested elsewhere (e.g., Kiesler and Kiesler, 1969), anything which leads a person to regard a counter-communication seriously is likely to lead to some attitude change.

So the hypothetical effect of commitment to the group—greater resistance or greater change—should depend entirely on whether the attack comes from within the group or without it. The first section of this chapter presents some data on the former problem: the effects of commitment to future interaction on reactions to disagreements within the group. The second part of the chapter deals with the effect of commitment to future interaction on reactions to violations of group norms.

Commitment to the Group and Disagreement with the Group

As we have suggested, it is necessary to take several variables into account when considering the effects of commitment to the group on reactions to intra-group disagreement. For example, consider the difference between reference groups and membership groups, a common distinction in the literature. Membership groups, of course, are indicated by those collections of people to which one actually belongs in some semiformal way. A reference group is one to which a person refers to gain evidence about correct values, opinions, and so forth. They may coincide; one may also be a member of a particular reference group or not.

When we discuss commitment to future interaction, we intend to mean something similar to the concept of membership group. Other variables intrude, however. For example, if a person is very attracted to a particular group, he may or may not be a member, but it would clearly be a reference group for him. Speaking loosely, if a group is functionally a reference group for an individual then it is likely to have influence over him, whether he is committed to future interaction with the group or not. Consequently, reasonably high levels of attraction to the group may obliterate or override any effects that commitment to future interaction may have in a given situation. For this reason, among others, we might expect commitment to the group to have an easily observable effect only with relatively low attraction to the group. The data of Kiesler and Corbin (1965) illustrate this hypothesis. They varied three levels of attraction to the group independently of two different levels of commitment to future interaction with the group. By manipulation, all subjects disagreed with the group about an issue central to the group's existence. Under these conditions, we would expect committed subjects to be more influenced by the group than uncommitted subjects, particularly when they are not very attracted to the group. Generally speaking, of course, the more attracted one is to the group, the more impact the group should have on the individual.* Discussion demands that we first consider the experimental procedure of Kiesler and Corbin in more detail.

THE KIESLER AND CORBIN EXPERIMENT

Procedure. Subjects participated in six-man groups. The alleged purpose of the experiment was to study how groups of strangers worked out certain tasks (subjects did not know each other). The group's function was to rate the 10 abstract paintings placed around the room. The subjects were told that prior to these discussion groups the paintings had been rated by a panel of experts and it was the group's purpose to arrive at a rating as close as possible to the one given by this panel.

Commitment to continue interaction with the group was manipulated by varying the probability that subjects could change to a different group if they wished. All subjects expected the experiment to continue over a total of four different hourly sessions. Committed subjects thought that they had little chance to change groups, even if they wished: They were explicitly told that the chances were small, about 5% (or 1 in 20), to change if they were dissatisfied. The uncommitted subjects, on the other hand, thought that it was a simple matter to change groups if dissatisfied; they were told that the chances were about 95% (or 19 in 20) of being able to change if they requested it.

This is a reasonable manipulation of commitment to future interaction. Subjects did not have to agree to any future interaction; all expected, before they arrived, that the experiment would last only the usual hour. The experimenter asked each if he would be willing to continue over the four sessions (naturally first approaching those who appeared most likely to agree) and no subject refused. Indeed, considering others around him are being good

* The finding that greater attraction to the group leads to greater impact of the group on the individual is typical in the literature (cf., Hare, 1962). The line of research described above began when I noticed that the so-called monotonic effect of attraction doesn't always occur. Sometimes the group has an immense impact on the unattracted member. A demonstration experiment (Kiesler, 1963) showed a U- or V-shaped relationship between attraction and influence, with both high and low attraction subjects being most influenced following disagreement with the group and moderately attracted subjects less influenced. This led to the Kiesler and Corbin experiment, which explicitly tested the commitment notion: a monotonic relationship between attraction and influence for subjects not committed to future interaction; and the U-shaped relationship for committed subjects. The major difference between committed and uncommitted subjects occurred when subjects were not very attracted to the group. This was expected on the basis of a combination of the commitment explanation of the Kiesler and Corbin experiment and the usual monotonic relationship. The attraction aspect of this research is, however, only tangential to the present discussion and line of thought. The reader wishing further detail on attraction itself and how it is related to other aspects of group interaction and influence is referred to the original experiments, plus Kiesler (1967; 1969), Kiesler and DeSalvo (1967), and Kiesler and Kiesler (1969).

sports and acquiescing, it would be difficult for a subject to refuse in the face of that subtle social pressure. In a sense it is only an illusion of choice (if it were not, surely some would refuse), but functionally it amounts to the same thing. Under these conditions subjects think that they are free to choose to continue or not, even though a casual observer, seeing a number of subjects in this setting, might raise an eyebrow.

As mentioned, this is a direct manipulation of the ease of undoing one's past behavior. Everything else is equated; only the ease with which one can shift out of the current group is varied. Only a difference in probabilities exists between the committed subjects and the uncommitted subjects. (Of course, both sets of subjects are committed to some degree, but we will call them committed and uncommitted for ease of presentation.)

In addition to commitment, attraction to the group was also varied, using a typical method of false feedback from others in the group. After introductions, each subject rose and told the others a little about himself. Later they discussed some of the paintings (without alluding to preferences). Each subject then rated each of the other five people in his group: how much he liked each and how much he thought each would contribute to the group. The introductions and discussions were employed only to give some credence to these ratings. Using the "waste basket technique," the experimenter glanced at the ratings, announced no one had been rejected and tossed them all in a waste basket by his desk. Later, at a suitable time, he retrieved false reports from the same container and passed them out to the subjects, casually remarking what the average seemed to be. In this manner one-third of the subjects, randomly determined, were considerably above average, one-third a little below average, and one-third quite a bit below average. These ratings indicated how the group rated the subject. However, in this case as usual (for this is a typical method of varying attraction), the subject's rating of the group followed accordingly.* This resulted in three levels of attraction to the group.

The dependent variable was opinion change, following disagreement with the group. Consequently we need a pre- and posttest of some opinion, interspersed with a discrepant group opinion. We accomplished this in the following way. Subjects first privately ranked the paintings for their esthetic appeal. These rankings were allegedly used to give each subject a group consensus, actually falsely derived. Later, all subjects ranked the paintings again. To give additional justification for the re-ratings, all subjects read a "fact-free" guide to modern painting, which presumably gave them food for thought and an excuse to change their opinions if they wished.

* The differences among the three conditions in rated attractiveness of the group are highly significant.

The discrepancy in opinion between the subject and the group was constant across subjects, "rigged" by manipulating the group consensus delivered to each subject. Regardless of how the subject ranked the paintings, we took whatever he had ranked as sixth (of 10) and placed that one first in the group consensus given him; his paintings ranked one through five were simply moved down in the group opinion to two through six, and paintings seven through ten remained unchanged. The dependent variable then was the change for each subject in the ranking of his sixth painting.

Results. The main results from the Kiesler and Corbin experiment are presented in Figure 7-1. As expected, commitment to future interaction had little effect for subjects whose attraction to the group was average or above. The differences between committed and uncommitted subjects in the high and average attraction conditions are not close to significance. We note in passing that the highly attracted subjects changed their evaluation of the sixth ranked painting much more following disagreement with the group than did the more moderately attracted subjects.

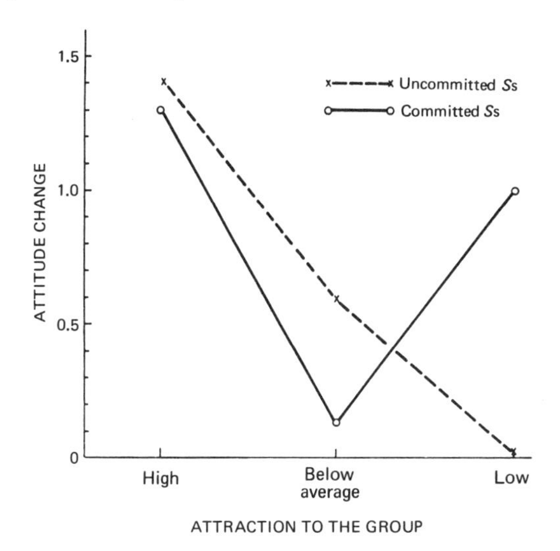

FIG. 7-1. The relationship of attraction to the group and commitment to continue in the group, to conformity to group norms (from Kiesler and Corbin, 1965).

The effect for commitment is concentrated in the low attraction condition, as expected. Subjects committed to continue the interaction with the group were more affected by a disagreement with the group than were subjects less committed to future interaction. Committed subjects elected to continue their association with the group even though there was small chance of changing later if they did not find it enjoyable. Later, they find themselves in disagreement with the group about a matter which, although perhaps not objectively important, was still central to the group's existence. Voluntarily committing oneself to future interaction unfortunately relieves one of the option of rejecting or devaluing the group later. Derogating a group with which one has freely allied himself is a difficult task (although clearly not impossible). These people face up to the discrepancy, re-think and re-evaluate their own opinions about the paintings and subsequently convince themselves that the group was right after all.

Through comparison with an extra control condition, not described here, we also found that committed but unattracted subjects came to evaluate the group more highly *after* they changed their opinions. Subjects committed to future interaction not only brought their opinions into line with those of the group but also changed their evaluation of the group so that it became more consistent with the commitment. Apparently they had to confront the conflict directly, however, since it was not until after opinion change occurred that the re-evaluation took place (see Kiesler and Corbin, 1965, for details).

These findings suggest a severe conflict for the subject, involving three salient cognitions: his disagreement with the group, his evaluation of the group, and the degree to which he must continue the association with the group. How one resolves the conflict should depend on the relative levels of each variable. A high level of attraction to the group appears to be the most prepotent variable. When a person highly attracted to others disagrees with them, it matters little whether he is also overtly committed to future interaction with them. The variable of attraction dominates the outcome. (Of course, at one level one is always committed to groups to which one is highly attracted. We have a difficult time doing without them, at least, since they are such a boon to our egos.)

When attraction is not a salient feature, then commitment to future interaction seems to dominate the outcome or resolution of the conflict. At least, commitment not only determines one's reaction to the discrepancy in opinion but also leads one subsequently to re-evaluate the group itself.

One can think of these subjects as being in a conflictful state, a conflict in which opinion change is not the most desired alternative. The subject changes his opinion if the surrounding circumstances force him to, but he seems to prefer a different resolution. This line of thought suggests several hypotheses about the Kiesler and Corbin paradigm. For example, if opinion change is really not a preferred alternative resolution, then the presence of an ally (who would really be a deviate-ally) should brighten the situation considerably. Having one person in the group as an ally should resolve the conflict or, at least, reduce it to a tolerable level. With an ally, the subject would not change his opinion presumably and would value his ally very highly.

But what if the subject were not aware of the ally until after he had resolved his conflict? Until after he had already changed his opinion? Would he resent this challenge to his resolution, or would he, with this new ammunition, revert back to his original opinion? The latter is a question of the stability of the effect of commitment that Kiesler and Corbin found. Rephrased, we ask: Given that the committed person is not resistant to intra-group attack and has changed his opinion, is his new opinion now well-formed enough to be resistant to outside attack? Viewed in yet a third way: Is the subject's resolution of the person–group discrepancy in attitude simply one of compliance, simply going along with the group, or does it represent true attitude change that can and will be defended?

These questions can be answered quite simply by an experiment in which the subject learns of another subject in the group who agrees with his original opinion. We can answer both questions above by varying whether the subject learns of the presence of this deviate-ally before he has resolved the conflict by changing his opinion or after. Such an experiment has been carried out by Kiesler, Zanna, and DeSalvo (1966) and is described below.

The Kiesler, Zanna, and DeSalvo Experiment

Procedure. The procedure was very similar to that of Kiesler and Corbin but with several exceptions. *All* subjects received a manipulation effecting low attraction to the group since this is the condition under which one expects commitment to have an effect. Commitment also was varied in a slightly different way. Committed subjects expected to continue in the same group over three different sessions. Uncommitted subjects were told that they could change groups if they wished and that they might be changed anyway. The ranking and re-ranking of the attitude objects was accomplished in the same way as Kiesler and Corbin, but the topic was different: The subject ranked the relative importance of certain qualities that boys like to see in girls (the subjects were high-school males). This ranking was actually done three times: one pretest and two posttests, which are described below.

The schematic representation of the experimental design and procedure is shown in Table 7-1. There it can be seen that there are three experimental variations and an uncommitted-control condition, four in all. The experimental conditions differ as to whether a deviate-ally existed or not (someone who agreed with the subject's original opinion) and, if a deviate-ally existed, whether his presence was made known before or after the subject changed his opinion.

The deviate-ally introduced himself in the following way. Each subject was allowed to send a message about anything he wished at two points in the experiment: once before the first posttest and once just before the second posttest. For convenience one can think of step 8 in Table 7-1 as ending the replication of the Kiesler and Corbin design. Step 6 shows the first message. All messages were intercepted, and at each point one of three messages was substituted: one supported the group decision, the second disagreed with it, and the third was irrelevant. The pro-group message said, "I agree almost completely with the group. I think that what they rank at the top really belongs there." In contrast, the anti-group (that is, pro-subject) message said, "I just can't go along with the group all the way. For example, I think that what the group ranked as number one should definitely be closer to the bottom." Of course, the subject thought number one should be lower as well; he had ranked it sixth himself. The irrelevant message said simply, "This note writing is sure a different way to discuss a problem."

As mentioned, step 8 in Table 7-1 ends the conceptual replication of the Kiesler–Corbin procedure, and step 6 shows the receipt of the first message. The late-deviate and the no-deviate conditions both received a message at that time supporting the group, as did the uncommitted-control group. The opinion for step 8 minus the opinion shown by step 3 in the Table, should indicate attitude change comparable to that obtained by Kiesler and Corbin. We expect the late-deviate and no-deviate conditions (which, incidentally, are procedurally identical at this point) to show more attitude change than the uncommitted-control condition. Except for the messages delivered, this comparison represents a conceptual replication of the two low attraction conditions in the Kiesler and Corbin experiment. The messages were intentionally identical for the three conditions (late, no deviate, and control) and, hence, would not affect between-condition differences (although, generally speaking, because of the pro-group messages, all three of these conditions should show more change than the comparable conditions in the Kiesler–Corbin experiment).

The early-deviate condition tests our conflict hypothesis. If the person is attempting to resolve a conflict among the variables of commitment, attraction, and disagreement with the group, then the presence of a deviate-ally should help resolve the conflict in favor of not changing one's opinion.*

* It should be obvious that this experiment was not intended to test a conflict hypothesis directly. The main intent of the experiment was to test the stability of the change produced in the Kiesler–Corbin experiment. There are a number of reasons why one might expect the early deviate condition not to show much change, and the conflict hypothesis is only one of them. The other possible explanations are excluded by neither the design of the experiment nor the data obtained.

TABLE 7-1

SCHEMATIC REPRESENTATION OF THE EXPERIMENTAL DESIGN (from Kiesler, Zanna, & De Salvo, 1966)[a]

Condition	Sequence of Events										
	1 Stay with Same Group	2 Rate Others	3 Rank Qualities	4 Accept-ance Manipu-lations	5 Subject Gets Group Consensus	6 Bogus Message from Other Subject	7 Irrelevant Infor-mation 1	8 Subject Gives Second Opinion (Private)	9 Bogus Second Message	10 Irrelevant Infor-mation 2	11 Subject Gives Third Opinion (Private)
No deviate	X	X	X	X	X	Pro group	X	X	Irrelevant	X	X
Late deviate	X	X	X	X	X	Pro group	X	X	Anti group	X	X
Early deviate	X	X	X	X	X	Anti group	X	X	Pro group	X	X
Uncommitted control	0	X	X	X	X	Pro group	X	X	Irrelevant	X	X

[a] X indicates the subject received that manipulation; 0 indicates he did not.

Subjects in the early-deviate condition should show little change then on the second opinion measure.

Steps 9 through 11 in Table 7-1 show the stability (or lack of it) of opinion change found in the first part of the experiment. For example, the no-deviate condition now receives an irrelevant message and the change observed from the second measure of attitude (step 8) to the third measure (step 11), merely gives a baseline of change or stability over time without anything intervening between the two measures that is directly relevant to the attitude in question. However, the late-deviate group, which should show attitude change on step 8, now has that change attacked. They receive a message attacking the group opinion and reasserting the subject's original opinion, the anti-group message. By comparing this change with the change shown by the baseline of the no-deviate condition, we may see the stability of the effect.

There is also a different way to look at stability, and that is to compare the total change of the late-deviate group with that of the early-deviate group. The early-deviate group has now received a pro-group message. It can be seen that in the experiment as a whole, the early- and late-deviate conditions had exactly the same steps; they simply received them in a different order.

Results. The data are presented in Figure 7-2 below.* The first points on the left represent the change shown by the subjects on the second measure, that is, the attitude evidenced on step 8 minus the pretest attitude (step 3). As mentioned, part of this is a conceptual replication of the Kiesler–Corbin low attraction conditions. The combination of the late-deviate and no-deviate conditions for change one is theoretically the same as Kiesler and Corbin's low attraction, committed condition. The uncommitted-control condition is theoretically equivalent to the Kiesler–Corbin low-attraction, uncommitted condition. As shown by Figure 7-2, Kiesler, Zanna, and DeSalvo replicated the main commitment finding of Kiesler and Corbin: Committed subjects changed more (towards the opinion held by the group) than did uncommitted subjects. Figure 7-2 also shows that the presence of a deviate-ally dissipated the effect completely. The early-deviate subjects not only changed less than the no-deviate subjects but also significantly less than the uncommitted-controls.

In summary, the critical finding of Kiesler and Corbin was replicated; committed subjects changed more than uncommitted subjects when faced with a disagreement with the group. However, the necessity for change, if we

* Figure 7-2 shows points corrected for a slight difference in opinion between the no- and late-deviate conditions at $change_1$ (step 8); a difference that could only be chance since the two conditions were procedurally identical at that point. The correction, however, is only for exposition and does not offset the completion of probability levels. See Kiesler, Zanna, and DeSalvo (1966) for details.

may use that phrase, was obviated by the presence of an ally who agreed with the subject's original opinion. A single corroborating opinion out of the five others enabled the subject to withstand the impact of the opinion discrepancy with the group.

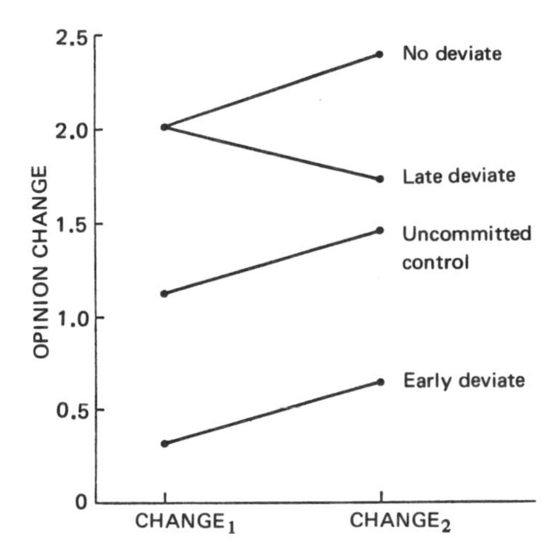

FIG. 7-2. Opinion change as a function of experimental condition for $change_1$ and $change_2$ (from Kiesler, Zanna, & DeSalvo, 1966).

$Change_2$ in Figure 7-2 shows the impact of the second message on each subject. The no-deviate subjects received an irrelevant message, and the late-deviate subjects were sent the anti-group message, the message that agreed with the subject's original opinion. One can see that the message had some impact on the late-deviate subjects: They agree with the group less at that point than do the no-deviate subjects (this difference is significant using the proper test, the interaction term; see the previous footnote). However, the late-deviate subjects still hold an opinion more similar to the group's than do the uncommitted-control subjects (the difference does not quite reach significance), in spite of the fact that the uncommitted-control subjects never received the attack message at all. In short, the change induced in committed subjects is relatively resistant (although not impervious, of course) to attack, even though the attack represents an opinion which the subject himself had advocated prior to his change.

This question of resistance to change on the part of committed subjects is demonstrated in a different way by comparing the late-deviate subjects to the early-deviate subjects. Each set of subjects, the late-deviate and the early-deviate, had the same messages sent to them and the same experimental operations. The messages were simply in a different order. The late-deviate batch first received the pro-group message, stated their opinion, and then received the anti-group message and then stated their opinion again. Subjects in the early-deviate condition had the order of the messages reversed. Yet the difference in opinions held by these two groups at the end of the experiment is highly different ($p < .0001$).

The expression of an opinion following the first set of manipulations (indicated in $change_1$) forced each subject to resolve his uncomfortable situation in some way. The late-deviate subjects, then faced with an apparently homogeneous but discrepant group opinion and committed to three more hours of interaction with the same group, reluctantly resolved their conflict by re-assessing their opinion and coming to agree more with the group's opinion. I say reluctantly, because look what happened to those subjects who had a deviate-ally before having to express their opinion. They didn't change at all.

The early-deviate subjects leaped at the chance to ally themselves with another who held the same deviate opinion. The ally resolved the conflict for them. Note, however, that although the anti-group message resolved the conflict for early-deviate subjects, it challenged the resolution of the conflict for late-deviate subjects. They had been forced to re-evaluate their opinion in light of their commitment and the discrepant group opinion—then they hear that someone in the group agrees with their original opinion. As true believers they should resent this reminder from the past.

Early- and late-deviate subjects should evaluate the deviate-ally quite differently, and they did. For example, one of the questions asked at the end of the experiment was, Which person do you like best in the group? In the early-deviate condition, 58% of the (55) subjects said they liked the deviate best. In the late-deviate condition, only 14.7% of the (80) subjects said they like the deviate best of the four or five others in the group. This difference in proportions is, of course, highly significant.

Discussion

The Kiesler–Corbin (1965) and Kiesler, Zanna, and DeSalvo (1966) experiments lend support to our preliminary notions about commitment to future interaction with a group. In both cases, commitment to future interaction led to increased attitude change following disagreement with one's group. Further, the change was not simply an overt response to the pressures of the moment, which could be withdrawn later. The change induced by commitment proved to be relatively resistant to subsequent attack. The differences in each experiment are statistically reliable, and they give an air of credence to our extrapolation of the commitment model to group effects. Nonetheless, there are a number of theoretical and empirical issues demanding resolution before one might wish to accept the extrapolation without reservation.

A central theoretical point in the extrapolation of the commitment model to group effects concerns the original choice to continue in the group. As we emphasized earlier in the chapter, an important assumption is that the subject is presented with a choice of whether to continue in the group or not. Choosing to continue for three sessions involves greater commitment than electing to continue with the others for only one hour, to use the Kiesler, Zanna, and DeSalvo method. Reasoning backward from the obtained data, we would have to say that this assumption is indirectly supported by the fact that the results of the experiment are as expected. On the other hand, the assumption has never been directly tested. To tie the group data together more explicitly would demand another experiment. Perhaps this small theoretical point could be solved by an experiment in which subjects are committed to the same length of time of interaction with the group, but the incentive (perhaps financial) is varied. If we are correct, then variation in incentive for continuing with the group should produce results similar to those obtained in the present two experiments.

To the extent that one freely chooses to engage in some behavior, one is ordinarily committed to it. Volition, however, does not define commitment, nor does it exhaust the possibilities for varying it. That is, in practice one could be highly committed to a group (or to some specific behavior) with little or no choice in the matter. These situations may be unusual but nonetheless potent. Consider four people sentenced to life imprisonment without parole, who share the same cell. Their expectation of future interaction is firm indeed, and should affect their overt behavior vis à vis one another, their strategies of dealing with each other, the ease with which the group could influence the individual, and their resistance to outside attitudinal attack. A similar, but not so potent, fate befalls college roommates, married couples, draftees, and even school children who remain class after class (or year after year) with their peers in the same setting while the teachers change. A strong case can be made, I think, for parallels between these situations and the commitment to future interaction in our studies. However, immediately comparable settings would be difficult (and unethical) to effect in the laboratory. The impact of the uncontrolled situations described above stems largely from the lack of available alternatives. To stretch the point slightly, one might assert that the hypothesized prisoners are not more or less committed; they really have no alternatives at all. Withdrawal from the group is literally impossible.

Volition is probably an important part of the typical laboratory study of commitment, where a high degree of extra-experimental control is neither feasible nor desired. But volition is not always critical to a variation of commitment. We shall discuss later the possibility of external commitment, where the committing circumstances are beyond the ken and reach of the individual.

To some degree we have exaggerated the cases of hypothetical prisoners and so forth. For the case of prisoners there is still the warden and guards. For the school children, the teachers are not completely in the background. What should happen in these situations probably depends on the power of the third party. Bettelheim (1958) describes the plight of prisoners of war held by the Germans during the Second World War. The salient enduring feature for these poor souls was not their fellow prisoners (who might be gone tomorrow) but, rather, the guards whose power and viciousness were omnipresent. For those who held hope of survival, it was the guards whom they could expect to continue their interaction with. Indeed it was the guard who could douse any ray of hope. Perhaps under these extraordinary circumstances we should not find surprising the prisoners' extreme orientation towards the guards and their subsequent imitation of them. Their attention to their fellows who shared their plight and the resistance that could have resulted from their cohesiveness was destroyed.

In a similar vein, Schein (1958) describes how, during the Korean War, the Chinese also tried to smash the cohesion within the group by creating an aura in which each man must necessarily suspect his fellow prisoners of possible collaboration. One could consider these people committed to both Chinese and fellow prisoners, but the commitment that was prepotent and salient was that to future interaction with the Chinese. They were the ones who held the key to each person's fate.

The hypothetical intra-group and extra-group effects also provoke interesting theoretical questions. We have said that commitment should make one less resistant to attack from inside the group but more resistant to attack from outside the group. Our research results support the former finding, but the latter statement is untested. The latter assertion is of interest since it represents the direct empirical extrapolation from the commitment effects on the individual; to wit, greater degrees of commitment produce greater resistance to attack. A simple experiment involving various levels of commitment and two directions of attack, from within and without the group should satisfy our curiosity on this point, however.

Commitment to continue interacting with group *x* should not affect one's resistance to outside attack if the attitude under attack is irrelevant to the group or one's membership in it. Turned around, the more central or important the attitude is to the group or one's membership, the greater the effect of commitment to continue in resisting outside attack.

In addition, one would think that in social reality it would be much easier to deny or distort the relationship of one's attitude or behavior to any particular group than it was in our experimental setting. For example, the sociologist or social psychologist would consider the number of informal groups to which a person belongs to be much larger than the number of formal groups of which he is a member.

The more informal the group the easier it would be to deny or distort the relationship of a particular attitude or behavior to continued interaction with them. If one can easily distort one's relationship to the group, then the necessity for attitude change following intra-group attack become less. Consequently, the attitude effects of commitment to future interaction might be nullified in uncontrolled situations; largely because attitude change is probably not the preferred alternative in such situations. But something will happen. That is, commitment to continue may not affect one's attitude in the face of attack, but it would initiate an active process of denial and distortion.

Many have emphasized the complexity of modern life and how frequently an individual has to face conflicting group memberships or conflicting roles within larger groups (see Gross *et al.*, 1958, on the conflicting roles of the school superintendent, for example). We can think of these situations as involving conflicting commitments as well. The outcome of a given influence setting may well depend on which commitment to which group is momentarily salient. Recall the data of Kelley (1955) previously discussed in which Catholic girls proved to be more resistant to an anti-Catholic communication when reminded of their ties to formal Catholicism.

We have discussed thus far the effect of commitment to future interaction upon one's reactions to influence attempts. It only stands to reason, however, that the same variable should affect one's covert reactions to the social behavior of another, and one's overt attempts to deal with that behavior. Three experiments by Kiesler, Kiesler, & Pallak (1967) explored this phenomenon and we shall mention them only briefly.

Commitment and Reactions to the Social Behavior of Another

All three experiments were concerned with one's reaction to violations of normative or expected behavior on the part of another. In the first experiment, a confederate behaved very casually in an experiment allegedly concerned with productivity in groups and individuals. Whether this behavior was appropriate or inappropprate was determined by the aura of the experiment. In one case, the experimenter himself was very casual: He appeared in Levis and introduced the experiment as just part of his bursury job. Thus, the confederate's unusual behavior (yawning, scratching, failing to follow directions) did not seem unduly inappropriate. In another condition, however, everything was very serious: The experimenter appeared in coat and jacket and announced that the project was part of his senior honors essay at Yale (a very serious business for the undergraduates).

As one dimension of the design, the confederate behaved either appropriately or inappropriately. Independently of this manipulation, each subject expected to be interacting with the confederate in a subsequent session or he did not. As expected, when the confederate's behavior was appropriate to the occasion, subjects committed to future interaction with him liked him better than subjects who did not expect subsequent interaction. Perhaps the uncommitted subjects interpreted his unusual behavior as bizarre, and the committed subjects interpreted it as cool. However, when the confederate's behavior was inappropriate, committed subjects liked him less than uncommitted subjects. For committed subjects, the odd behavior of the confederate had implications for future interaction, making the anticipation of interacting with this person in a future session unpleasant, and they justifiably disliked him for it. For uncommitted subjects, the odd behavior had no implications for the future, and they were more tolerant.

The other two experiments dealt with the committed subject's willingness or desire to correct the other's behavior when he has violated normative rules of behavior—in this case, committed a social faux pas. A faux pas also has implications for future interaction, and we suspected that the committed individual, more than the uncommitted, would try to change the other's behavior, to bring his faux pas up so as to lessen the probability of its future occurrence. But we thought that he would only do this privately, not in the presence of other people. To be corrected in the presence of others is embarrassing and resented. For the committed person to mention the faux pas publicly would only incur the wrath of the other and as a result, also threaten the smoothness or pleasantness of the anticipated future interaction.

To test these ideas, experiments two and three of Kiesler, Kiesler, and Pallak had a similar design. Half of the subjects in each experiment were committed to some future interaction (with another person of a dyad) and half were not. During the progress of the experiment, all of the subjects overheard the confederate making a nasty remark about secretaries ("God-damn . . . these secretaries have got to be the least talented people in the whole world."). Naturally, before the confederate had arrived for the experiment, the female experimenter had let it slip to half of the subjects that she had recently been a secretary. Consequently, the negative remark of the confederate was a classic faux pas for these subjects, much like commenting on a boring party to an attractive woman and in the presence of others who know she is the hostess.

Within the elaborate subterfuge of the experiment, there was a point at which each subject could send his partner-confederate any message he wished. We simply computed the number of times the remark about the secretaries was brought up and negatively referred to. When there had been no mention of the experimenter having been a secretary, only 1 in 20 subjects even mentioned the remark of the confederate's. When, however, it was a faux pas, 20% of the uncommitted subjects and 62.5% of the subjects committed to future interaction with the confederate made negative reference to the remark.

In the third experiment, we gave subjects both a public and a private opportunity to mention the remark. We found that uncommitted subjects were perfectly willing to bring up the confederate's gaucherie in front of the experimenter, but the committed subjects did it privately.

In short, commitment to future interaction not only has implications for the acceptance or rejection of influence attempts from others but also for one's evaluative impressions of others (see also, Darley & Berscheid, 1967; Berscheid, Boye, & Darley, 1968; Mirels & Mills, 1964; and Davis & Jones, 1960 on this point) and one's strategy in dealing with others.

Commitment to future interaction has not yet been as firmly tied to the concept of commitment to some particular behavior as one might prefer. It mains, however, a fruitful area of inquiry and research.

VIII

COMMITMENT AND SELF-ATTRIBUTION

The previous six chapters review the evidence concerning the effects of commitment on attitudes and behavior. In general we have interpreted commitment as a behavioral phenomenon which effectively freezes attitudes or makes them more resistant to change. It is "the pillar around which the cognitive apparatus must be draped." I find it intuitively appealing to see commitment as a behavioral action which solidifies cognition; which, in essence, can affect one's definition of self. At one level of thought, this view not only adequately describes the data we have obtained, but also fits rather well with traditional, if imprecise, ideas about commitment from both layman and professional. However, at another level of thought, and I won't say that it is a deeper one, this explanation is unsatisfactory. One is compelled to go further and is still nagged by the omnipresent, But why?

To my mind, explaining a psychological datum is not a discrete action but, rather, a process. At each level of explanation one can, and usually does, continue to ask why something happens. I do not mean that this process of questioning is one of reductionism, for I think we will find that micro-biological explanations of social behavior are no more (but perhaps no less) satisfying than the ones currently in vogue. I mean simply that through the process of questioning we learn more about a particular phenomenon, about different aspects of the same phenomenon, and perhaps about different variables which affect it. In short, I reject the notion of a single ultimate explanation, while at the same time endorsing the process of searching for it. It is the search that pays the dividends in theory and power of explanation rather than the wishful hope for a single ultimate answer.

The present case is no exception to the rule of continued questioning. In Chapter II a model for commitment was presented. It is an axiomatic model, one in which formal assumptions are made in order to see where they lead us. The axioms are reasonably well tied to other research results, but they are still axioms with no more properties than we are willing to give them. It is also a *descriptive* model rather than an inferential one. It purports to represent a psychological process rather than posit variables with properties of their own which might underlie the process.

For further questioning then, one can go in one (or both) of two directions. First, one can accept the current model as adequately representing the process of commitment and then search for the variables which presumably underlie or mediate this process. Or, one can look askance at the current model and search for other possible processes, other possible descriptions of commitment. One might come up with either a slightly different picture of commitment or an alternative explanation of our data, perhaps even unrelated to the commitment concept.

The present chapter considers one such alternative process, a very interesting one and one which we have briefly mentioned before: the notion that one infers one's attitude from one's behavior. Recall that in Chapter II, we mentioned this notion as one of two guesses about the phenomenological process underlying the effect of a committing act. The other was trying-on-for-size: the idea that when one is faced with a (counter-) communication one tries the new attitude on for size; one thinks whether it is possible to accept the advocated attitude, whether it fits with one's definition of self and one's past, as it were. These two processes are not mutually exclusive. They could take place at the same time and both could contribute to the observed effect of behavior on belief. The fact that they are not mutually exclusive, of course, does not preclude exclusion on other grounds. That is, the fact that both could operate at the same time and influence our data does not necessarily imply that both, or either, are related to the data we have presented. In short, the following discussion of inferring one's belief from one's behavior is only tangential to the acceptance or rejection of the alternative process of trying-on-for-size.

Before, we mentioned that belief inference might be a variable mediating the effects of commitment, and we did not present it as an alternative process. However, the implications of belief inference for commitment become clearer if we give it the formal status of an alternative explanation or rival hypothesis.

in this way we can be more specific about the issues and possible interpretations.

The hypothesis that one infers his beliefs from a consideration of his past behavior is not new and has been discussed at some length in the literature. Therefore, proper discussion requires that we first consider what others have said. There are three main sources of theorizing about belief inference that we should think about before we consider the application of this notion to the present data on commitment. These are the theoretical discussions by Jones and Davis (1965), Bem (1965; 1967), and Kelley (1967).

Jones and Davis: Correspondent Inferences

The theoretical insights provided by Jones and Davis (1965) are perhap, not directly relevant to the data at hand, but they provide a good beginning for our discussion and an interesting context within which to place it. The central concern of Jones and Davis is inferences about others' attitudes motivations, and dispositions, rather than one's own. To provide predictability in one's environment and smoothness in social interaction, people wish to interpret others' behavior: "The person-perceiver's fundamental task is to interpret or infer the causal antecedents of [others'] action. . . . The cognitive task of establishing sufficient reason for an action involves processing available information about, or making assumptions about, the links between stable individual dispositions and observed action [p. 220]."

Thus, one wishes to interpret others' behavior because it is useful to do so, and one infers particular dispositions or attitudes from others' behavior. Which personal characteristics one assigns to the other depends on the circumstances surrounding his behavior and, of course, on the behavior itself. A correspondent inference or correspondence "refers to the extent that the act and the underlying characteristic or attribute are similarly described by the inference [p. 223]."

Suppose one person harms another. Do we infer from the vicious act that the harm-doer is a vicious person? In other words, do we make a correspondent inference? Whether we do or not, Jones and Davis tell us, depends upon the circumstances, the setting in which the vicious behavior occurs. When the circumstances or setting dictate or force the behavior, we do not infer a harmful intent. A captured U.S. Naval Commander who signs a propaganda statement for the enemy is not called a traitor by his fellow men if it is shown that his intent was not to be harmful to his country but, instead, to save the lives of other captured men under his command. What else could he do? we ask. He had no choice. As the circumstances force the behavior we become less likely to make an inference of disposition that is correspondent with the behavior.

According to this view, commitment may be one of the behavioral inputs from which observers infer attitudes or dispositions. A high degree of commitment could lead the observer to infer that the other either holds the attitude implied by the committing act or that the act is important to him somehow.

This model can also be applied to an observer's interpretation of particular experiments. Take the Festinger and Carlsmith (1959) experiment, for example. In that experiment, subjects lie to a confederate. Some subjects are paid one dollar and some twenty dollars to tell another that a dull and boring task was really fun and enjoyable. With the Jones and Davis theory we can see how an observer would interpret this act. The observer should say that when the subject was paid twenty dollars for the counter-attitudinal act, circumstances dictated the behavior. That is, the behavior itself would give one no clue to the stable dispositions of the actor. However, when the actor was paid only one dollar for the counter-attitudinal act, then the observer would be more likely to make an inference of intent that is correspondent with the act. That is, when only one dollar was paid, the observer would be more likely to say that the actor did not think the task was really boring, that he must have thought it fun. Why else would he do it?

The same reasoning might be applied to any behavior, dissonant or consonant, except that the behavior must be *unusual.* That is to say, if to the observer's way of thinking anyone would have behaved the same way under similar circumstance, then the behavior gives no clue to the dispositions underlying it. If it's popular behavior in some sense, then one will not make a correspondent inference. If it is behavior that clearly comes within some "role" specified to the actor, then the observer will not make a correspondent inference.

We note that Jones and Davis make it quite clear that they are talking about the inferences being made by observers about the dispositions or attitudes of actors, on the basis of the latter's behavior. They do not propose that one makes the same inference or goes through the same process when observing his own behavior. Indeed, they go to some length to point out the differences between observers and actors. For example, the actor has information about his own attitude. The observer does not; that is what he is inferring, in fact. On the other hand, the actor may see himself responding to a unique set of circumstances in which he must chart a path among the unknown. The observer has the advantage there. He not only has the actor's behavior on which to make an inference, but he also knows (or at least has some idea) how he himself would react under the same circumstances. He thus can make a judgment of typicality of the behavior—how usual it would be for the circumstances—much more confidently than can the actor.

The question at hand, however, is whether or to what extent subjects in our commitment experiments are inferring their beliefs from observing their own behavior. It is a question of actors inferring from knowledge of their own behavior. In this sense, the theory of Jones and Davis is not directly relevant to the present discussion, as previously mentioned. On the other hand, the notion of attributing attitudes and dispositions to others is much better documented than that of attributing attitudes to self. The theory and data of Jones and Davis give a reasonably well-documented context within which to place the subsequent discussion. One possibility, of course, is that the process of attributing attitudes to others and that of attributing to self are identical. This is essentially what Bem (1965; 1967) proposes.

Bem: Attributions to Self and Others

Bem's theory is loosely based on Skinner's (1953; 1957) model of the acquisition of verbal descriptive statements, and its unique feature is its proposed similarity of inferences about others and those about self. A preliminary assumption is that it is very difficult for society to teach an individual anything about his internal states and how to label them since the stimuli are private and not available to the socializing public. Bem suggests that learning how to describe one's inner states is imperfect. As a result, "many of the self-descriptive statements that appear to be exclusively under the discriminative control of private stimuli may, in fact, still be partially controlled by the same accompanying public events used by the training community to infer the individual's inner states [1967, p. 185]." This leads to the notion that "the individual's belief and attitude statements are functionally equivalent to those that an outside observer would attribute to him. They are 'inferences' from the same evidence [1965, p. 217]." That is, a person who behaves in a particular way should use that behavior as data for an inference about his own true attitude in exactly the same sense and with the same outcome as the outside observer who watches him perform the act. The actor knows no more and no less than the observer.

The idea that observers and actors have exactly the same evidence and that they go through the same process to arrive at an inference about the attitude of the actor is rather naive, in my view. There are occasions for which the evidence is the same, but not usually or perhaps even often. Nonetheless, the idea led Bem to carry out some interpersonal replications, as he calls them, of dissonance experiments. In these studies, the observer was given a skeletal outline of the position of one subject in a dissonance experiment (person *x* was offered one dollar to do so-and-so, and he agreed), and he was then asked to guess what the subject's attitude was. The guesses of the observers reproduced the dissonance responses: the less the subject was paid, the more observers thought that the behavior reflected the subject's attitude. This led others to protest that the skeletal outline did not at all reflect the information that a subject in a dissonance experiment possessed. A series of experiments (Jones, Linder, Kiesler, Zanna, & Brehm, 1968; Piliavin, Piliavin, Loewenton, McCauley, & Hammond, 1969) showed that the more closely the observer's information approximated that of the "real" subject, the less similar their responses became.

I think the evidence shows that observers and subjects do not possess the same information and they are not making the same sort of inference about attitude. To the extent that Bem's theory rests on this single assumption of isomorphism between observer and subject, it is demonstrably false.* On the other hand—and more appropriate to the present discussion—it is interesting to note that the notion that people may infer their own attitude from their behavior remains unscathed. Indeed, there is evidence that under some conditions at least, people do infer their own attitudes from their own behavior. Some of this evidence is presented after the following brief discussion of Harold Kelley's paper on attribution.

Kelley: Attribution Theory

Like that of Jones and Davis, Kelley's theory of attitude attribution is based on the phenomenological writings of Fritz Heider (e.g., 1958). For Kelley, attribution is the "process of inferring or perceiving the dispositional properties of entities in the environment [p. 193]," including oneself. The main difference between Jones and Davis and Kelley is one of emphasis. Jones and Davis emphasize the *uniqueness* of the stimulus (e.g., object perceived, behavior of the other, outcome of the behavior of the other) in order that one may infer motivation or intentionality of the other. On the other hand, Kelley's subject is pictured as deciding between self-motivation or object attribute; between liking something because it is intrinsically good (an object attribute), which means that all others would like it too, or liking it because of your own attitudes or motivations, which means that all others may not like the object. Kelley therefore emphasizes the *consistency* of self's and others' behavior toward the object.

Like Bem, however, Kelley also discusses attribution to self. His predictions

* For example, Jones and Nisbett (1971) say, "There is a pervasive tendency for actors to attribute their actions to situational requirements, whereas observers tend to attribute the same actions to stable personality traits [p. 2]."

are very similar to those of Bem. In general, the greater the feeling of subjective volition, or the fewer the restraints involved in behaving in a certain way, the more likely the individual is to infer that the behavior reflected his own true belief. Going one step further, he "suggests the interesting possibility of defining volition in terms of perception of acting according to one's own intention [p. 218]."

Much of the effort of both Bem and Kelley in explicating self-perception or self-attribution of attitude goes toward offering an alternative explanation of dissonance effects. Of course, these (dissonance) data provide the biggest challenge to the attribution theorist. The present analysis is also concerned with dissonance effects although, for reasons explained in Chapter III, we have largely avoided using dissonant topics and dissonant behavior in our experiments. As mentioned, the purpose of the present chapter is to inspect attribution theory for possible alternative explanations or hints of underlying variables for the experiments we have thus far described in this monograph. Consequently, we will resist joining the controversy over dissonance theory and concentrate on the matter at hand. What insights does attribution theory offer us in understanding commitment? The easiest and most precise way of finding out is to stick very closely to the data.

Attribution Explanations of Commitment Effects

There are several possible explanations of obtained commitment effects that we should consider. Let us take the Kiesler and Sakumura experiment as our prototype commitment study and see how one might look at those results with attribution theory.

Immediate Inference

One possible explanation is that prior to the counter-communication subjects in the one-dollar conditions used their behavior to infer a true attitude and the five-dollar subjects did not. In Bem's explanations of dissonance experiments, larger amounts of money are considered mands and lesser amounts, tacts. With a larger amount of money, one infers that the behavior is due to the money offered. With less money one infers that the behavior must reflect one's true attitude. If this were the case for the Kiesler–Sakumura experiment as well, then subjects in the one-dollar condition would become more extreme attitudinally and five-dollar subjects would not. Five-dollar subjects would be less likely to use the behavior as a clue to their true attitude. If the counter-communication were equally effective for both groups of subjects, the final results of Kiesler and Sakumura would be obtained, with one-dollar subjects changing less overall than five-dollar subjects.

This explanation of immediate inference can be ruled out because of the data for the control conditions in the Kiesler–Sakumura experiment. Recall that there was no difference between one-dollar and five-dollar conditions for the controls. The behavior itself had no immediate effect on belief as a function of payment, contrary to what this first explanation must imply. Hence, one may conclude that subjects in the Kiesler–Sakumura experiment did not infer their attitude from their behavior, at least not immediately.

Backward Inference

If subjects did not infer their attitudes as a function of payment immediately, how about later—a backward inference, as it were? Suppose one- and five-dollar subjects both performed the behavior without a second thought because it didn't seem important at the time and it didn't seem to have any hidden implications. Later, however, they read the counter-communication and reviewed their position. At that time, perhaps, the one-dollar subjects might infer that their former behavior reflected their true attitudes; five-dollar subjects would not make the same inference because of the contingencies involved. This explanation would lead one to expect precisely the data Kiesler and Sakumura obtained: no difference between the control conditions and the one-dollar experimental condition showing less change after attack than the five-dollar experimental condition.*

This backward inference explanation cannot be easily disposed of, but at the same time, it seems a little unlikely. For example, the Salancik and Kiesler experiment described in Chapter VI suggests that the commitment manipulations do have an immediate effect either on the organization of cognitions or their salience to the subject. This experiment implies a factor immediately at work which subsequently mediates the commitment effect observed. The backward inference explanation suggests a completely passive subject who does not think about his behavior at all at the time it is performed. If he did think about it, then the one-dollar subject should infer that the behavior reflected his true attitude immediately, according to attribution theory. In sum, the Salancik and Kiesler data do not rule out an explanation based on backward inference, but they do reduce it to a status somewhat less than compelling.

Innocuous Inference

Is it possible that the one-dollar subject inferred that the behavior must have reflected his true attitude but that the behavior fit so well with his

* An explanation similar to this is proposed by Nisbett and Valins (1971). They suggest that in the Kiesler–Sakumura experiment the behavior–attitude link was made salient by the counter-communication.

previously expressed attitude (e.g., on the pretest) that the inference did not lead to a change in expression of attitude; in short, an inference but no immediate effect? If both one- and five-dollar subjects express the same attitude but only the one-dollar subject infers that it is his true or real attitude, then that could account for the increased subsequent resistance of the one-dollar subjects to counterattack. Inference of true attitude might lead to greater confidence in the validity of the attitude or simply increased salience of the attitude itself. Either one would lead to increased resistance to attack. We might call this hypothesis the innocuous inference explanation since an inference is presumably drawn but no effect on attitude is seen.

An experiment by Kiesler, Nisbett, and Zanna (1969) provides evidence on this point although that was not among its primary purposes. Its primary question was why there has been no observed effect in commitment experiments (in the control conditions) as a function of payment when Bem maintains (by implication) that there should be. Kiesler, Nisbett, and Zanna suggested that consonant behavior is not very disturbing to the individual and that one needs some cue that it is relevant to attitude before the behavior will be used to infer attitude. In this experiment, subjects agreed to

> . . . be experimenters in a study allegedly designed to determine the optimal number of arguments to use in a persuasive communication. They were to point out the importance of combatting air pollution to passersby in the street and urge them to sign an anti-air pollution petition. A confederate was asked to deliver similar arguments about the importance of promoting auto safety. When the experimenter asked subject and confederate if they were agreeable to delivering arguments on their assigned topics, the confederate delivered the experimental manipulation, saying either that he was glad to promote a cause he believed in or pleased to participate in an experiment that might have scientific value. The confederate thus served as a model for the subject: in one case he implied that the sort of behavior to which the subject was committed was relevant to belief and in the other case he drew no such implication. The experimenter then asked subject and confederate, before leaving to carry out their arguments, to respond to several opinion items, including items assessing attitudes toward air pollution. In order to determine whether commitment to the behavior produced attitude change by itself, in the absence of a cue linking behavior to belief, a control condition was included in the design. This condition was composed of subjects who merely observed the experimental situation and did not expect to perform the behavior [p. 322].

Some subjects, then, received a cue that their behavior was relevant to attitude and others did not, and in both cases the procedure and expressions were overheard by a witness. The data from this experiment are presented in Table 8-1. (There was no difference at all between the two witness conditions, and hence, they are grouped together in the table.) It can be seen that, when the person was only committed to some consonant behavior, it did not affect his attitude. The mean attitude of the belief–irrelevant condition was very similar to that of the witness control conditions. However, when there was an indirect cue that the behavior was relevant to attitude, subjects became attitudinally more extreme.*

TABLE 8-1

OPPOSITION TO AIR POLLUTION
(from Kiesler, Nisbett, & Zanna, 1969)[a]

Condition	Mean Score	*t*
Belief relevant	37.00 (15)	
Belief irrelevant	31.75 (16)	
Witness	30.52 (27)	
Relevant vs. irrelevant		2.28[b]
Relevant vs. witness		2.66[c]
Irrelevant vs. witness		<1

[a] *N*'s are in parentheses. Range of possible scores is from 4 (minimal opposition) to 44 (maximal opposition).
[b] $p < .05$.
[c] $p < .02$.

When the subject did infer that his behavior reflected true attitude, he became more extreme. This finding implies, with regard to the innocuous inference explanation of the Kiesler–Sakumura experiment, that a similar thing should have happened there. The explanation based on innocuous inference requires an inference but no immediate effect. However, the Kiesler, Nisbett, and Zanna experiment suggests that if an inference had occurred, then there would indeed have been an immediate effect. The implication is that if one-dollar subjects had made an inference about attitude, they would have become more extreme as a result, prior to the receipt of the countercommunication. Of course, data for the Kiesler–Sakumura control conditions show no such effect. Given the data of Kiesler, Nisbett, and Zanna, the explanation of innocuous inference, although not explicitly ruled out, is not easily defensible.

Parenthetically, we may ask why the subjects in the Kiesler, Nisbett, and Zanna experiment became more extreme if the behavior were really consonant. I think it is because of the momentary salience of particular aspects of the consonant behavior. For example, I have a positive attitude toward a democratic system of government. To paraphrase Winston Churchill, I think

* Kiesler and Zanna (1969) found that the cue had no effect when the behavior was clearly inconsistent with one's attitude.

that it is a terrible system but that there is none better. In other words, I am in favor of it, but I am also aware of many negative features. On the other hand, I could construct a positive communication regarding democracy in which I would agree with every single assertion. It would be consistent with my attitude, but if it did not contain many negative statements, it would not be identical with my attitude. This is probably a good representation of the consonant behavior we have induced our subjects to perform: consistent with their attitudes, but not identical to them. (Indeed, if one tried to make the behavior identical, then one would have to tailor a different behavior for each subject—a laborious and methodologically weak technique.)

Consequently, in each of these experiments, the behavior demanded is similar to the subject's attitude, but since it has few or no negative aspects *vis à vis* the attitude object, the net result of the behavior is that it is a little more extreme than the subject's attitude would strictly imply. If the subject is to use only the induced behavior as a basis for his inference, then the expression of his attitude should be a little more extreme than it would otherwise be. Then, too, positive aspects of attitude could be more salient, in our case. Salient positive features of attitude should lead to a more extreme expression of attitude.

A Different Kind of Inference?

There is yet a fourth explanation of commitment effects, based particularly on Kelley's theory of attribution. It requires a slightly different interpretation of an inference, however. We might call the way we have been using the term, a *strong inference*. It either occurs or it doesn't; yes or no. An alternative might be called a *weak inference*. Consider a case where all subjects make an inference from behavior to attitude, but one's confidence in his inference varies from subject to subject. This notion fits well with Kelley's theory since he implies that people continue to test what their attitudes are. The main variable for Kelley is consistency in response. If I behave consistently toward an object over time, modality, and situation, and others do not, then I can confidently infer that I have a certain attitude toward the object. (If others always behave the same as I toward the object, I would alternatively conclude that my feelings depended somehow on innate qualities of the object rather than on self-dispositions.)

Suppose, then, that the subject is always observing his own behavior looking for clues to his dispositions or attitudes, in general trying to make sense out of his environment, as both Kelley and Heider suggest. At one level, he is always making an inference, but it is a weak inference, and he tests it according to certain rules: the test of consistency in particular. In the Kiesler–Sakumura experiment there are two pieces of behavior that would be subjected to test, in this view: the consonant behavior and the pretest. The pretest of attitude, of course, was carried out under identical conditions and, hence, would not affect any differences between conditions. However, subjects were differentially paid for the consonant behavior. Let us further assume that the consonant behavior does not occasion much thought and induces no change. It is not until the subject is confronted with the counter-communication that he begins to question himself about what his attitude really is. Subjects in the one-dollar conditions have two relevant pieces of behavioral information on which to make their judgment: They freely expressed their opinion and they also carried out attitudinally relevant behavior freely or, at least, for a very small payment. In this sense, the five-dollar subjects have only one piece of behavior on which to make their inference: the pretest. The consonant behavior is less relevant since it was performed under conditions which do not necessarily imply a certain attitude, i.e., a large payment for their services. This difference in consistency of response would lead, in Kelley's view, to a difference in confidence about one's attitude. Thus, when dealing with the counter-communication the one-dollar subjects would be more confident of what their true attitudes are than would the five-dollar subjects. Greater confidence in one's opinion should lead to greater resistance to attack (as a great deal of evidence shows).

Thus, the notion that subjects make a weak inference of attitude based on their previous consistency of response toward the attitude object leads to a reasonable explanation of the Kiesler–Sakumura results. Using the same logic, one could also explain the data of Kiesler, Pallak, and Kanouse (1968) described in Chapter III. Recall that their design involved the orthogonal manipulation of commitment and dissonance. Using Kelley's idea of confidence based on previous consistency of response, we could guess several things. When commitment is low and dissonance is high, the person should lean on the dissonant behavior for his inference. When commitment is high and dissonance low, the consonant behavior provides the subject with the best clue to his true attitude. When both commitment and dissonance are at high levels (but inconsistent), perhaps the two pieces of behavior should cancel each other out. If one has freely performed both a consonant behavior and a dissonant act, then, in a sense, neither behavior provides a clue to attitude about which one could be confident. If the reader's memory is good, he will recognize that these guesses from Kelley's theory have replicated the data of Kiesler, Pallak, and Kanouse.

How would these ideas be applied to our data described in Chapters IV and V, in which five different studies showed a boomerang effect under conditions of high consonant commitment and weak attack? Here the task is a little more difficult. One obvious possibility is that subjects knew that their attitudes would be attacked. If a subject agrees to perform some consonant behavior, and at the same time knows that he will be attacked, then he should infer that he has a well-formed, and probably extreme, opinion. That is, conditions of high commitment and preknowledge of attack should produce a boomerang effect. However, in those studies (i.e., Kiesler and Mathog, Kiesler *et al.* and Jones and Kiesler), it is difficult to maintain that subjects knew that they would be attacked. That is, if they knew they would be attacked, then control groups should show the same inference as experimental groups, since they should have the same information. Indeed, in the Jones and Kiesler experiments the second independent variable is not attack, but forewarning of attack. Consequently, this argument comes down to asserting that those subjects were forewarned of a forewarning, which makes little sense.

Attribution theory seems not to provide a very powerful explanation for the boomerang effect, unless one could argue that the attack was somehow anticipated. Indeed, Kelley suggests that, in general, the problem of unanticipated consequences is a tough one for attribution theory. It has been shown that unanticipated consequences of a behavioral act can affect both one's own attitude (e.g., Brehm, 1959; Jecker, 1964), and attribution to others (e.g., Walster, 1966). It is difficult for a broad theory of attribution such as Kelley's to account for these findings. According to Kelley, Jones and Davis get around this problem by dealing only with cases where the subject (the one being observed) can be presumed to have foreknowledge of the consequences of his behavior. Bem (and dissonance theory, as well) bypasses the problem by discussing only those stimuli present at the time of the behavior.

I think that in all of our experiments one has to accept the notion that the attacks were not anticipated by the subjects. If they were anticipated, then we should have found that the behavior affected attitude; there should have been a corresponding difference between the control conditions, which does not occur. In this sense, attribution theory, although promising, does not adequately account for our commitment data.

In Kelley's clever hands, attribution theory can account for rather a good deal of the current literature on attitude change. However, he has painted with a broad brush, and many of the details have not yet been filled in. It may well be that after we learn more about the process of attribution, filling in some of the detail and cracks in the current model, we shall be able to apply a theory of attribution to the present data in a more satisfactory fashion. (The fact that it provides a neat explanation of the Kiesler–Sakumura experiment suggests promise here.)

However, in our posed alternative explanations of the commitment data here, we have been taking attribution theory quite literally; it is whatever

Kelley and others specifically say it is. One could be a little more creative though and ask if there is any way to twist attribution theory so that it would account for these data more adequately. Rephrased, can we force greater theoretical contact between commitment and attribution? I think we can, but it requires, first, that we make the distinction between strong and weak inferences more clearly and, second, that attribution is seen more as a test for consistency than as an inference per se. In the following discussion, we try to clarify these issues and then show how a suitable theoretical translation could be made.

Weak Inferences and Strong Inferences

As we have discussed, the concepts of weak and strong inference do not have the same explanatory power with regard to our commitment data. The notion of strong inference, i.e., the idea that one literally infers his attitude from his behavior, is not a compelling explanation of our data on a priori grounds. We considered three hypotheses based on strong inference, i.e., the concepts of immediate, backward, and innocuous inference, and concluded that data already accrued rendered them relatively implausible. On the other hand, a process we have described as a weak inference provided us with some interesting theoretical leads even though it too lacks the power to explain much richness of detail in our data. The concepts of strong and weak inference have quite different implications and, in fact, rest on somewhat different theoretical grounds. It may be worthwhile to consider the distinction between strong and weak inferences in greater detail.

Bem appears to be the prime advocate of the strong inference. He puts heavy emphasis on immediately preceding behavior, overlooking other information the person may have about himself, opinions he holds, and the world around him. To Bem, this other information is based on internal cues, to which the person has only imperfect access at best. It is his orientation to behavior alone that leads Bem to assert that the observer and the actor make inferences from precisely the same information. However, it is obvious that the observer and the actor do not have the same information. For example, an observer may see a subject in a dissonance experiment being offered one dollar (or twenty dollars) to perform some behavior that is atypical or unusual in Jones and Davis's terms. What does the observer know? He knows that the behavior is atypical (the subject himself is often assured of this in dissonance experiments), he knows the subject was offered a certain amount of money, and he knows that the subject agreed to perform the behavior. But that is all that the observer knows.

What does the subject, the actor, know? First, he knows all that the observer knows (although the actor may be at a slight disadvantage when judging the atypicality of his behavior), but he knows a few other things besides. For example, he might know any or all of the following: (*a*) that he put a certain mark on his pretest form a few minutes before, (*b*) that he had upheld a certain opinion of this issue in a college bull session, (*c*) that he has behaved in certain ways related to this attitude in the past, (*d*) that his parents and/or friends believe a certain way on the issue (and that they expect him to do the same), (*e*) that he has openly expressed an opinion on this issue on a number of occasions, (*f*) that he holds other opinions on related issues that are inextricably connected to this opinion, (*g*) that the very mention of the issue arouses a certain emotion in him, i.e., he feels there is something intrinsically valid to his attitude, and so forth. What the actor knows that the observer does not, will vary from person to person and situation to situation. But probably in no case do the actor and the observer have exactly the same information on which to base an inference about attitude.

In sum, the theoretical position of strong inference leads to an over-reliance on only one source of information, i.e., one's own behavior, while slighting other acknowledged sources of information. Bem asserts that in response to the question, "Do you like brown bread?," the subject might reply, "I guess I do, I'm always eating it." This nicely reflects the information the observer might have as well. However, as Jack Brehm (personal communication) has suggested, the subject is more likely to respond, "Yes, I do like brown bread, because it smells and tastes so good." The actor has access to much more information than simply his own behavior on which to base an attitude. In short, a theoretical assertion of strong inference leads one to a position that, at worst, is demonstrably false and, at best, over-emphasizes a single source of information out of several.*

In contrast, the notion of weak inference stresses consistency of response over several sources of information, such as modality (e.g., seeing, hearing, smelling, tasting) or time (behaving similarly over several occasions). In this view, one does not infer his attitudes from his behavior in any straightforward fashion. Whereas strong inference implies a specific process, "I did behavior x under conditions y, therefore I must believe z," weak inference could be defined as a test for consistency over several sources of information or a check for prior stability of attribution, to use Kelley's term.

One could consider the weak inference as not an inference at all, literally speaking, but an assessment of one's attitude, based on all the sources of information at one's disposal including past behavior and its "emitting cir-

* This is not to say, however, that a strong inference never occurs, but that it occurs much less frequently than a weak inference, and that it does not have the breadth of explanatory power that the concept of weak inference does.

cumstances." Given such a broad interpretation, it is possible to fit both the notions of trying-on-for-size and inferring-one's-belief-from-one's-behavior into different aspects of the same process. To check the fit of a possible new attitude, one inventories previous behaviors, verbalizes attitudes, checks relationships to other attitudes and behavior, recalls what friends and attractive others believe, and so forth. In this manner one could determine whether it is possible or feasible to adopt a new attitude (perhaps in response to a counter-communication). However, after the assessment, the individual also has all the information necessary to state his present attitude and his confidence in it; his confidence depending on the stability of prior attribution. Moreover, a reappraisal of prior attributions should lead to especial salience of cues to attitude, such as that used in the experiment by Kiesler, Nisbett, and Zanna (1969).

Suppose an individual completes his assessment of the past (and the cognitive present, as well) and finds that his prior attributions are very stable, so stable, in fact, that it would be extremely difficult to adopt a new attitude, as perhaps implied in a forewarning or a counter-communication. What would he do? All of the information he holds that is consistent with his opinion should be very salient following his attribution assessment. It seems to me plausible that he should argue (to himself) against the opposite opinion. (Of course, this arguing should be particularly effective if one is only forewarned of an impending attack rather than faced with the detailed attack itself.) If the attack is not devastating, then the person's (subvocal) arguments might make him even more attitudinally extreme than he formerly was—the boomerang effect.

This train of thought provides us with some insight into the boomerang effect observed in the five experiments described in Chapters IV and V. However, it is necessary to consider commitment as an especially stable attribution, which seems eminently reasonable. Commitment is defined as the pledging or binding of the individual to behavioral acts, and its main effect is to make an act more difficult to undo, deny, distort, or reinterpret. We have suggested that a committing act is one the individual must live with and face up to. That a committing act would produce an extremely stable attribution that would, perforce, subsequently affect alternative attributions to self and others is simply another way of saying what we have been stating all along. It is really a theoretical translation, rather than an alternative explanation.

We can continue this translation by applying it to another study of theoretical interest, that of Salancik and Kiesler described in Chapter VI. Recall that in that study we found that commitment had an immediate cognitive effect such that committed subjects were more likely to remember word-pairs consistent with their attitude than were uncommitted subjects. Recall also that this effect was not predicted by commitment theory although it is perfectly consistent with it. With a little twisting, we may give it equal status for our revision of attribution theory. It may simply be that when a person performs an act which carries with it some aspect of self-responsibility, i.e., some commitment, he looks momentarily at his prior attributions as a small check for consistency. If the act involves greater self-responsibility, i.e., if it carries greater commitment with it, the person may wish to be a little more certain of his prior attributions and check a little further than would a person not so committed. If so, then the ties or connections between this act and others that may have occurred in the past would be more salient for the person in the high commitment condition than in the low. Greater salience of other cognitive connections or prior attributions could easily mediate the retention of consistent word-pairs.

In sum, by considering commitment to be an especially stable attribution, we may derive a contact between the present theory and research and Kelley's brilliant exposition on attribution. Indeed, in one view, commitment might be a special case of attribution theory: the "Psychology of Especially Stable Attributions," as it were. This view is not to be denigrated, since it has several advantages.

One advantage is that the present pocket of research we have been describing can be placed in perspective, into a broader context of attitude development and change. Secondly, the ease of translation across theoretical lines is provocative in terms of potential research.

Moreover, the translation from commitment theory to attribution theory and back, gives some insight into both models. We are provided with ideas about the process underlying our results, which at the time were rather formally derived. We think we have something to add to attribution theory as well. For example, the contact between commitment and attribution depends upon a particular view of attribution. The distinction between strong inference and weak inference was the initial impetus, and it may ultimately provide us with some insight into the process involving attribution as well. Our results on the boomerang effect and the organization-salience effect noted by Salancik and Kiesler cannot be easily derived from attribution theory, as we discussed earlier. (Recall that we have not even mentioned the effect of commitment on interpersonal interaction as well.) However, given a certain interpretation of attribution, then these results are consistent with it and may lead to more precise digging at the issues.

IX

IMPLICATIONS AND RELATED ISSUES

In the previous chapters we have presented our case on the psychology of commitment. In doing so, however, we felt it necessary to keep rather close to the data and the issues they raise directly. We have tread a very narrow path through the conceptual thicket, generally ignoring the many byways to generalizations, broader issues, and connections to other research, however tempting. And they were tempting. But commitment is a complicated concept with many connotations and even more applications, and we wanted to be as logically precise about the issues as we could. In sticking to the case at hand, we've left a number of loose ends. The present chapter is devoted to a discussion of several of these.

Commitment and the Illusion of Freedom

Our data imply that one's commitment to some behavior follows from one's perception that he was free to have acted otherwise. Commitment was directly manipulated by varying choice in the Kiesler, Pallak, and Kanouse experiment, but the perception of choice is closely related to other variables such as the amount of financial incentive, as used by Kiesler and Sakumura. One's perception that he has freely elected to act in some way should certainly contribute to the degree to which he feels committed to the act. Having elected to act in a particular way should make him feel more personally responsible for his behavior. And Heider (1958) suggests that one's perception of self-responsibility is the very core of commitment. Thus, one's perception of freely choosing to behave in a certain way (and its concomitant, one's feeling of self-responsibility for the behavior) would undoubtedly be an important input for any theory of commitment.

Choice also is a critical input for other theories as well. For example, in dissonance theory, choosing to behave in a way that is inconsistent with one's attitudes creates dissonance. And the greater the choice, the greater the dissonance. Similarly, in attribution theory, choice affects the attribution of attitudes to self and others. The greater the choice self (or another) had in doing something, the more likely one is to attribute an attitude consistent with the behavior to self (or another).

A problem arises with regard to choice when attribution theorists attempt to account for results of some dissonance experiments. In the Kiesler and DeSalvo (1967) experiment, for example, the subject chose to work on a dull and boring task at the request of an unattractive group. The knowledge that one has agreed to work on the task is inconsistent with the knowledge that one knows the task to be dull and boring. The fact that one was asked to do so by a group of unattractive others should only increase the dissonance (indeed, in that experiment the attractiveness of the inducing group was varied as the manipulation of dissonance). However, in the typical dissonance experiment, everyone (or almost everyone) actually performs the dissonant behavior. It is this fact that creates some discomfort for the attribution theorist.

In attribution theory (e.g., Kelley, 1967), the person is seen as motivated to attribute causes for environmental effects. "A major application of the theory concerns the processes by which the typical observer infers a person's motivations from his actions [p. 193]." With regard to self-attribution, the person presumably is often in conflict between wanting to attribute the cause for his behavior to the environment ("I was forced to do it.") or to self ("I really wanted to do it.") Kelley assumes a bias toward attribution to the environment. (See, also, Heider, 1958 for a more detailed exposition on this point.) That is, the individual would prefer to attribute the cause of his behavior to something in the environment than to some disposition in himself. Kelley goes even further and differentiates among actions with positive outcomes:

> Am I to take my enjoyment of a movie as a basis for an attribution to the movie (that it is intrinsically enjoyable) or for an attribution to myself (that I have a specific kind of desire relevant to movies)? . . . The attribution to the external thing rather than to the self requires that I respond *differentially* to the thing, that I respond *consistently*, over time and modality, and that I respond *in agreement* with a con-

> sensus of other persons' responses to it. In other words the movie is judged enjoyable if I enjoy only it (or at least not all movies), if I enjoy it even the second time, if I enjoy it on TV as well as at the drive-in theater, and if others also enjoy it. If these conditions are not met, there is indicated an attribution to the self . . . [p. 194].

According to Kelley, before one's behavior would lead one to attribute an attitude to self, one would have to know that others would not behave the same way in similar circumstances. However, in dissonance experiments everyone in the high-dissonance condition complies and acts inconsistently with his attitudes. The point is, if everyone does it, how could the dissonance data be explained by attribution theory? If everyone would act the same way in the same circumstances, one should contribute the cause of the behavior to the environment rather than to self. There should be no self-attribution.

Of course, the subjects don't know that everyone else complies with the experimenter's request; that's the whole point. Were the subject's to know the extent of compliance, that would be an additional cognition consistent with the behavior and would therefore reduce the dissonance. A consensus of others agreeing to perform the same behavior would both imply pressure to act in the same manner oneself and provide a consensual validation for the behavior. For dissonance theory, one critical input for the arousal of dissonance is the *perception* of choice. Whether this perception is veridical or not, i.e., whether it would accord with the way an outside observer would interpret the same event, is simply irrelevant. But it is not irrelevant to attribution theory. Recall Bem's assertion that the observer and the subject make inferences from the same information. We have argued against this point of view, suggesting that for any given situation the observer and the acting self do not necessarily have the same information nor would they often have the same information. As we have mentioned, when we do give the observer more of the information that the subject in the dissonance experiment has, he ceases to make the same inference about the subject's final attitude (e.g., Jones *et al.*, 1968; Piliavin *et al.*, 1969).

This puzzle may only exist for the particular attribution theorist who wishes the observer's inference always to be in accord with the subject's. The rest of us may simply take this as another instance of the importance of phenomenology, i.e., of assessing the way the subject sees the world, in predicting how one will ultimately behave.

In discussing Bem's interpretation of dissonance phenomena, Kelley tries to take this apparent paradox seriously and refers to the *illusion of freedom.** To grasp the term one must assume that in dissonance research the subject

* We do not mean to suggest that Kelley endorses the view that the process and outcome of inference in observer and subject are identical. He apparently does not.

is not really free to refuse to perform the act because *no one does refuse*. It is only when one feels free to do otherwise but one is not objectively free to do so that one can refer to the illusion of freedom. Because this term has broad implications and possibly could be applied to commitment research, I would like to pick at this point a little.

In what sense is this freedom an illusion? I would argue that either it is not an illusion or almost any perceived freedom is an illusion. In either case the term loses its impact. Let's take an example. In our society, one is presumably free to vote in an election for any candidate he wishes. And most people perceive themselves free to do so. But suppose that I as an outside observer try to predict how a small group of randomly selected people would vote. I first might look at a number of correlates of voting behavior. To begin, I might check how each individual's father and mother voted. That, in itself, is a fairly good predictor. Next, I might determine the religion of the subjects and the candidates (there are some data suggesting that Catholics will vote for Catholics, for example: Converse & Campbell, 1960). I might then inquire about the subject's immediate environment: How did his wife and colleagues vote in the last several elections? Does he feel strongly about any of the issues being debated in the current election? I could continue on with this process without ever asking any subject a question directly by checking bias in the newspapers, magazines, and television shows the subject has access to, and on and on and on.

Suppose at the end of this elaborate process I was able to predict in every case how the subjects in my sample would vote. The subjects might feel free to vote for whichever candidate they chose, but I would know in advance which one each would choose. Would you say that they had an illusion of freedom? If so, then most of the freedom of all of us is illusory. Because, in a sense, a combination of our previous learning history and the impact of contemporaneous events compels us to behave in certain ways. At least a good deal of the day-to-day behavior of each of us could be predicted in advance by an astute observer, given exhaustive knowledge of our past and the events currently impinging on us.* There is no question about it. We are influenced by the way we have been brought up, by the newspapers we read, by the opinions of our colleagues, and by our immediate environment as we currently perceive it. In this sense, to the extent that our behavior could be predicted by an outside observer, we are not free, because everyone else in the same situation and with the same background would behave in the

* In its extreme form, this is a completely deterministic point of view. But it is not necessary to adopt the extreme viewpoint to see the logic of the argument. The argument only demands that some of the behavior of each of us could be predicted by a knowledgeable other. And that I think we all accept.

same way. If we adopt this as our criterion, then almost any perceived freedom is an illusion. If we reject this as a criterion, then the perceived freedom to act otherwise in the dissonance experiments is not illusory either, since one's perception of freedom would be the critical issue.

Why such a detailed argument over a picayune point? Mostly because of the connotations of the word "illusion," implying to my mind that if a subject's freedom were of that variety, it would be superficial and unreal, a figment of the experimenter's imagination that could not be applied or generalized elsewhere. My argument is that it is not an illusion in any sense of that word. It is real to the subject, and it guides his behavior. It could only be illusory in the sense that all of our perceived freedom is illusory or with reference to a criterion that the subject's perceptions and those of the observer must match up. The former is meaningless because it is too broad and covers all possibilities; and the latter is a theoretical assumption that is not supported by the evidence.

As mentioned, in some of our experiments we varied commitment to some behavior by manipulating one's perceived freedom to act otherwise. In each case the behavior was consistent with the subject's attitude, and surely, everyone with the same attitude would also have acted the same way. (Occasionally the subject even thinks that everyone has a similar attitude on that issue). By Kelley's criterion, these subjects had only an illusion of freedom. (Indeed, since the subjects often perceive that all others would have acted similarly, perhaps they should feel no freedom at all.) But is it scientifically useful to refer to this perceived freedom as illusory? For the reasons stated above, I would argue that the concept adds little to our understanding of the choice manipulations. The concept is only useful if one wants to argue for the (to my mind, implausible) view that the process of attribution for subject and observer is identical.

One could make a similar argument and counterargument for the assertion that in our experiments the subjects are not really committed but only have the illusion of commitment. For the same reasons as outlined above, this argument adds little to our understanding of the process of commitment. For example, although we have never done the experiment, it is unlikely that observers could reproduce the results of our commitment studies. In the first place, observers would probably think that the committing act would have some impact on the subject's existing attitude (they might wonder why else we would ask them). However, if observers were informed that the behavior had no impact on existing attitude, they likely would not think that it made any difference in reacting to subsequent events either. So the subject and observer inference process is probably not identical for consistent behavior either.

This is not to say, however, that the degree of commitment in our studies is irrevocable or even very high. Our commitment manipulations do the job for us, i.e., they provide us with conservative tests of our hypotheses, but they are not (nor are they intended to be) widely applicable. For example, suppose we paid heavy smokers either one dollar or five to go without smoking for a day. My guess is that there would be little difference between conditions in the percentage of subjects who subsequently gave up smoking. Even if there were a difference, the percentage of subjects in the one-dollar condition who gave up smoking would not be very high. In short, the small difference in financial incentive would not have a major impact in such an important realm of behavior. But because this intentionally rinky-dink manipulation *could* be swamped by other considerations does not imply that we cannot manipulate commitment with financial incentives. It simply means that it is not a very powerful manipulation. By the same token, if a person is very opposed to war and killing, we could not reasonably expect that giving him a raisin reward for killing another in combat would have much effect on his behavior, even though the raisin reward might well be effective in other situations (e.g., toilet training in children).

We argue then that referring to a choice manipulation as an illusion of freedom is not very meaningful and only confuses the issues. The concept implies that either (almost) all freedom is an illusion or the process and outcome of inference are identical for observer and actor. One implication is all-inclusive and the other unsupported. By the same token, extending the concept to propose an illusion of commitment is equally misleading. Our manipulations of commitment are certainly real to our subjects. On the other hand, that the manipulations are real does not imply that they are extremely powerful and could be applied anywhere without regard to other competing influences.*

A Note of Caution for the Behavioral Engineer

Historically, one can trace many of the ideas in this monograph to Kurt Lewin's early work on commitment and decision-making. It is also related to Leon Festinger's theory of cognitive dissonance and Harold Kelley's conceptualization of attribution theory. Given the large body of related data, one could urge the following empirical generalization upon the behavioral engineer: If you want someone not only to behave in a particular way but also to believe accordingly, then induce the behavior under conditions of

* For further discussion of the generalizability of typical experimental operations to applied settings, see Janis (1968) and Janis and Mann (1968) on the relationship between commitment and the stages of decision-making.

very little apparent external pressure. Give the person the feeling that he was free to do otherwise if he wished. Make him think that he was responsible for his own behavior.

As described in Chapter I, one could interpret the effects of participation in group decision-making, say, as dependent upon the perception that one was not forced to behave in a particular way. Participating in making decisions which affect him gives one the perception that he is responsible for his own behavior. In this way the group leader can commit the members to certain behaviors consistent with the goals of the leader. In these early experiments and in many applied settings, the group leader is a very subtle force inducing the members to accept particular goals for themselves, while at the same time leading them to think that they personally were responsible for the final decision.

Note the similarity between this description of the leader's role in group decision-making and the high-choice condition in dissonance experiments. Indeed, a high-choice manipulation consists of inducing a subject to perform some predetermined behavior while at the same time giving him the impression that he is totally responsible for the behavior. This description fits whether the behavior involved is consistent or inconsistent with one's previous beliefs.

The note of caution alluded to above refers to an often neglected fact in this analysis: The person must perform the preselected behavior. If he doesn't, the experimenter-leader is worse off than when he started. For example, Zanna (1969) assigned subjects the task of tape-recording a speech consistent with their beliefs. Some subjects were offered the opportunity to write and record a speech advocating a more extreme view; others were not given this option. By design, none of the experimental subjects agreed to write the more extreme speech (partly because it was just too much time and trouble; the moderate speech was already prepared). Later, however, those subjects who declined to write an extreme speech attributed a more moderate view to themselves than did the subjects who were not offered that opportunity. Of course, the experimental subjects refused to write the speech by design of the experimenter, but the implication is clear. Suppose we try to induce someone to carry out some behavior as a method of increasing his commitment. If we succeed, fine. We would expect the sort of results described in this monograph. However, if we fail, if the other refuses to act as intended, we are not left with a null effect but rather the opposite effect. The subject we tried to commit may now be less resistant to counter-propaganda than before, more open to opposing views.

In a study done under my direction, Steinglass (1968) found a similar effect in a more typical dissonance paragdim. Subjects were offered either fifty cents or two dollars and fifty cents to write a counter-attitudinal essay. Using a very subtle manipulation, Steinglass induced the subjects either to agree or refuse to write the essay. When subjects complied, the usual dissonance results were found: Those offered the smaller incentive changed their attitudes more in the direction to be advocated in the essay than did subjects promised the larger incentive. In the refusal condition, the results were quite different. These subjects tended to react against the counter-attitudinal essay, to become more extreme in their attitudes. However, as expected, this boomerang effect was much stronger for the subjects who were offered the larger incentive than those offered the smaller one.

Consequently, we might say that if we are successful in inducing the subject to act in some way, whether it is consonant or dissonant with his prior beliefs, then the less the perceived pressure, the greater effect that the behavior will have on his attitudes. On the other hand, if we fail, if the subject refuses to act as we wish, then the subject will react against our influence attempt and the greater the pressure, the greater his reaction.

The behavioral engineer should not only be certain that his target does act but also that the action is the one the engineer had in mind. Suppose you have carefully arranged the situation so your subject will perform behavior *a* but will feel free to have done otherwise—the proper conditions for a powerful influence attempt. Suddenly, you find that the subject indeed felt free to choose. In fact, he chose not *a* but, rather, *b*, a behavior quite inconsistent with behavior *a*. You're sunk. But this is exactly what can happen when one reifies such concepts as pressure to behave and group-participation.

I've always had the fantasy that something along these lines went on with the community participation programs. My Thurberesque vignette goes something like this. Around election time, the government decides it will do something for the ghetto. About the time they are ready to implement the program, some budding young social scientist remembers Kurt Lewin and leaps to his feet. "Ah," he says, "But if we impose these programs on them from above, even though they are only for their own good, they will resent it. We must give them the feeling that they are participating in the decisions that affect them." Everyone looks mildly askance until the politician observes, "That way, if the programs fail, we can't be blamed." Then everyone agrees that, indeed, people in the ghetto deserve to participate in decisions that affect them. So they give the money to the ghetto and tell the residents, "You decide what to do with it." The next morning they wake up to find that half of the money has been spent on anti-establishment programs and the other half on lawsuits to change other existing programs. And stock in the generality of social science experiments plummets.

The point is that if you let workers participate in the decision of how to increase production, you may likely find that they are more accepting of the ultimate decision and more motivated to implement it. However, if you let workers decide *if* production will be increased, you are in for a sad surprise. Reducing the pressure to behave in a certain way is an advantage to the behavioral engineer only if the behavior intended is actually carried out. Probably, the development of the community participation programs is unrelated to my fantasy. I'd like to think that it is unrelated, but I have the sneaking hunch that some reification of group-participation played a part. The data fit too well.

Factors Affecting the Degree of Commitment

Choice

One's perception of choice, i.e., one's feeling that he was free to have acted otherwise, must be a central feature of any exposition on commitment. Just how central it must be, we don't know. In some of our experiments we have manipulated choice directly. In most, some other manipulation of commitment was used, but perhaps one could make the argument that other translations of commitment are mediated by feelings of choice or one's perception that one is responsible for one's own behavior (and hence, one must somehow accommodate to the behavior).

For example, we have argued that the amount of incentive offered for a particular behavior is closely related to a perception of pressure to behave. The more one is offered to act, the less option one feels one has. Perhaps, this argument might go, incentive does not affect commitment directly but only in so far as it affects one's perception of choice. Further, one might hypothesize that feeling responsible for one's own behavior in turn mediates the effects of choice. In this view, when one freely elects to carry out some act, he is committed to it *because* he is responsible for it. Incentive would therefore affect one's commitment to the act only when it affects one's perception of choice.

This argument is interesting because it amounts to a slightly different definition of commitment and interpretation of its effects. Essentially, the hypothesis implies that commitment should be equated with self-responsibility and that choice is the main (perhaps only) way to manipulate it. The other ways we have used to vary commitment could be fit into the same scheme. Consider the public–private distinction, for example. If one can remain anonymous, it is difficult to refuse to tape-record a speech that one endorses. Many of the objections to recording a public speech are irrelevant when one's identity will not be known by the audience. Because no one will know who it is, one can't refuse because of possible embarrassment, or a feeling of invasion of privacy, or the possibility that the opinion is incorrect. It's possible, therefore, that subjects in a private condition perceive that they had less freedom to refuse than subjects in a public condition. Consequently, the degree of perceived choice could vary between public and private conditions just as it might between incentive conditions. The public–private manipulation might also directly affect one's feeling of responsibility for his behavior. When the speech is to be made public, there are implications of the behavior not present for the private condition. One might be called upon to defend or explain the position advocated in the speech, for example. Since one will be held more responsible for the speech by others, it is only logical that one should feel more responsible as well.

How well could anticipation of future interaction fit into this scheme? We don't know, largely because, at this point, at least, we can't say whether the effects of future interaction are dependent upon one's perception of choice or not. In Chapter VII, we argued that it was related to choice, but we don't have the data to back that up, and it's not the only analysis that one could make of those data.

In Chapter VIII, we suggested that it might be profitable to view commitment as an especially stable attribution. We mentioned that more data are needed before one could tell just how profitable a view it was. We are now opening up another possibility: Perhaps commitment could be seen as one's perception that he is responsible for his own behavior.

The major advantage of the view that commitment is determined by the perception of responsibility for one's own behavior is that it posits a mediating or underlying variable for effects of commitment. One is committed because he feels responsible for his past behavior. The committed self is more resistant to attack because of the implications of change. The uncommitted self changes his belief when under attack. Change for the committed self would involve not only a new opinion but also some change in his self-view. Since he is more responsible for behavior inconsistent with the new opinion, he must somehow explain that, if only to himself. Many of the explanations are not complimentary: His is stupid, he made a mistake, he acted without forethought, and so forth. The skeletal outline of this view is (*a*) change for committed subject involves explaining his previous behavior, (*b*) these explanations are largely demeaning to self, (*c*) the attack is therefore resisted. Further, since commitment implies only responsibility for one's behavior, the committing act would not necessarily demand any immediate change in belief, a notion consistent with our data. Although untested, this explanation of commitment is provocative and worthy of pursuit.

EXTERNAL COMMITMENT

Rosenbaum (Rosenbaum & Zimmerman, 1959; Rosenbaum & Franc, 1960) conducted two studies in which he varied what he called "external commitment." In each case, this involved an outsider attributing an attitude to the subject. In Rosenbaum and Franc, the person's attitude was guessed by a "professional person" on the basis of having read an essay written by the subject. In one condition, this guess was congruent (actually identical) with the subject's initial opinion, in another it was incongruent (three steps away on a six-point scale), and in yet a third condition no external attribution was made. Rosenbaum and Franc found that subjects in the congruent commitment condition were more resistant to attack than the controls and that subjects in the incongruent commitment condition were less resistant to attack than the controls. Rosenbaum hypothesized that external commitment acts analogously to self-commitment and that its effects are the same.

One is struck by the similarity of these effects to what one might expect from a manipulation of self-commitment.* However, one can ask the same question of these data that we have asked ourselves about many of the experiments in this monograph: What was the effect of the commitment manipulations alone? Unless we can demonstrate that there was no immediate effect of the commitment manipulations on attitude, we cannot leap to the inference that the commitment manipulations conferred resistance on existing attitude. In this case, one would suspect that the commitment manipulations, i.e., the act of another attributing an attitude to oneself, had a persuasive impact on the subject which mediated the effects of the attack. (The attack actually consisted of knowledge of where the "professional" other put his marks on the attitude scale.)

That is, we might expect the attribution to have an effect as a persuasive quasi-communication. If so, the congruent attribution would intensify attitude and the incongruent attribution would lead to a partial abandoning of one's position. Add an assumption that the control mean would regress somewhat towards neutrality and we have exactly the array of means that Rosenbaum and Franc found. But our reasoning took into account only events prior to attack, and Rosenbaum and Franc measured attitude only after attack. Thus one could argue that the manipulation of external commitment did not confer resistance but, rather, affected attitude directly. If so, the differences between conditions occurred before the attack and the effect of the subsequent attack might even have been uniform across conditions.

* In fact, by my calculations of Rosenbaum and Franc's data, there was a higher frequency of boomerang responses in the congruent commitment condition than in the incongruent commitment condition (CR = 2.04; $p < .05$), much like the Jones and Kiesler experiment.

In sum, in order to draw an inference about differential resistance to attack following commitment, one must assess the impact of the commitment manipulation prior to attack (see Chapter II).

Whether the criticism of the experiment is valid or not, the underlying theoretical notion is intriguing. Suppose a person was trying to choose among several alternative courses of action (or anticipated choosing among them at some time in the future). Suppose further that through chance and unforeseeable events all but one of these alternatives are eliminated from consideration (for example, one may not have the money to go to college or the training to obtain a job one wanted to consider). The person is then left with one alternative, not because he chose it but, rather, because the other alternatives are no longer open for consideration. Could we say that our hypothetical person was committed now?

The answer is probably yes, but only under very limited circumstances. If the conclusion were really inescapable that the other alternatives were closed, the person might well display some of the effects we expect under conditions of commitment (e.g., resistance to outside attack, belief bolstering when challenged, etc.). Usually however, one would think that the individual would rather avoid the implication that he must resign himself to his fate and would resist the conclusion that the alternatives are, in fact, really closed. Brehm (1966) has addressed himself to this question. He suggests that people want to retain an impression of behavioral freedom and that when choice alternatives are eliminated from consideration whether by design or chance, the person experiences an uncomfortable state called "reactance" and he will actively work to restore his freedom. I suspect that reactance is the typical result of an elimination of choice alternatives and the perception of external commitment is rather rare.

External commitment is rare because people much prefer to be in charge of their own destiny. But when one's environment is effectively controlled by outside forces, then acting as if one's behavior were really self-derived is one of the few alternatives left open. For example, Bettelheim (1958) describes the position of the inmate of a Nazi prison camp. An extremely large chunk of the prisoner's behavior is both observable and controllable. Almost all of one's behavior is prescribed. Bettelheim pictures the prisoner as ultimately acting as if his behavior were self-derived. But the only way open to him is to act like the Nazi, and indeed, he acts more Nazi than the Nazis.* One sees a similar sort of reaction in the military training camps for recruits. Again, a vast part of one's behavior is prescribed in the training camp (things loosen up a bit later). In my own experience, I found the

* Bettelheim, of course, describes this reaction as identification with the aggressor. We are suggesting that the phenomenon may be more general than he thought.

percentage of recruits displaying hyper-military behavior quite large. That is, people behaved in a military fashion even when it was not demanded nor suggested (e.g., marching from one's bunk to the bathroom, saluting other recruits). In behaving the same way in freer settings, one retains the perception of choice or self-responsibility in more prescribed situations.

However, in no case would one say that everyone reacts to the closed environment by ultimately accepting it and then overdoing it. Another response suggested by both Bettelheim and Schein (1958) is extreme apathy, bordering on psychotic withdrawal, so severe that it sometimes resulted in death (Schein, 1958). Over-adoption of the prescribed behavior is not the only alternative, perhaps not even the preferred one.

Possibly, commitment to future interaction has an effect similar to external commitment. Although we previously suggested that choice may be a critical intervening variable in mediating the effects of commitment to future interaction, suppose, for the sake of argument, that it is not. For example, choice might increase the effects of future interaction, without being a critical determinant of them. That is, we might obtain similar (but less dramatic) effects without the subject perceiving that he chose to interact with the group in the future.

Without choice, commitment to future interaction has the flavor of external commitment. When the subject dislikes the group, as in the Kiesler and Corbin experiment, the preferred alternative presumably is to withdraw, to cease the interaction. However, the environment (the experimenter) eliminates this alternative by setting the conditions for unavoidable future interaction. The subject then behaves as if that were what he wanted in the first place. In the Kiesler and Corbin experiment the subjects who were committed to future interaction but found the group unattractive ended up liking the group very much and adjusting their opinions to those of the group, much like the committed and highly attracted subjects.

The implications of commitment to future interaction are somewhat different, depending on whether one's perception of choice is critical to the effect or not. However, this issue could be solved by an experiment in which commitment to future interaction and one's perception of choice in the future interaction are independently varied. If choice were critical, the implications for other research described here would be obvious. But if choice were not critical, the concept of external commitment would take on new meaning and importance.

Effort

In none of our experiments have we manipulated the amount of effort the subject expends in carrying out some behavior. Since, intuitively, effort should make such an obvious contribution to commitment, the reader may have wondered about the omission. We agree that effort is an important variable. Increasing the effort expenditure of the subject should exaggerate the impact of almost any commitment manipulation.

As it turns out, effort is a variable central to several theories. In learning, it is postulated that the more active response is more readily learned. Indeed, the field of programmed learning is based partly on that premise (for example, see Fry, 1963). In attribution theory, effort should not only serve as a link between behavior and attitude, it probably simultaneously makes the linkage salient. In dissonance theory, the amount of effort expended on a counter-attitudinal activity directly affects the degree of dissonance aroused (see Aronson, Carlsmith, & Darley, 1963; and Zimbardo, 1965). Even Hitler (1941) recommends active behavioral participation to commit the members of the in-group: "Followership demands only a passive appreciation of an idea, while membership demands an active presentation and defense . . . [p. 849]."

Broadly conceived, effort should have a dramatic impact on behavioral commitment, and for a variety of theoretical reasons. However, its effects are heterogeneous; when manipulated, it has a number of consequences, in addition to a contribution to commitment. In our research we were trying to pin down the theoretical core of commitment, ruling out alternative explanations and controlling for other relevant variables. At that preliminary point of inquiry, effort could not be operationalized simply enough. For every way of operationally defining effort, we could think of five very plausible explanations for the predicted effects.

Consequently, the reader should not infer that one's effort is not an important determinant of one's feeling of commitment. It is. Certainly every consideration points in that direction. We were sure that effort would affect commitment, but we wanted to be able to say precisely *why* it would do so, and an experiment with four or five possible explanations is not very satisfying. These issues are unimportant to a person who wants to apply these concepts in a more practical setting. There one is interested in *if* something works, not why. In application, forget the agony of the experimentalist who searches for precise explanations. Pragmatically, make certain that your subject not only acts but that his action also requires a lot of effort.

When Does Behavior Imply Attitude?

Psychological Implication

The nature of the relationship between behavior and attitude is a problem for most theories about attitudes and their change. These theories assume that at least under some circumstances, a certain behavior will imply a particular attitude. Heider might say, for example, that the statement "I *bought* a sports car" (a behavior) implies "I *like* sports cars" (an attitude). Or, as in one dissonance experiment (Aronson, 1961), "I worked hard to achieve some end" (a behavior) implies that "I value the end product" (an attitude). Or in attribution theory, "I often eat brown bread" (a behavior) implies that "I like brown bread" (an attitude) (see Bem, 1967).

In each case, the ability of the theory to predict attitude given the behavior rests on the validity of the implicative statement. If owning a sports car does not imply enjoying it, then knowledge of the former would not help one in predicting the latter. To the extent that the implicative statement is valid and other things are equal, one could predict the attitude from a knowledge of the behavior. Of course, each theory posits other variables that affect the validity of the implication. For example, if brown bread happens to be the only type available, then the act of eating it does necessarily imply that one prefers it to other varieties.

How does one arrive at these statements of implication between behavior and attitude? Previously, the statements have typically been based on the individual investigator's knowledge of the naive psychology of his culture. The more astute he was about naive psychology, the better could he predict attitude from behavior.

Recently there has been more direct interest in psychological implication. Both Aronson (1968) and Abelson (1968) have proposed similar methods of deriving implicational statements. Aronson proposes that we give the subject a simple statement of a situation (Jones is a famous author) and then ask him what his expectations are of related events (Does Jones beat his wife?). Relative to dissonance theory, the stronger the a priori expectation, the greater the dissonance that would be produced were the expectation disconfirmed. Abelson suggests a similar technique, which he calls the "Naive Question Game." He would feed the subject an outcome (Joe likes Bill) and then ask for an antecedent event (How come?). In a sense, Abelson and Aronson are working at opposite ends of the statement "*X* implies *Y*." Aronson asks, "Here is *X*, does *Y* suggest itself (or how likely is *Y*)?" while Abelson asks, "Here is *Y*, did *X* precede (or cause) it?" Both men, however, are trying to propose methods of specifying psychological implication in advance, other than simple intuition.

In our own work on commitment, the question of psychological implication is also important to the theoretical derivation. However, we have avoided the issue by setting up experimental situations so that either the implication is obvious or the attitude is not only implied but inherent in the behavior. In Kiesler and Sakumura, the subject made a speech for or against lowering the voting age to 18. The behavior is the act of making the speech. But the content of the speech expresses an attitude, and the connection between the behavior and attitude is clear. The behavior and attitude are so interwoven in fact and in implication that it is difficult to separate one from the other. To separate them, the subject must say "I made the speech, but I do not endorse the position advocated." Such compartmentalization is difficult to maintain. If it becomes necessary to resolve the issue, it is much easier to tell oneself or others such things as: "I was forced to make the speech"; "the speech does not really endorse that attitudinal position"; "I only meant it in principle, I didn't mean that a reduction in voting age should occur now"; or a complicated one that I have heard, "I only said that if one is old enough to be drafted, he is old enough to vote. I intended the speech only as a statement against the draft, not in favor of a younger voting age."

Theoretically, commitment makes these distortions and reinterpretations of the act and its implications for attitude more difficult. But the a priori implications of act for attitude are quite clear. The experimental work thus far carried out on commitment cannot be faulted on the grounds that there is some ambiguity about psychological implication. The assumption of the cognitive corollary (see Chapters II and III) that there is a direct relationship between act and attitude has not been violated.

The question of generalizing to uncontrolled situations is something else, however. There the cognitive corollary may or may not be valid. In uncontrolled settings, then, the commitment model, no less than other theoretical statements, loses some of its predictive power. As do other theories, it needs some method of specifying in advance the connection between behavior and attitude. Therefore, we endorse wholeheartedly the attempts of Aronson, Abelson, and others to develop techniques of assessing psychological implication.

The study of inconsistent behavior has not demanded great precision about psychological implication. The statement, "*X* is inconsistent with *Y*," often remains the same from condition to condition. For example, in Aronson and Carlsmith's (1963) experiment on severity of threat, the subject in each experimental condition was faced with the dilemma, "I find that toy very attractive, but I am not playing with it." Dissonance was varied by means of the severity of the experimenter's admonition not to play with the favored toy; the threat was either severe or mild. In this way dissonance could be varied without modifying the basic implicational statement. In fact, in most of the research on inconsistent behavior the basic implicational statement remains constant from condition to condition.

BEHAVIOR SCALING

It would be useful, especially in the study of consistent behavior, if we could vary the implicational statement in some precise and measurable way. Then, in one condition, the statement, "*X* implies *Y*," could be used and in another condition could be the statement, "*X'* implies *Y'*." If we were able to match a behavior to one's attitude in this manner, new research topics would open up. For example, we could study the interactive effects of commitment and extremeness of opinion. Within each commitment condition, we could vary the extremeness of opinion without affecting (or confounding) the degree of commitment. In the present state of affairs, we could not reassure a critic about a possible confound if such an experiment were attempted.

What I am suggesting is that in addition to developing techniques of assessing situational implications, work should be encouraged in *behavior scaling*. One could try to scale behaviors much in the same way that we scale attitudes now. Of course, as we mentioned in Chapter I, other things affect how we behave besides one's attitudes. (One could turn this around and suggest that factors other than our past history of behavior also affect how we express our attitudes on a scale.) But it would still be useful to know, other things equal, what particular attitudes are implied by each of an array of behaviors. To do so the typical approach must be reversed. Instead of asking, "This person has attitude *X*, how will he behave?," we would ask, "This person acted in a particular way, how must he think or believe or feel?" It does not seem unlikely that, at least for particular settings, we could usefully apply typical methods of scaling attitudes (e.g., whether Guttman, Thurstone, or Likert; each would probably suffice) to scaling an array of behaviors. Of course, when considering possible behaviors for scaling, not all would ultimately be reliable indicators of attitude and many would have to be discarded. The same thing is true of attitude scaling where one may start with a pool of two or three hundred items to develop a 24-item Thurstone scale.

Whatever one's theoretical orientation, ultimately one would like to be able to apply his findings to the real world, which for the most part means an application to an uncontrolled setting. And whether dealing with commitment, dissonance, or whatever, we probably won't be asked to make predictions about a group of people who have all performed the same behavior, but where something else varied. More likely, we will be asked what will happen when people have behaved differently. In which case, over a variety of theoretical orientations, one would have to know something about the psychological implications of the behavior before he could be at all confident about his prediction of subsequent events. The prediction would require some scaling of behavior, whether it is implicit or explicit.

Individual Differences in Commitment

How general are our findings? Can we predict that everyone will behave and believe in the predicted way? Obviously not. A particular variation of commitment would have more impact on one person than another. Some of these variations in impact could be attributed to other contemporaneous events affecting one's interpretation of the act: Did the manner of the experimenter appear affected to Mr. Jones and thereby offend him? Some of the variation is due to historical factors prior to the act: What was the person's attitude before action? How much did he know about the issues? Who else agrees with him? What is his interpretation of the implications of the act? All of these could easily affect whether a committing act would affect an individual in the predicted way.

More stable attributes of the person should also be influential. Consider Rotter's distinction between internal and external locus of control (Rotter, 1954). The variable underlying the distinction is characterized as a generalized expectancy regarding the relationship between one's own behavior and reinforcement; whether one perceives his outcomes in social situations to be contingent on his own behavior or determined by outside forces. One would suspect that any given behavior would be less committing to a person with a stable perceived external locus of control than to one more internally oriented. Those with the external orientation should feel less responsibility for their own behavior, which probably would directly affect the degree of commitment engendered by a particular act. Consequently, one's expectancy of internal versus external control should exert considerable influence over the impact of commitment. Further, internal–external control could affect whether the person will act at all (Gore & Rotter, 1963) in response to inducements from the environment. In uncontrolled settings, this notion should be of especial interest.

Without bothering to detail a list, we can confidently agree that a number of personality variables might well partly control whether one acts, and if so, the degree of commitment produced by the act. Also, some people have probably been *taught* to attend to behavior, theirs and others', more closely and to endorse more enthusiastically the idea that behavior and self-definition are intertwined. For example, people who have grown up in a small town are probably more attentive to the behavior of self and others and hold self and others more responsible for their behavior. Part of this is the small-town folk-culture, but it is assisted by an environment where one's behavior is typically under the scrutiny of familiar others. Since the individual may know everyone and is himself readily observable, all the inconsistencies and implications of his behavior come home to haunt him.

Concluding Remarks

Our data indicate that when discussing the concept of commitment and its effects, it is not necessary to depend upon such variables as social support, familiarity with the issue, extreme opinions, and so forth. Surely these variables contribute to one's perception of self-commitment and exaggerate effects otherwise produced, but they are not critical. In none of our experiments did these variables play any role, yet predicted effects occurred in every case. Consequently, questions of whether these well-researched variables are either identical to commitment or critical to its effects are laid to rest. They obviously contribute, but they are not decisive.

Another old saw that I hope we have laid to rest is the assumption that commitment is somehow dichotomous; that one is either committed or uncommitted, but never in between. In almost every experiment described in this monograph, we manipulated the *degree* of commitment. This point seems important to me, not only in terms of the implications for theory, but also in terms of what kind of research one is going to do. In many experiments on commitment in the experimental literature, a very gross manipulation has been used. One either decides something or he does not; he writes an essay or he does not; he passes out petitions on the street or he fills out a "filler" questionnaire. These manipulations are complex, and a number of differences exist between experimental conditions besides some presumed degree of commitment (note the relationship to the previous paragraph). It should not surprise us then that when we review the literature in which the term commitment has been used, we find a very heterogeneous set of conclusions. In our experiments, everyone performs the same behavior, and the committing circumstances are arranged so as to have little or no immediate impact on the subject.

We have observed Campbell's dictum and have tried to triangulate in on our concept. That is, we have deliberately manipulated it in a variety of ways, to make certain that our findings were not dependent on, or particular to, a specific set of operations. Consequently, we can say with some confidence that the effects observed have some generality across operations.

One way to think of the commitment effects reported in this monograph is that they are an experimental demonstration of Lewin's notion of the freezing effect of behavior. Viewed in this way, one might more readily see some of the points of connection between this relatively isolated batch of data and such related concepts as dissonance, decision-making, and attribution. Indeed, I hope that the present monograph eventually contributes to at least a partial understanding of these related concepts.

Some of our research (particularly Chapters IV and V) is directly related to the process by which people become attitudinally more extreme and adopt more extreme behavior. Given the increasing polarization of opinion in our society today, we desperately need a deeper understanding of the processes underlying the development of extreme behavior and attitudes. Although I would not suggest that our research represents more than a small ripple on a very large pond, at least I am enthusiastic about it and hope to follow up some of the leads in the near future.

REFERENCES

Abelson, R. P. Psychological implication. In R. P. Abelson *et al.* (Eds.), *Theories of cognitive consistency: A sourcebook*. Chicago: Rand McNally, 1968. Pp. 112–139.

Abelson, R. P., Aronson, E., McGuire, W. J., Newcomb, T. M., Rosenberg, M. J., & Tannenbaum, P. H. (Eds.), *Theories of cognitive consistency*. Chicago: Rand McNally, 1968.

Adams, J. A. *Human memory*. New York: McGraw-Hill, 1967.

Allyn, J. & Festinger, L. The effectiveness of unanticipated persuasive communications. *Journal of Abnormal and Social Psychology*, 1961, **62,** 35–40.

Alverson, H. The social and organizational antecedents of job satisfaction among black South African industrial workers. Unpublished doctoral dissertation, Yale University, 1968.

Apsler, R. & Sears, D. O. Warning, personal involvement, and attitude change. *Journal of Personality and Social Psychology*, 1968, **9,** 162–166.

Aronson, E. The effect of effort on the attractiveness of rewarded and unrewarded stimuli. *Journal of Abnormal and Social Psychology*, 1961, **63,** 375–380.

Aronson, E. Dissonance theory: Progress and problems. In R. P. Abelson *et al.* (Eds.), *Theories of cognitive consistency: A sourcebook*. Chicago: Rand McNally, 1968. Pp. 5–27.

Aronson, E. & Carlsmith, J. M. Effect of severity of threat on the devaluation of forbidden behavior. *Journal of Abnormal and Social Psychology*, 1963, **66,** 584–588.

Aronson, E. & Carlsmith, J. M. Experimentation in social psychology. In G. Lindzey and E. Aronson (Eds.), *Handbook of social psychology*. Vol. II. Reading, Mass: Addison-Wesley, 1968. Pp. 1–79.

Aronson, E., Carlsmith, J. M., & Darley, J. M. The effects of expectancy on volunteering for an unpleasant experience. *Journal of Abnormal and Social Psychology*, 1963, **66,** 220–224.

Aronson, E. & Mills, J. The effect of severity of initation on liking for a group. *Journal of Abnormal and Social Psychology*, 1959, **59,** 177–181.

Ausubel, D. P. Cognitive structure and the facilitation of meaningful verbal learning. *Journal of Teacher Education*, 1963, **14,** 217–221.

Barker, R. G. (Ed.) *The stream of behavior.* New York: Appleton-Century-Crofts, 1963.

Bem, D. J. An experimental analysis of self-persuasion. *Journal of Experimental Social Psychology*, 1965, **1,** 199–218.

Bem, D. J. Self-perception: An alternative interpretation of cognitive dissonance phenomena. *Psychological Review*, 1967, **74,** 183–200.

Berscheid, E., Boye, D., & Darley, J. M. Effects of forced association upon voluntary choice to associate. *Journal of Personality and Social Psychology*, 1968, **8,** 13–19.

Bettelheim, B. Individual and mass behavior in extreme situations. In E. E. Maccoby, T. M. Newcomb, & E. L. Hartley (Eds.), *Readings in social psychology.* (3rd ed.) New York: Holt, 1958. Pp. 300–310.

Brehm, J. W. Post-decision changes in the desirability of alternatives. *Journal of Abnormal and Social Psychology*, 1956, **52,** 384–389.

Brehm, J. W. Increasing cognitive dissonance by a fait-accompli. *Journal of Abnormal and Social Psychology*, 1959, **58,** 379–382.

Brehm, J. W. *A theory of psychological reactance.* New York: Academic Press, 1966.

Brehm, J. W. & Cohen, A. R. *Exploration in cognitive dissonance.* New York: Wiley, 1962.

Campbell, D. T. The indirect assessment of social attitudes. *Psychological Bulletin*, 1950, **47,** 15–38.

Campbell, D. T. Recommendations for APA test standards regarding construct, trait, or discriminant validity. *American Psychologist*, 1960, **15,** 546–553.

Campbell, D. T. & Stanley, J. C. Experimental and quasi-experimental designs for research on teaching. In N. L. Gage (Ed.), *Handbook of research on teaching.* Chicago: Rand McNally, 1963. Pp. 171–246.

Caplan, N. Treatment intervention and reciprocal interaction effects. *Journal of Social Issues*, 1968, **24,** 63–88.

Charters, W. W., Jr., & Newcomb, T. M. Some attitudinal effects of experimentally increased salience of a membership group. In E. E. Maccoby, T. M. Newcomb, & E. L. Hartley (Eds.), *Readings in social psychology.* (3rd ed.) New York: Holt, 1958.

Coch, L. & French, J. R. P., Jr. Overcoming resistance to change. In D. Cartwright and A. Zander (Eds.) *Group dynamics.* (2nd ed.) Evanston, Ill.: Row, Peterson, 1960. pp. 319–344.

Cofer, C. N. & Appley, M. H. *Motivation: Theory and research.* New York: Wiley, 1964.

Cohen, A. R. A dissonance analysis of the boomerang effect. *Journal of Personality*, 1962, **30,** 75–88.

Converse, P. & Campbell, A. Political standards in secondary groups. In D. Cartwright & A. Zander (Eds.), *Group dynamics.* (2nd ed.) Evanston, Ill.: Row-Peterson, 1960. Pp. 300–318.

Darley, J. M. & Berscheid, E. Increased liking as a result of the anticipation of personal contact. *Human Relations*, 1967, **20,** 29–40.

Davis, K. E. & Jones, E. E. Changes in interpersonal perception as a means of reducing cognitive dissonance. *Journal of Abnormal and Social Psychology*, 1960, **61,** 402–410.

Deutsch, M. Field theory in social psychology. In G. Lindzey & E. Aronson (Eds.), *Handbook of social psychology.* Vol. 1. (2nd ed.) Reading, Mass.: Addison-Wesley, 1968. Pp. 412–487.

Deutsch, M. & Collins, M. *Interracial housing.* Minneapolis: University of Minnesota Press, 1951.

Deutsch, M. & Gerard, H. B. A study of normative and informational social influence upon individual judgment. *Journal of Abnormal and Social Psychology*, 1955, **51,** 629–636

Ewing, T. N. A study of certain factors involved in changes of opinion. *Journal of Social Psychology*, 1942, **16**, 63–88.
Festinger, L. *A theory of cognitive dissonance*. Stanford, Calif.: Stanford University Press, 1957.
Festinger, L. *Conflict, decision, and dissonance*. Stanford, Calif.: Stanford University Press, 1964.
Festinger, L. & Carlsmith, J. M. Cognitive consequences of forced compliance. *Journal of abnormal and Social Psychology*, 1959, **58**, 203–211.
Fitzgerald, D. Cognitive versus affective factors in the learning and retention of controversial material. Unpublished doctoral dissertation, University of Illinois, 1962.
Fitzgerald, D. & Ausubel, D. P. Cognitive versus affective factors in the learning and retention of controversial material. *Journal of Educational Psychology*, 1963, **54**, 73–84.
Freedman, J. L. & Fraser, S. C. Compliance without pressure: The foot-in-the-door technique. *Journal of Personality and Social Psychology*, 1966, **4**, 195–202.
Freedman, J. L. & Sears, D. O. Warning, distraction and resistance to influence. *Journal of Personality and Social Psychology*, 1965, **1**, 262–265.
Freedman, J. L. & Steinbruner, J. D. Perceived choice and resistance to persuasion. *Journal of Abnormal and Social Psychology*, 1964, **68**, 678–681.
Fry, E. B. *Teaching machines and programmed instruction*. New York: McGraw-Hill, 1963.
Gerard, H. B. Deviation, conformity, and commitment. In I. D. Steiner & M. Fishbein (Eds.), *Current studies in social psychology*. New York: Holt, Rinehart and Winston, 1965. Pp. 263–277.
Gerard, H. B. Basic features of commitment. In R. P. Abelson *et al.* (Eds.), *Theories of cognitive consistency: A sourcebook*. Chicago: Rand McNally, 1968. Pp. 456–463.
Gerard, H. B. & Mathewson, G. C. The effects of severity of initiation on liking for a group: A replication. *Journal of Experimental Social Psychology*, 1966, **2**, 278–287.
Gilson, C. & Abelson, R. P. The subjective use of inductive evidence. *Journal of Personality and Social Psychology*, 1965, **2**, 301–310.
Goffman, E. *The presentation of self in everyday life*. Garden City, N.Y.: Doubleday, 1959.
Gore, P. M. & Rotter, J. B. A personality correlate of social action. *Journal of Personality*, 1963, **31**, 58–64.
Green, B. F. Attitude measurement. In G. Lindzey (Ed.), *Handbook of social psychology*. Vol. 1. (1st ed.) Reading, Mass.: Addison-Wesley, 1954. Pp. 335–369.
Gross, N., Mason, W. S., & McEachern, A. W. *Explorations in role analysis: Studies of the school superintendency role*. New York: Wiley, 1958.
Hare, A. P. *Handbook of small group research*. Glencoe, Ill.: Free Press, 1962.
Harvey, O. J., Hunt, D., & Schroder, H. *Conceptual systems and personality organization*. New York: Wiley, 1961.
Heider, F. *The psychology of interpersonal relations*. New York: Wiley, 1958.
Hitler, A. *Mein Kampf*. New York: Reynal & Hitchcock, 1941.
Hollander, E. P. Conformity, status and idiosyncrasy credit. *Psychological Review*, 1958, **65**, 117–127.
Hovland, C. I. Reconciling conflicting results derived from experimental and survey studies of attitude change. *American Psychologist*, 1959, **14**, 8–17.
Hovland, C. I., Campbell, E. H., & Brock, T. C. The effects of "commitment" on opinion change following communication. In C. I. Hovland *et al.* (Eds.), *The order of presentation in persuasion*. New Haven, Conn.: Yale University Press, 1957. Pp. 23–32.
Husek, T. R. Persuasive impacts of early, late, or no mention of a negative source. *Journal of Personality and Social Psychology*, 1965, **2**, 125–128.

Janis, I. L. The psychological effects of warnings. In G. W. Baker & D. W. Chapman (Eds.), *Man and society in disaster*. New York: Basic Books, 1962. Pp. 55–92.

Janis, I. L. Stages in the decision-making process. In R. P. Abelson *et al.* (Eds.), *Theories of cognitive consistency: A sourcebook*. Chicago: Rand McNally, 1968. Pp. 577–588.

Janis, I. L. & Gilmore, J. B. The influence of incentive conditions on the success of role-playing in modifying attitudes. *Journal of Personality and Social Psychology*, 1965, **1**, 17–27.

Janis, I. L. and Mann, L. A conflict-theory approach to attitude change and decision-making. In A. G. Greenwald, T. C. Brock, & T. M. Ostrom (Eds.), *Psychological foundations of attitudes*. New York: Academic Press, 1968. Pp. 327–360.

Jecker, J. D. The cognitive effects of conflict and dissonance. In L. Festinger, *Conflict, decision, and dissonance*. Stanford, Calif.: Stanford University Press, 1964. Pp. 21–30.

Jones, E. E. *Ingratiation*. New York: Appleton-Century-Crofts, 1964.

Jones, E. E. & Davis, K. E. From acts to dispositions. In L. Berkowitz (Ed.), *Advances in experimental social psychology*. Vol. 2. New York: Academic Press, 1965. Pp. 219–266.

Jones, E. E. & Gerard, H. B. *Foundations of social psychology*. New York: Wiley, 1967.

Jones, E. E. & Nisbett, R. E. The actor and the observer: Divergent perceptions of the causes of behavior. In E. E. Jones, D. Kanouse, H. H. Kelley, R. E. Nisbett, S. Valins, & B. Weiner (Eds.), *Attribution: Perceiving the causes of behavior* (to be published, 1971).

Jones, R. A., Linder, D. E., Kiesler, C. A., Zanna, M., & Brehm, J. W. Internal states or external stimuli: Observers' attitude judgments and the dissonance-theory/self-persuasion controversy. *Journal of Experimental Social Psychology*, 1968, **4**, 247–269.

Katz, E. & Feldman, J. J. The debates in the light of research. In S. Kraus (Ed.), *The great debates*. Bloomington, Ind.: University of Indiana Press, 1962. Pp. 173–223.

Kelley, H. H. Two functions of reference groups. In G. E. Swanson, T. M. Newcomb, & E. L. Hartley (Eds.), *Readings in social psychology*. (2nd Ed.) New York: Holt, Rinehart, and Winston, 1952. Pp. 410–414.

Kelley, H. H. Salience of membership and resistance to change of group-anchored attitudes. *Human Relations*, 1955, **8**, 275–290.

Kelley, H. H. Attribution theory in social psychology. In D. Levine (Ed.), *Nebraska symposium on motivation*. Lincoln, Neb.: University of Nebraska Press, 1967. Pp. 192–240.

Kelley, H. H. & Volkart, E. H. The resistance to change of group-anchored attitudes. *American Sociological Review*, 1952, **17**, 453–465.

Keniston, K. *The uncommitted: alienated youth in American society*. New York: Dell, 1965.

Kiesler, C. A. Attraction to the group and conformity to group norms. *Journal of Personality*, 1963, **31**, 559–569.

Kiesler, C. A. Conformity and commitment. *Trans-Action*, 1967, June, 32–35.

Kiesler, C. A. Commitment. In R. P. Abelson *et al.* (Eds.), *Theories of cognitive consistency: A sourcebook*. Chicago: Rand McNally, 1968. Pp. 448–455.

Kiesler, C. A. Conformity. In J. Mills (Ed.), *Experimental social psychology*. New York: MacMillan, 1969. Pp. 233–306.

Kiesler, C. A., Collins, B.E., & Miller, N. *Attitude change: A critical analysis of theoretical approaches*. New York: Wiley, 1969.

Kiesler, C. A. & Corbin, L. Commitment, attraction, and conformity. *Journal of Personality and Social Psychology*, 1965, **2**, 890–895.

Kiesler, C. A. & DeSalvo, J. The group as an influencing agent in a forced compliance paradigm. *Journal of Experimental Social Psychology*, 1967, **3**, 160–171.

Kiesler, C. A. & Kiesler, S. B. *Conformity*. Reading, Mass.: Addison-Wesley, 1969.
Kiesler, C. A. & Kiesler, S. B. Role of forewarning in persuasive communications. *Journal of Abnormal and Social Psychology*, 1964, **68,** 547–549.
Kiesler, C. A., Kiesler, S. B., & Pallak, M. S. The effect of commitment to future interaction on reactions to norm violations. *Journal of Personality*, 1967, **35,** 585–599.
Kiesler, C. A., Nisbett, R. E., & Zanna, M. P. On inferring one's belief from one's behavior. *Journal of Personality and Social Psychology*, 1969, **11,** 321–327.
Kiesler, C. A., Pallak, M. S., & Kanouse, D. E. Interaction of commitment and dissonance. *Journal of Personality and Social Psychology*, 1968, **8,** 331–338.
Kiesler, C. A. & Sakumura, J. A test of a model for commitment. *Journal of Personality and Social Psychology*, 1966, **3,** 349–353.
Kiesler, C. A. & Zanna, M. P. Inferring one's beliefs from one's behavior as a function of belief relevance and discrepancy of behavior. Paper presented at the Eastern Psychological Association Meetings, Philadelphia, 1969.
Kiesler, C. A., Zanna, M. P., & DeSalvo, J. Deviation and conformity: Opinion change as a function of commitment, attraction and presence of a deviate. *Journal of Personality and Social Psychology*, 1966, **3,** 458–467.
Kleck, R. E. & Wheaton, J. Dogmatism and responses to opinion-consistent and opinion-inconsistent information. *Journal of Personality and Social Psychology*, 1967, **5,** 249–252.
Latanè, B. & Darley, J. M. *The unresponsive bystander—why doesn't he help?* New York: Appleton-Century-Crofts, 1970.
Lewin, K. Group decision and social change. In T. M. Newcomb & E. L. Hartley (Eds.), *Readings in social psychology*. New York: Holt, 1947. Pp. 330–344.
Lewin, K. & Grabbe, P. (Eds.) Problems of re-education. *Journal of Social Issues* (August) 1945, **1,** No. 3.
Lieberman, S. The effects of changes in roles on the attitudes of role occupants. *Human Relations*, 1956, **9,** 385–402.
Marlowe, D., Frager, R., & Nuttal, R. L. Commitment to action-taking as a consequence of cognitive dissonance. *Journal of Personality and Social Psychology*, 1965, **2,** 864–868.
Marlowe, D. & Gergen, K. J. Personality and social interaction. In G. Lindzey & E. Aronson (Eds.), *Handbook of social psychology*. Vol. 3. (2nd Ed.) Reading, Mass.: Addison-Wesley, 1969. Pp. 590–665.
McGuire, W. J. The nature of attitudes and attitude change. In G. Lindzey & E. Aronson (Eds.), *Handbook of social psychology*. Vol. 3. (2nd Ed.) Reading, Mass.: Addison-Wesley, 1969. Pp. 136–314.
McGuire, W. J. & Millman, S. Anticipatory belief lowering following forewarning of a persuasive attack. *Journal of Personality and Social Psychology*, 1965, **2,** 471–479.
Mead, G. H. *Mind, self and society*. Chicago: University of Chicago Press, 1934.
Meyerson, M. The ethos of the American college student: Beyond the protests. *Daedalus*, 1966, Summer, 713–739.
Mirels, H. & Mills, J. Perception of the pleasantness and competence of a partner. *Journal of Abnormal and Social Psychology*, 1964, **68,** 456–459.
Moore, W. E. & Feldman, A. S. *Labor commitment and social change in developing areas*. New York: Social Science Research Council, 1960.
Nabokov, V. *The eye*. London, England: Panther, 1966.
Nisbett, R. E. & Valins, S. Inferring one's beliefs and feelings from one's own behavior. In E. E. Jones, D. Kanouse, H. H. Kelley, R. E. Nisbett, S. Valins, & B. Weiner (Eds.), *Attribution: Perceiving the causes of behavior* (to be published, 1971).

Osgood, C. E. Cognitive dynamics in the conduct of human affairs. *Public Opinion Quarterly*, 1960, **24,** 341–365.

Papageorgis, D. Anticipation of exposure to persuasive message and belief change. *Journal of Personality and Social Psychology*, 1967, **5,** 490–496.

Pelz, E. Bennett. Discussion, decision, commitment, and consensus in "group decision." *Human Relations*, 1955, **8,** 251–274.

Piliavin, J. A., Piliavin, I. M., Loewenton, E. P., McCauley, C., & Hammond, P. On observers' reproductions of dissonance effects: The right answers for the wrong reasons? *Journal of Personality and Social Psychology*, 1969, **13,** 98–106.

Rokeach, M. *The open and closed mind.* New York: Basic Books, 1960.

Rokeach, M. *Beliefs, attitudes and values.* San Francisco: Jossey-Bass, 1968.

Rosenbaum, M. E. & Franc, D. E. Opinion change as a function of external commitment and amount of discrepancy from the opinion of another. *Journal of Abnormal and Social Psychology*, 1960, **61,** 15–20.

Rosenbaum, M. E. & Zimmerman, I. M. The effect of external commitment on response to an attempt to change opinions. *Public Opinion Quarterly*, 1959, **23,** 247–254.

Rosenberg, M. J. When dissonance fails: on eliminating evaluation apprehension from attitude measurement. *Journal of Personality and Social Psychology*, 1965, **1,** 28–43.

Rotter, J. B. *Social learning and clinical psychology.* Englewood Cliffs, N.J.: Prentice-Hall, 1954.

Sarbin, T. R. & Allen, V. L. Role theory. In G. Lindzey & E. Aronson (Eds.), *Handbook of social psychology.* Vol. 1. (2nd ed.) Reading, Mass.: Addison-Wesley, 1968. Pp. 488–567.

Schein, E. H. The Chinese indoctrination program for prisoners of war: A study of attempted brainwashing. In E. E. Maccoby, T. M. Newcomb, & E. L. Hartley (Eds.), *Readings in social psychology.* (3rd ed.) New York: Holt, 1958. Pp. 311–334.

Sears, D. O., Freedman, J. L., & O'Connor, E. F. The effects of anticipated debate and commitment on the polarization of audience opinion. *Public Opinion Quarterly*, 1964, **28,** 615–627.

Secord, P. F. & Backman, C. W. *Social psychology.* New York: McGraw-Hill, 1964.

Segalman, R. The Protestant ethic and social welfare. *Journal of Social Issues*, 1968, **24,** 125–141.

Shaw, M. E. & Wright, J. M. *Scales for the measurement of attitudes.* New York: McGraw-Hill, 1967.

Sherif, C. W., Sherif, M., & Nebergall, R. E. *Attitude and attitude change.* Philadelphia: Saunders, 1965.

Skinner, B. F. *Science and human behavior.* New York: MacMillan, 1953.

Skinner, B. F. *Verbal behavior.* New York: Appleton-Century-Crofts, 1957.

Star, S. A., Williams, R. M., Jr., & Stouffer, S. A. Negro infantry platoons in white companies. In E. E. Maccoby, T. M. Newcomb, & E. L. Hartley (Eds.), *Readings in social psychology.* (3rd ed.), New York: Holt, 1958. Pp. 596–601.

Steinglass, K. Attitude change as a function of differential inducements and acceptance or rejection of a discrepant act. Unpublished Junior Honors thesis, Culture and Behavior Major, Yale University, 1967.

Webb, E. J., Campbell, D. T., Schwartz, R. D., & Sechrest, L. *Unobtrusive measures: Nonreactive research in the social sciences.* Chicago: Rand McNally, 1966.

Walster, E. Assignment of responsibility for an accident. *Journal of Personality and Social Psychology*, 1966, **3,** 73–79.

Weiner, B. Effects of motivation on the availability and retrieval of memory traces. *Psychological Bulletin*, 1966, **65,** 24–37.

Whiting, J. W. M., Kluckhohn, R., & Anthony, A. The functions of male initiation ceremonies at puberty. In E. E. Maccoby, T. M. Newcomb, and E. L. Hartley (Eds.), *Readings in social psychology*. (3rd ed.) New York: Holt, 1958. Pp. 359–370.

Winer, B. J. *Statistical principles in experimental design*. New York: McGraw-Hill, 1962.

Wolpe, J. *Psychotherapy by reciprocal inhibition*. Stanford, Calif.: Stanford University Press, 1958.

Zanna, M. P. Inference of belief from rejection of an alternative action. Unpublished manuscript, Yale University, 1969.

Zimbardo, P. G. The effect of effort and improvisation on self-persuasion produced by role-playing. *Journal of Experimental Social Psychology*, 1965, **1,** 103–120.

SUBJECT INDEX

A